PALGRAVE STUDIES IN CULTURAL AND INTELLECTUAL HISTORY

Series Editors

Anthony J. La Vopa, North Carolina State University

Suzanne Marchand, Louisiana State University

Javed Majeed, Queen Mary, University of London

The Palgrave Studies in Cultural and Intellectual History series has three primary aims: to close divides between intellectual and cultural approaches, thus bringing them into mutually enriching interactions; to encourage interdisciplinarity in intellectual and cultural history; and to globalize the field, both in geographical scope and in subjects and methods. This series is open to work on a range of modes of intellectual inquiry, including social theory and the social sciences; the natural sciences; economic thought; literature; religion; gender and sexuality; philosophy; political and legal thought; psychology; and music and the arts. It encompasses not just North America but also Africa, Asia, Eurasia, Europe, Latin America, and the Middle East. It includes both nationally focused studies and studies of intellectual and cultural exchanges between different nations and regions of the world, and encompasses research monographs, synthetic studies, edited collections, and broad works of reinterpretation. Regardless of methodology or geography, all books in the series are historical in the fundamental sense of undertaking rigorous contextual analysis.

Published by Palgrave Macmillan

Indian Mobilities in the West, 1900–1947: Gender, Performance, Embodiment
By Shompa Lahiri

The Shelley-Byron Circle and the Idea of Europe
By Paul Stock

Culture and Hegemony in the Colonial Middle East
By Yaseen Noorani

Recovering Bishop Berkeley: Virtue and Society in the Anglo-Irish Context
By Scott Breuninger

The Reading of Russian Literature in China: A Moral Example and Manual of Practice
By Mark Gamsa

Rammohun Roy and the Making of Victorian Britain
By Lynn Zastoupil

Carl Gustav Jung: Avant-Garde Conservative
By Jay Sherry

Law and Politics in British Colonial Thought: Transpositions of Empire
Edited by Shaunnagh Dorsett and Ian Hunter

Sir John Malcolm and the Creation of British India
By Jack Harrington

Music and Empire in Britain and India

Identity, Internationalism, and Cross-Cultural Communication

Bob van der Linden

palgrave
macmillan

First published in 2013 by
PALGRAVE MACMILLAN®
in the United States—a division of St. Martin's Press LLC,
175 Fifth Avenue, New York, NY 10010.

Where this book is distributed in the UK, Europe and the rest of the world,
this is by Palgrave Macmillan, a division of Macmillan Publishers Limited,
registered in England, company number 785998, of Houndmills,
Basingstoke, Hampshire RG21 6XS.

Palgrave Macmillan is the global academic imprint of the above companies
and has companies and representatives throughout the world.

Palgrave® and Macmillan® are registered trademarks in the United States,
the United Kingdom, Europe and other countries.

ISBN: 978–1–137–31163–4

Library of Congress Cataloging-in-Publication Data

Linden, Bob van der.
    Music and empire in Britain and India : identity, internationalism, and
cross-cultural communication / Bob van der Linden.
        pages cm.—(Palgrave studies in cultural and intellectual history)
    Includes bibliographical references and index.
    ISBN 978–1–137–31163–4 (alk. paper)
        1. Music—Social aspects—India—History—19th century. 2. Music—
Social aspects—India—History—20th century. 3. Music—Social
aspects—Great Britain—History—19th century. 4. Music—Social
aspects—Great Britain—History—20th century. 5. Music—India—19th
century—History and criticism. 6. Music—India—20th century—History
and criticism. 7. Music—Great Britain—19th century—History and
criticism. 8. Music—Great Britain—20th century—History and criticism.
9. Music—Great Britain—Indic influences. 10. Music—India—Western
influences. I. Title.
ML3917.I4L56 2013
780.9171′241—dc23   2013005943

A catalogue record of the book is available from the British Library.

Design by Newgen Knowledge Works (P) Ltd., Chennai, India.

First edition: August 2013

10 9 8 7 6 5 4 3 2 1

To the memory of my father

Contents

Illustrations

Preface

This book is the result of my double background as a historian of modern South Asia, especially of colonial Punjab, and a practiced musician with an ever-growing fascination for (ethno) musicology. My budding interest in South Asian music was boosted when I traveled to India and Pakistan for the first time in 1989. I really got into it, however, during subsequent research periods in Indian and Pakistani Punjab. I still have clear memories, for example, of some musical events that I greatly enjoyed during the late 1990s in Lahore: the Muslim Sufi devotional music (*qawwali*) sung at the shrine of the city's patron saint, Datta Ganj Baksh; the *dhol* drums at the shrine of Baba Shah Jamal; and the girls singing and dancing erotic dances (*mujra*) to the harmonium and *tabla* (north-Indian hand-played drums) in the red-light district. Conversely, I was touched by the tranquil music sung and played at the holiest Sikh shrine, the Golden Temple, in Amritsar, though at that time of course it never entered my mind that I would eventually write about Sikh sacred music. Later, in 2000, during a research period in the British Library in London, the piano suite *Impressions from the Jungle Book* (1912) by Cyril Scott (1879–1970) set me on the track of British modernist composers with an interest in non-Western music and Indian music in particular. Scott not only brought to my attention his lifelong friend, the eccentric Australian American pianist, composer, and proto-ethnomusicologist, Percy Grainger (1882–1961), but also the couple Maud MacCarthy (1882–1967) and John Foulds (1880–1939). Finally, the name of the Dutch pioneer in South Asian ethnomusicology, Arnold Bake (1899–1963), already haunted me for some years as being someone whose life and work I should look into. It was Bake's relationship with the Bengali poet, playwright, novelist, short story writer, essayist, composer, painter, and Nobel Laureate, Rabindranath Tagore (1861–1941), that made me realize the importance of folk music research as a concurrent imperial phenomenon in metropolis and colony.

I am thankful to Arvind Mandair and Balbinder Singh Bhogal for inviting me to the first ever conference on Sikh sacred music, "The Hermeneutics of Sikh Music (*rag*) and Word (*shabad*)," held at New York's Hofstra University, May 21–23, 2010. Given the centrality of music to the Sikh tradition, it remains surprising that this subject is critically discussed only now, and it certainly feels exciting to be involved in the emergence of a new and important field for study. Special thanks here also to Bhai Baldeep Singh for his support and Pashaura Singh for inviting me to the conference, "Dialogues with/ in Sikh Studies: Texts, Practices and Performances," University of California, Riverside, May 10–12, 2013. In addition, the New York conference gave me the opportunity to visit Percy Grainger's former house in White Plains. There, I had a wonderful day with Stewart Manville, who showed me around the house where he had lived with his wife and Percy's widow, Ella, and time had stood still. To listen to Stewart's stories about the Graingers in particular was an unforgettable experience. The chapter on Scott received a boost after Robbert Muuse and Micha van Weers contacted me to write the liner notes for their debut recording *Songs of Quest and Inspiration: Cyril Scott— Ralph Vaughan Williams* (2011). It was entirely because of this project that I began to study Scott's songs, and I generally learned a lot from these two wonderful musicians. More immediately, I am indebted to Desmond Scott for his overall advice and helpfulness regarding the chapter about his father; Chris Bayly for his comments upon an earlier version of this book and warm hospitality in Cambridge; and Joep Bor for his critical remarks upon a penultimate edition of the text and our delightful discussions. The criticism of one anonymous reader of the manuscript also was useful (the other reader, Jeffrey Richards, wanted the book to be published straightaway). Needless to say, I remain responsible for any errors or misjudgments that remain. Earlier versions of sections of this book appeared in *Sikh Formations: Religion, Culture, Theory*; the *Journal of Global History*; and *British Music: The Journal of the British Music Society*.

Introduction

Partly because of academic disciplinary boundaries, music largely remains a neglected subject in the historiography of the British Empire. It is not mentioned at all for example in the five volumes of *The Oxford History of the British Empire* (1998–1999) and its subsequent companion series, including *India and the British Empire* (2012), or *The New Imperial Histories Reader* (2010).[1] This book, however, emphasizes that the imperial encounter partially also was a sound exercise and that music is an essential topic for the discussion of processes of (national) identity formation, as well as transnational networks and patterns of cross-cultural communication between colonizer and colonized. In the main, *Music and Empire in Britain and India* is concerned with the ways in which some rational, moral, and aesthetic motives underlying the institutionalization and modernization of "classical" music every so often resembled each other in Britain and India, and which at the time led to the use of the term "musical renaissance" in both countries. Furthermore, it looks at "internationalism in music" by discussing some subversive internationalist countermovements against the dominant nationalist musical establishments as well as the openness of some Britons and Indians to the possibility of learning from each other. Along the lines of the concern of the so-called new imperial history,[2] the book adopts a relational view on the music histories of Britain and India. In particular, it looks at shared influences and complicities, which at the time generally were played down by the national music establishments. To a great deal, in fact, it investigates music in Britain and India that "was deliberately intended to counter or subvert imperial ideology, or could in retrospect be interpreted as doing so."[3]

Significantly, the idea to investigate musical parallels, networks, and interactions within "webs of empire" that were interdependent and mutually constitutive in metropolis and colony is a novel contribution to the (ethno)musicological literature.[4] Besides an earlier article of mine,[5] as far as I know, the British ethnomusicologist Martin Clayton is the only other person who paid attention to the

1

"relationships between movements of musical revival and reform in England and India, and the mutual effects of their interpenetration."[6] On the other hand, *Music and Empire in Britain and India* in some ways builds further upon the late Gerry Farrell's seminal *Indian Music and the West* (1997).[7] So, for example, my discussion of the role of Theosophy among Western internationalists can be seen as an antecedent to his fascination with the interest into India of the Western hippies of the 1960s. However, while Farrell mainly investigated the impact of Indian music on "popular" Western music since the eighteenth century, I look at the historical interactions between Indian and Western agents in the sphere of modern Hindustani music making against the dissimilar backgrounds of musical Orientalism among modernist British "classical" composers; (Theosophical) internationalism; *Rabindra Sangit*; Sikh sacred music; and the making of the modern discipline of ethnomusicology. Also, more than Farrell, I underline the intellectual importance of the imperial encounter to the making of modern Indian music in the context of long-term historical processes such as modernization, imperial knowledge formation, and identity politics.

Furthermore, this book aims to be an addition to the intellectual history of the discipline of ethnomusicology, which during the first half of the twentieth century was known as "comparative musicology." Though Joep Bor rightly emphasized that the history of Indian ethnomusicology goes back to the late eighteenth century,[8] ethnomusicologists generally share the opinion that their discipline distinctly developed since the late nineteenth century and especially during the early twentieth century.[9] On the whole, I think that the institutionalization of the modern scientific discipline of comparative musicology should be seen against the background of a wide configuration of late nineteenth-century ideas (evolutionism, folk music research, anthropology, and so on) and technological developments (the phonograph, recordings, and so on) because these made researchers, more than before, aware of music worldwide from a comparative and, indeed, imperial perspective. While looking at metropolis and colony in one analytic field, *Music and Empire in Britain and India* particularly underlines the importance of the transnational linkage between the English folk song movement and the emergence of comparative musicology simultaneously in Britain and India. No doubt, some of the main protagonists of this book (Arnold Bake, Ananda Kentish Coomaraswamy, Arthur Henry Fox Strangways, Maud MacCarthy, and Rabindranath Tagore) were different from earlier Indian music researchers because in their writings and/or performances they asked for greater attention for Indian (folk) music from Indian and Western audiences. In this context, Arnold Bake too is presented as the pioneer in Indian ethnomusicology because of his knowledge of Indian (folk) music practice, extensive fieldwork, recordings, films, photographs, comparative writings on Indian music, and numerous lecture-recitals around the world.

All in all, I take music as a lens through which to examine societal and intellectual change, assuming that it is closely embedded in society and formative to its construction, negotiation, and transformation in terms of consensus and conflict. Indubitably, there is a deep-rooted connection between music and collective identity, whether national or international. Through music, people recognize identities and places, and the boundaries that separate them. Music may be local, marking the differences between national groups (as in the case of folk music as the spirit of that so-difficult-to-define concept "the nation"), or it may be universal, facilitating cross-cultural communication. One of my central assumptions is that members of the British and Indian musical elites simultaneously began to study their respective musical (folk) traditions in the context of processes of (national) identity seeking, and institution building. Obviously the book's subject is wide ranging and the essayistic chapters solely concentrate on a select number of individuals and themes that have preoccupied me during the last decade or so. What follows therefore is tentative rather than definitive and, to further this important topic, I hope that other researchers will take up personalities and ideas that I did not include.

National musical renaissance, folk music research, and empire

In Britain, the word "folk song"' was included in dictionaries only from the late nineteenth century onward.[10] As the founding father of the early twentieth-century English folk music revival, Cecil Sharp (1859–1924), put it: "The word folk song was added to the language when we had a use for it, and not before."[11] To a great extent, the English folk song movement had its origin in the nationalism and imperial rivalry of the so-called English musical renaissance. Though the next generation would track down the foreign sources of many

English folk songs, composers like Ralph Vaughan Williams (1872–1958) romantically sought their salvation in folk music to create a national music in opposition to centuries of Austro-German musical hegemony.[12] As he wrote in *National Music* (1934):

> Now what does this revival mean to the composer? It means that several of us found here in its simplest form the musical idiom which we unconsciously were cultivating in ourselves, it gave a point to our imagination; far from fettering us, it freed us from foreign influences which weighted on us, which we could not get rid of, but which we felt were not pointing in the direction in which we really wanted to go. The knowledge of our folk-songs did not so much discover for us something new, but uncovered for us something which had been hidden by foreign matter.[13]

Thus, as argued by Meirion Hughes and Robert Stradling in their controversial *The English Musical Renaissance 1840–1940: Constructing a National Music* (2001) and Jeffrey Richards in his pioneering *Imperialism and Music: Britain 1876–1953* (2001), the British elite constructed a national and imperial music that became hegemonic in the public domain through such institutions as the Royal Academy of Music, the Royal College of Music, the Novello music publishing company, *The Musical Times*, George Grove's *Dictionary of Music and Musicians*, Henry Wood's Promenade Concerts and the British Broadcasting Corporation (BBC), a private enterprise founded in 1922, which gained a monopoly on broadcasting after it was nationalized five years later.[14] During the more than 40 years that Charles Villiers Stanford taught composition at the flagship of English musical nationalism, the Royal College of Music, and Cambridge University, he educated nearly 200 composers who were crucial to the "English musical renaissance," including Vaughan Williams and Gustav Holst (1874–1934). Principally, these composers together produced an imperial musical idiom, which was meant for, and played at official occasions such as coronations, jubilees, exhibitions, tattoos, Armistice Day, and Empire Day, and generally had a great influence on British popular music (operettas, ballets, films, music halls, ballads, shanties, hymns and marches). A great number of them eventually also worked or toured as performers in imperial settlement colonies like Australia and South Africa.[15]

While the institutionalization and canonization of modern British music largely was the result of processes of national identity and state formation, recent research shows how in many ways something similar took place in British India, as Indians self-consciously defined themselves as modern musical subjects.[16] Comparable to what happened in Britain, Indian music reformers defined and institutionalized the national "classical" north-Indian (Hindustani) and south-Indian (Carnatic) music traditions in terms of (staff) notation, music schools, canonical composers and repertoire, concert arrangements, national music conferences, and so on. All this gave Indian music the respectability longed for by the often English-educated developing Indian middle classes, who generally looked down upon folk music from a Western evolutionary perspective, while they associated it with tribal and low-caste groups. Thus, despite the fact that Indian music most probably remains the cultural domain that was least influenced by Western thought, this book emphasizes that many aspects of the "classical" Indian music traditions were modernized, whereby the anti-imperial goals of its creators, ironically, often overlapped with those of the British civilizing mission. Because of these modernizing efforts, Indian music practice certainly experienced profound changes, which aesthetically perhaps remain best epitomized, as Walter Kaufmann did already made clear decades earlier, by the gradual decline in the use of microtonal alterations.[17] At the same time, of course, it should be emphasized that the "Indian musical renaissance" had a multiple intellectual lineage, incorporating Western ideas alongside, for example, a reinterpretation of the ancient *marga* ("classical") versus *desi* ("nonclassical") distinction in music.

Unquestionably, theories about the national and racial basis of culture as well as the evolutionary ideas of Vaughan Williams's greatuncle Charles Darwin and especially Herbert Spencer, who both wrote about the origins of music, were important to the mapping of the world with "folk music," which increasingly took place in the name of nationalism and a search for "authenticity."[18] In *The Evolution of the Art of Music* (1893), the prominent British composer of *Jerusalem* (1916)-fame,[19] Charles Hubert Parry, emphasized that the maturity of the music of different races depended "on the stage of each race's 'mental development.'"[20] According to this evolutionist scheme, contemporary Western classical music had developed from "primitive" music and of course was the highest stage to be reached. Parry's thoughts greatly influenced Cecil Sharp and, Parry's student at the Royal College of Music, Vaughan Williams. While writing about the evolution and racial origins of folk song, for example, they emphasized the distinction between "individual" classical music and "communal"/"racial" folk music.[21] In chorus, ironically in the face of their opposition to Austro-German musical hegemony, they propagated the use of "authentic" folk song in education to improve the English national spirit under the influence of such German thinkers as Johann Gottfried Herder and Georg Wilhelm Friedrich Hegel.[22] Then again, comparative musicologists in search of the origins of European music based their theories on evolutionary models such as that of the "contemporary ancestor," which assumed that the origins of music were to be found among non-Western musicians. As a result, both British folk song collectors and comparative musicologists increasingly analyzed "primitive" music through the so-called Greek modes.[23] Though these theories about the origins of music and "a universal folk scale" (pentatonic at first) already existed in some form or the other since the Enlightenment,[24] their meaning undeniably changed under the influence of late nineteenth-century evolutionism, for example, through ideas about evolving modal scales and the relationship between music and race, respectively.

Since 1877, the study of European folk music and non-Western music was boosted by Thomas Edison's invention of the phonograph, because it made it possible to listen to fieldwork recordings for transcription and analysis. From then onward, besides collections of instruments, photographs, and notations by the ear, two-to-four-minute samples of music on wax cylinders became part of the musicologist's stock-in-trade. Around the same time, comparative musicologists became gradually aware of the fact that non-Westerners had advanced musical practices and theories of their own. Here the role of the tone-deaf British physicist and phonetician Alexander John Ellis, who in Britain generally is known as the father of ethnomusicology, needs to be mentioned. In his article "On the Musical Scales of Various Nations" (1885), he challenged Western assumptions of natural tonal and harmonic laws, and indeed of cultural superiority, by arguing that musical scales were the product of cultural invention. In addition, musicologists increasingly began to contest evolutionary and racial models through the anthropological idea that the world consisted of a variety of different cultures: individual peoples with distinctive values, ways of life, modes of expression, and, indeed, music traditions. Charles Samuel Myers, who was also an eminent psychologist, was the first Briton to record non-Western music during his only significant music research trip: the famous Cambridge anthropological expedition to the Torres Strait, which lies between Northern Australia and New Guinea, in 1898–1899.[25] He never visited India but studied collections of cylinder recordings made in Ceylon by Charles and Brenda Seligman (1907–1908), and in South India by Edgar Thurston and K. Rangachari (ca. 1905). In his article "The Study of Primitive Music" (1912), Myers compared the recordings he made in the Torres Strait with the recordings of the Vedda people of Ceylon and developed a theory of "individual differences." As he wrote in the concluding paragraph: "Probably the Vedda and the Miriam [Torres Straits] songs represent (in two different forms!) the simplest primitive music that has hitherto been recorded."[26]

Musicologists such as Myers largely belonged to a much wider group of contrarians in metropolis and colony who more or less adhered to "primitivism." As Partha Mitter wrote in relation to primitivism in art:

Primitivism was not anti-modern; it was a critical form of modernity that affected the peripheries no less than the West. Primitivists did not deny the importance of technology in contemporary life; they simply refused to accept the teleological certainty of modernity.[27]

While the term "primitivism" overall designates the Romantic longing for the "innocence" of premodern existence, it simultaneously is replete with ambiguities and contradictions. In the West, the very flexibility of primitivism offered endless possibilities, including "going native" and a radical questioning, as in Percy Grainger's case, of Western civilization. Alternately, it allowed Indians certain modes of (anti-imperial) empowerment, though in doing so, as I will discuss in relation to Rabindranath Tagore, it simultaneously turned "the outward 'gaze' of the West" toward themselves. Finally, it is worth remembering that the primitivizing process had begun with imperial expansion. Anthropologists, artists, musicologists, and others created "the myth of the timeless 'noble savage,'" even as the colonial rulers suppressed tribals through "brutal counter-insurgency measures."[28]

Arthur Henry Fox Strangways, comparative musicology, and national "Hindu" music

Arthur Henry Fox Strangways (1859–1948), who shared ideas and advice with Myers, was another Briton who favored relativism and mutual respect in relation to non-Western music.[29] Most probably he remains the best-known British scholar of comparative musicology, and he is particularly important to this book because he played a role in the history of folk music research in Britain and India at the same time. Fox Strangways was part of the British music establishment. He was a prominent member of the Folk Song Society from 1908, a music critic for *The Times* (1911–1925) and *The Observer* (1925–1939), and the founder-editor of the journal *Music and Letters* for 17 years since 1920. Among his friends, he counted Cecil Sharp, of whom he wrote a biography together with Maud Karpeles, and Vaughan Williams, whose work and that of other English national composers he advocated. Simultaneously, however, Fox Strangways became fascinated with Indian music after reading a translation of the Sanskrit music theory treatise, *Sangit Darpan* (ca. 1625). He went to India in 1904 and more extensively in 1910–1911, partly also to visit his brother, who lived in Punjab for 31 years. He traveled throughout the subcontinent and made many wax-cylinder recordings. He stayed at the Santiniketan School, about a hundred miles northwest of Calcutta (now Kolkata), which in 1918 became Visva-Bharati (University) and was founded by Rabindranath Tagore, who in his eyes was the personification of Indian music "in its broadest sense."[30] In 1910, Fox Strangways was one of the founders of the India Society, London, which promoted

> the study and appreciation of Indian culture in its aesthetic aspects, believing that in Indian sculpture, architecture, and painting, as well as in Indian literature and music, there is a vast unexplored field, the investigation of which will bring about a better understanding of Indian ideals and aspirations, both in this country and in India.[31]

As the secretary of this society, he came into contact with a cosmopolitan circle of people with an interest in India, including the Ceylonese English art historian Ananda Kentish Coomaraswamy, who played a prominent role in the propagation of Indian art and music in the West, and to whom I will return later; the Indian art historian and educator Ernest Binfield Havell;[32] the painter William Rothenstein, who introduced Tagore and his work in Britain; and the Irish poet, dramatist, and Nobel Laureate William Butler Yeats. In fact, Fox Strangways acted as Tagore's unpaid literary agent and played a crucial role in securing him a lucrative contract with MacMillan for

Gitanjali (Song Offerings), the work that was first published by the India Society in 1912, and led to Rabindranath's sudden world fame after his winning of the Nobel Prize for literature in 1913. During the early 1930s, Arnold Bake also delivered a few lectures at the India Society, which were published in the society's journal *Indian Art and Letters*.[33]

Over the years, Fox Strangways published several articles on Indian music, including one for George Grove's *Dictionary of Music and Musicians*, which was later revised by Arnold Bake. Yet, he remains best remembered for his magnum opus *The Music of Hindostan* (1914), of which the India Society bought copies to distribute to its members. Besides a detailed analysis of *raga* (generalized melodic practice), *tala* (rhythmic cycle), and form in Indian music, this classic of Indian ethnomusicology includes a musical diary of his Indian sojourn. With its attention to devotional songs, street cries, beggars' songs, grinding songs, and so on, it remains the earliest large-scale engagement with Indian folk music, containing numerous music transcriptions in staff notation, including some of Tagore's songs, of which he strangely enough made no recordings. Unfortunately for this book, he did not make any reference to Sikh sacred music, though he stayed with his brother in Punjab for some time. Generally, Fox Strangways made comparisons between Indian and Western classical and folk compositions, sometimes in the light of their common Aryan background, which in hindsight are odd. He also envisaged an unbroken link between ancient Sanskrit music theories and contemporary Indian music practice and, in doing so, did not recognize that Hindustani music to a great extent was the result of the encounter between the existing Indian music traditions and Persian–Central Asian music. So he attempted to reconstruct the 22 microtonal divisions of the ancient Indian octave, known as *shrutis*. In fact, because the division of 22 *shrutis* over 7 tones in an octave presents a mathematical problem, *shruti* intonation ever since has been an imperial trope in the discussion between Western and Indian musicologists and musicians about the "difference" in Indian music.[34] Fox Strangways's contribution was that he replaced the idea of a conscious division of the octave into 22 parts with a theory "based on the simple division of a vibrating string length, resulting in a just scale."[35]

To a great extent, *The Music of Hindostan* was organized around trajectories of evolution and decay in music worldwide. Fox Strangways saw similarities between music-theoretical treatises of classical India and Greece. He argued that Indian music was based on the same intonational principles as ancient Greek music but that it had remained more genuine to its source than Western music, since the latter had adopted harmonization based upon equal temperament. Following the theory of the contemporary ancestor, he further emphasized that Indian (folk) music represented a living fossil that Westerners could use to reflect on their own music history:

> The study of Indian music is of interest to all who care for song, and of special interest to those who have studied the early stages of song in mediaeval Europe or ancient Greece. For here is the living language of which in those we have only dead examples. It is hardly possible in the case of modern European Folk-song to study melody pure and simple, for we have no large body of such song of which we can certainly say that it was not influenced at all by the current conception of harmony. But here is melody absolutely untouched by harmony, which has developed through many centuries tendencies which have the force of laws; and the examination of these enables us to some extent to separate the respective contributions of melody and harmony to the final effect in or own music.[36]

Likewise, he often referred to the Orientalist idea of an ancient Hindu Golden Age in music. As so many Western Orientalists and Indian musicians/music researchers since the late eighteenth century up to the present, he believed in the myth, for which the famous Orientalist William Jones (see later) was responsible,[37] that Indian "Hindu" music making was in a state of decline, while on the contrary it went through a period of profound change and was very much alive.[38] As he wrote in 1936:

> Hindu music, its mere time and tune, is a marvel of intricate detail, or was till this generation. An indifference, perhaps an unconscientiousness, has latterly come in with regard to detail: the modes, once reputed infinite, have dropped in practice to some dozens; the thirty-five kinds of time are reduced to a quarter of what they were.[39]

As to be expected against the background of these ideas, he paternalistically declared the Western harmonium to be a "serious menace to Indian music" because it undermined "authentic" music making.[40]

No doubt, Fox Strangways had a great deal of empathy for Indian music. Yet, he found it aesthetically different, mainly because of its "spirituality."[41] At the same time, he believed that it was equal and comparable to Western music, and that some day, after an understanding of it had been reached, there would emerge "an aesthetic which will show us what music is really doing in the world."[42] The point is that he more or less accepted the individuality of Indian (folk) music and aesthetics, and aimed to translate this for Western audiences. In doing so, he paved the way for Western musicologists such as his friend, Arnold Bake, who, together with his wife, temporarily lived in his London house during the early 1930s, when the two men worked together on a full translation of *Sangit Darpan*, as a follow-up of the Dutchman's PhD dissertation and first book, *Bijdrage tot de Kennis der Voor-Indische Muziek* (1930), of which the text is in English. In fact, in 1937, at one of Bake's lectures in London, perhaps because he was impressed by the Dutchman's knowledge of Indian music and culture, Fox Strangways self-critically looked back at his time in India and came to the conclusion that he had been "a mere globe-trotter," who "had to depend on whoever came, so to speak, and of course they were a very miscellaneous crew."[43]

While the preoccupation with Indian (folk) music of Fox Strangways and Bake largely should be seen against the background of the work of Cecil Sharp and the English folk song movement, they and other comparative musicologists interested in Indian music certainly were also aware of the questions brought up by the earlier research into the Hindustani and Carnatic music traditions and accordingly wrestled with them. In the case of Hindustani music, which remains central to this study, the main issues appeared mostly through the works of four key scholars: William Jones, N. Augustus Willard, Sourindro Mohun Tagore (1840–1914), and Vishnu Narayan Bhatkhande (1860–1936).[44] In the first English essay on Indian music, *On the Musical Modes of Hindus* (1792), which was often reprinted and fundamentally reconfigured the study of north-Indian music, William Jones not only portrayed the myth of Hindustani music being on the verge of extinction but, moreover, like many other Orientalists glorifying Sanskrit sources, directly connected this view with the loss of the "Hindu" music of a supposedly Golden Age. While in fact the majority of musicians in northern India were Muslim, he undeniably "was prejudiced and had little sympathy for Muslim scholarship."[45] In contrast, Willard, who was an Eurasian and played several

Indian instruments himself, has been repeatedly praised in histo-riography because, unlike Jones, he gathered the information for his *A Treatise on the Music of Hindoostan: Comprising a Detail of the Ancient Theory and Modern Practice* (1834) directly from Indian musi-cians rather than from ancient (Sanskrit) texts as was common at the time. At the same time, however, as Katherine Butler Schofield recently emphasized, he literally translated and paraphrased Indo-Persian treatises on music, and therefore perhaps can also be seen as "the last great Indo-Persian theorists of Indian music history."[46] In the footsteps of these two pioneering figures, then, Hindustani music was modernized by Indian music reformers, who set out to establish a "classical" tradition that was on par with that of Europe by demon-strating its rational, scientific status.

An elder relative of Rabindranath Tagore, Sourindro, was the first modern Indian musicologist. In 1871, he founded one of the first schools of Indian music in Calcutta. His *Universal History of Music* (1896) probably is the first history of "world music" written by a non-Westerner, and according to Martin Clayton its organization was influenced by Charles Hubert Parry's *The Evolution of the Art of Music*.[47] Tagore's anthology of eighteenth- and nineteenth-century literature about Indian music written in English, *Hindu Music from Various Authors* (1882), which also includes the earlier mentioned works by Jones and Willard, remains useful to this day. On the whole, Tagore was fundamental to the dialogue on music between Indian and Western writers on music, partly because he corresponded with many Western authors on music, including Alexander John Ellis, who for his "On the Musical Scales of Various Nations" mostly relied on Sourindro's publications.[48] At the same time, he was a Hindu nation-alist, who, like Jones and Willard, adopted the notion of Hindustani music being in a state of decay and dedicated his life to its revival. Around 20 years later, Vishnu Narayan Bhatkhande sought to revive and redefine "Hindu" music but simultaneously challenged the con-temporary orthodox idea that the practice and theory of Hindustani music could be directly traced to ancient and medieval music theory treatises.[49] He looked down upon the music practice of professional Muslim musicians but nonetheless believed that Hindustani music had benefitted from Muslim influence.[50] From 1916 onward, he organized a series of All India Music Conferences with the goal of preserving, promoting, and modernizing Hindustani music, which were attended by both Hindu and Muslim scholars and musicians.[51]

North-India's most famous music scholar became especially known, nonetheless, because of his *that* system of *raga* classification, which is based upon 12 semitones rather than the 22 *shrutis* and to this day remains the only standardized *raga* classification system. It found an outlet in the six volumes of his *Kramik Pustak Malika* (1919–1937), a collection of 1800 compositions gathered from various contemporary performers from different lineages. Through this standard reference work, which was many times reprinted, and other writings, his *raga* classification system and his notation system in syllabic script, which replaced all other existing systems, Bhatkhande ever since dominantly influenced the teaching and performance of Hindustani music in India and elsewhere.

All in all, as a result of the imperial encounter, Indian national music reformers mostly were concerned with "how that music had been in the past and how it should be in the future, rather than how it existed in the present."[52] Hence, their activities generally confronted the interests of the (largely Muslim) musicians of the traditional musical lineages, whom they attacked not only for "their so-called unsystematic pedagogy, but also for holding hostage, through their secrecy, music's national future."[53] Nonetheless, the traditional musicians coped with the modernizing attacks and, ever since, the uniqueness of Hindustani music "lies in the fact that with very few exceptions, and unlike other fields such as painting and art, the leading performers of Indian classical music are not trained in modern schools of music" but in the refashioned lineages (the so-called *gharanas*).[54] Even so, the number of Muslim musicians steadily declined because of the "Hindu" music politics of Tagore, Bhatkhande, and others, including Vishnu Digambar Paluskar (1872–1931),[55] and of course due to the partition of British India. As I will discuss in Chapter 5, the case of the Muslim musicians (*rababis*) within the tradition of Sikh sacred music also fits in this context. Unsurprisingly, the concept of "Hindu" music as a tool of self-agency for the Hindu elite also generally led to a negative evaluation of the Persian–Central Asian musical contributions to Hindustani music.

Internationalism: The Theosophical Movement, Indian nationalism, and music

To a great deal, this book concerns what today is labeled "transnational history" because of its involvement with cosmopolitan identities; the flow of people, musical instruments, and ideas between Britain and India, and the British Empire at large; the formation of international communities and organizations; and the ideology of internationalism, which went hand in hand with the rise of nationalism and imperialism. Rather than the concept "transnational history", however, I have chosen for the term "internationalism" (the doctrine that the common interests of nations are greater and more important than their differences) in the title, because its meaning, like that of "cosmopolitanism" (the ideology that one belongs to all parts of the world, free from national limitations or attachments), "developed concurrently with the ideas and movements discussed here."[56] Above all, I will highlight the ambiguities within the internationalist thoughts of Indian music reformers, British musical modernists, ethnomusicologists, and so on. This to underline that internationalism, despite its overall optimism toward the idea of social and intellectual progress, has "no absolute moral or political value," but, on the contrary, is a "floating category,"[57] which may be compatible with imperial politics and tropes, as well as with the left-wing and progressive, and indeed the "self-questioning" that since late nineteenth century became increasingly common among a great number of Western and non-Western writers, artists, and intellectuals. Also, it should be clear that internationalist values sometimes varied in metropolitan or colonial contexts, and internationalists often were highly critical about each other or themselves.

To different degrees, Arthur Henry Fox Strangways, Arnold Bake, Cyril Scott, Percy Grainger, Maud MacCarthy, and John Foulds interacted with a loosely linked network of Western internationalist writers, artists, musicians, and politicians such as Annie Besant, George Bernard Shaw, H. G. Wells, and W. B. Yeats, who found common ground with Rabindranath Tagore, Ananda Kentish Coomaraswamy, and similar Indians. Overall, internationalists lived and worked in, and drew inspiration from, more than one culture, Western and/or non-Western. Even if they did not know each other personally, they generally knew each other's work. Often they participated in countercultural activist groups like the India Society, the Theosophical Society, and the Arts and Crafts Movement, which were influential simultaneously in Britain and India. In particular, internationalism was a cultural priority among Westerners living in India, "who, neither sympathetic to the continuance of British colonial rule nor keen on seeing a violent takeover by extreme nationalists, favoured a more spiritual successor to the inevitable demise of empire."[58] Especially in the wake of the First World War, Western and Indian internationalists shared a common front against urban industrial capitalism, the ideology of progress, and sometimes even Western civilization at large. Many internationalists were Irish. Yeats, for instance, was a member of the Theosophical Society and later of the Hermetic Order of the Golden Dawn. He had a great interest in India and helped Tagore with his translation of *Gitanjali*, a collection of mostly songs set by the poet to music. In turn, Tagore found helpful correspondences for his own work in Irish literature and music, especially in its folk influences.[59]

Obviously, the Theosophical Society remains the most important internationalist movement to this book. This is, on the one hand, because Theosophical ideas, including those about music, had a decisive effect on Scott, MacCarthy and Foulds, and on the other, because Theosophists advanced Indian nationalist politics (Theosophist Allen Octave Hume was instrumental in organizing the first meetings of the Indian National Congress during the 1880s) and, more immediately, had some influence on the making of south-Indian national music and dance. The society was founded in 1875 in New York by Madame Helena Blavatsky and Henry Steel Olcott. It claimed to bring a new enlightenment based on the ancient wisdom of "spiritual" India. Mainly on the basis of Blavatsky's writings, often as expanded by later writers, and Orientalist interpretations of Buddhist and Hindu sources, Theosophists investigated the "spiritual" element in human beings and the world, so as to promote "universal brotherhood of man," irrespective of race, creed, color, or sex. Contradictorily, they leaned toward the unity of the Indo-European tradition (Aryanism) and overall followed an evolutionary, hierarchical, and racial worldview. They often advanced their ideas in a polarizing manner as being superior to Western rational science and, generally, as an international movement, had a role in the development of radical antiestablishment and anticolonial politics at once in metropoles and colonies. After being confronted with Western science and Christianity, Indian reformers and nationalists were especially attracted to the Theosophists because, unlike the missionaries, they judged British imperial rule negatively. On the contrary, they praised the Brahmanism of the Vedic age and reinterpreted it in scientific evolutionary terms.

In 1877, the Theosophical Society moved to India and established its headquarters in Adyar, near Madras (now Chennai). After the deaths of Blavatsky and Olcott, Annie Besant, who was born in London of Irish parents, became the society's president from 1907. Earlier, she was a close friend of the staunch socialist George Bernard Shaw and affiliated to the socialist-reformist Fabian Society, whose members in its early years were as interested in "spirituality" as in politics.[60] In 1890, however, she turned her back on the Fabians and, to the disgust of Shaw, joined the Theosophists. In India, Besant founded Central Hindu College (1898), which later became Benares Hindu University, learned Sanskrit, and made a scholarly translation of the *Bhagavad Gita* (1905). She became much involved in the revival and dissemination of the Hindu tradition, Indian social reform (female education in particular), and Indian nationalist politics. During the First World War, she modeled a Home Rule League on the Irish example and actually was elected president of the Indian National Congress in 1917. Indeed, since the *swadeshi* (own country) campaign, a Bengali equivalent of Ireland's Sinn Féin, which followed the British division of Bengal into a Hindu and a Muslim part in 1905, Indian elites increasingly established links with their Irish counterparts, investigating strategies of both parliamentary pressure and armed insurrection.

By and large, the Theosophist reading of a Hindu Golden Age, and especially the superior place therein of the Brahmin caste, worked as a catalyst in the definition of nationalist Carnatic music and dance by the Madras Brahmin elite, for whom these art forms came to represent the "authentic" and "spiritual" Hindu self.[61] What should be stressed in relation to the revivalism of these south-Indian arts, as well as Theosophical internationalism in general, is the critical role of two Theosophical couples: James and Margaret Cousins, and George and Rukmini Devi Arundale. At the expense of Besant, the Irish James and Margaret Cousins traveled to India in 1915. Both were internationalists, Theosophists, and well-known public figures in Ireland. Among other things, Margaret had founded the Irish Women's Franchise League and supported Irish independence. James was a writer, critic, and Irish nationalist, who published widely on Theosophy and was part of the Irish literary revival that included Yeats and James Joyce. As a follower of the Arts and Crafts Movement, he took up the cause of the Bengal School of *swadeshi* art and in general propagated Indian ideals in the fields of art, literature, and education. This was not so much to promote a mood of nationalism but because he believed that India, as the "mother of Asian culture," could provide an answer to the problems of the world. He became an avid supporter of Tagore and, as a committed Theosophist and internationalist, urged that the horrors of the World War demanded a model of world unity "expressive of spiritual oneness."[62] Even so, because of some passionate articles that he wrote in *New India* about the Easter Rising of 1916, mounted by Irish Republicans to end British rule in Ireland and establish the Irish Republic, he was not only dismissed by Besant but also closely monitored by the British authorities, "who regarded him as a subversive radical threatening to extend support to Indian insurgents."[63] Between 1917 and 1937, Margaret Cousins had a leading role in Indian feminism, whereby she followed a mystical internationalist vision for world womanhood. She became well known as a campaigner for women's rights and, in 1922, was appointed the first woman magistrate in the subcontinent. She organized the first All India Women's Conference (1927) and coordinated the All Asia Woman's Conference (1931) in Lahore, because she believed that the world and the West, especially, "needed a dose of the spirit of Asian womanhood to counter and heal an excessively masculinist, capitalist, Western world order."[64] She was convinced that the successes of her efforts to further the case of Indian women (suffrage, schools, and so on) were the effect of the "time spirit," which Indian women manifested.[65]

Yet, besides being a reformer and politician, Margaret was also a musician, who studied at the Royal Irish Academy of Music in Dublin and graduated in 1902 with a Bachelor of Music from the Royal University of Ireland. In 1918, when Tagore spent a few days at Besant Theosophical College (1915) in Madanapalle,[66] of which James Cousins was the principal, he wrote down the English translation of *Jana Gana Mana* (since 1950 the national anthem of India) and together with Margaret made a setting to music that is followed till this day. In 1920, when the maharaja of Mysore, Nalvadi Krishnaraja Wodeyar, the greatest patron of (Western) music in south-India, organized a concert for the celebration of Ludwig van Beethoven's centenary in Bangalore, Margaret played a Beethoven Piano Concerto with the Palace Orchestra.[67] In her *Music of the Orient and the Occident: Essays Towards Mutual Understanding* (1935) and other writings, she emphasized that Indian music had reached a much higher level of development than European music, partially because of its "spirituality." On the whole, she played a role in the institutionalization, modernization, and teaching of Carnatic music. In 1917, in response to the movement for national education, which included among its members Besant and Tagore, a National University was set up in Madras, with Tagore as chancellor. Together with members of the Madras Brahmin elite, Cousins established a music curriculum. She not only emphasized the significance of music notation to spread "scientific" music but also underlined the value of music for the "spiritual" revival of the Indian nation. In 1933, she was particularly proud when the first woman graduate in music came out of the University of Madras.

While Margaret Cousins saw Indian music as a "spiritual" vehicle for national regeneration, other Theosophists like Besant were far more exotic in their understanding of (Indian) music as they explicitly came up with theories that related the medium to the Pythagorean concept of "the music of the spheres," which followed the idea that the planets and stars moved according to mathematical equations that corresponded in musical vibrations on earth.[68] In a lecture about the relationship between religion and music, delivered in Madras in 1908, Besant specifically connected musical vibrations to "the occult power of sound" and the creation of a higher consciousness.[69] Interesting to mention, especially because of the typical esoteric idiom of the program note, is *A Yoga in Sound* (1938) composed for piano by George Arundale, who in 1934 became the third president of the Theosophical Society (Margaret Cousins, in fact, described Indian music as "an instrument of yoga"). Arundale wrote that he composed the piece, which was published by the Theosophical Society in Adyar, as an individual way to bridge the gulf between the inner and outer worlds, whereby some material was supplied by the *devas*.[70] With the opening of the G-octave tremolos, he interpreted the cosmic thunder-sounds that permeate all life and "constitute the Damru roll so wonderfully depicted in the ancient Hindu scriptures." Halfway through the piece, then, he used the notes of *deva* invocation and music generally (E and Bes). The *devas*, in response, built a bridge in music signified by a "Chord of Fulfilment" (Fis, Fis, Ais, Cis, and Fis) to enable the yoga force to flow and make Union (figure I.1). I mention the esoteric concepts of "the music of the spheres," "the occult power of sound," and *deva* music here because, together with other Theosophical notions, they eventually influenced Scott, Foulds, and other British modernist composers.

Conversely, the Theosophical movement influenced the remaking of the south-Indian dancing style, Bharatanatyam, into a national "classical" Indian dance. In 1917, Arundale, who earlier had been

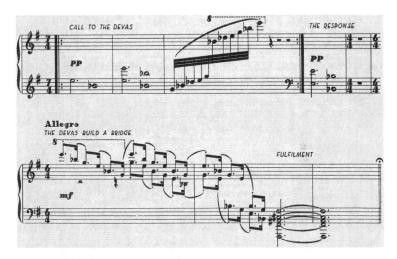

Figure I.1 George Arundale, *A Yoga in Sound*, 1938, communication with the *devas* (Courtesy Theosophical Publishing House).

the principal of Central Hindu College in Benares, was appointed as the principal of the training college for teachers of the National University in Madras. Alongside Besant, he was interned in that same year for his involvement in the Home Rule League. In 1920, he married the 26-year-younger Theosophist, dancer, and choreographer Rukmini Devi, who was "the first Brahmin woman to perform dance in modern South Asian history" and who became the most important revivalist of Bharatanatyam.[71] The Arundales were acquainted with the Cousins and as two increasingly influential Theosophists traveled all over the world. In 1936, the couple established Kalakshetra (*kshetra*, womb or place, of *kala*, arts) at Adyar, as a cultural academy for the preservation of "authentic" and "spiritual" Indian music and dance. With the continuous support of her husband, Rukmini Devi advocated the cause of Bharatanatyam, besides that of female reform and Indian culture and freedom at large. After initial protests from the Brahmin orthodoxy against its performances on stage, she appropriated the dance from the devadasi (temple dance) community to which it had been confined for many centuries. In line with the British civilizing mission, she removed the erotic elements from the dance and transformed it into a puritanical art form. As a modernizer, she introduced new combinations of musical instruments, set and lighting design elements, and customs and jewelry inspired by temple sculptures. In congruence with the Victorian idea of the "sensitive" and "intuitive" female spirit, Rukmini Devi emphasized the special relationship between women and the fine arts. As a result, a new kind of female dancer emerged: one who was "an individual interpreter, rather than merely a hereditary practitioner of the art."[72] Moreover, in the Indian independence movement and then in the nation-building project of "integration" that followed the partition, many Indians came to see Bharatanatyam as the country's national "classical" dance. As part of this very same process, Nataraja (*raja*, king, of *natanam*, of dance), the primarily south-Indian appearance of the Hindu god Shiva as "cosmic dancer" became "the central icon and master metaphor for the revival of dance and, arguably, for the Indian nationalist movement as a whole."[73] In fact, central to this re-sanctification of a recently secularized dance and the overall popularization of Nataraj as "the symbol of the synthetic grandeur of ancient (specifically Hindu) Indian art, science, and religion" was Ananda Coomaraswamy's *The Dance of Shiva* (1928).[74]

All in all, the Theosophical Society was a self-conscious and well-organized internationalist movement that strengthened Indian nationalism (in music) through its solidarity, as Theosophists confirmed the growing self-confidence of the colonized in terms of the imperial trope of Eastern "spirituality" versus Western materiality. Otherwise, the society's mutual influence on Indian and Irish politics, as in the cases of Besant and the Cousins, remains an intriguing example of what Elleke Boehmer labeled "resistance in interaction," that is, "the development of national selfhood *in the context of* inter-relationship."[75] Ironically, however, while Theosophy in the West emerged as an antiestablishment movement, opposed to Christianity in particular, over time the movement defended orthodox revivalism in both India and Ireland, and, in the case of James Cousins, who eventually became a Hindu, even advanced Aryan Indo-Irish analogies.[76]

Two Indian internationalists: Ananda Kentish Coomaraswamy and Rabindranath Tagore

These are the days of nation building. Yet how many "nationalists" are in truth "denationalists" in their lives and aspirations! They want to be "free," to compete with Europe on her own lines,

to be "progressive," "advanced," to gain political power and material success. It is not with these that the future of India lies. It lies
in the lives of those who are truly Indian at heart, [...] who believe
that India still is (and not merely may be, when duly "educated")
the light of the World, who today judge all things by Indian standards, and in whom is manifest the work of the shapers of India
from the beginning until now.

> (Ananda Kentish Coomaraswamy,
> *Essays in National Idealism*, 1909).[77]

What irony of fate is this that I should be preaching co-operation
of cultures between East and West on this side of the sea just at the
moment when the doctrine of non-co-operation is preached on
the other side?

> (Rabindranath Tagore, Letter to C.F. Andrews,
> Chicago, March 5, 1921)[78]

The two famous early twentieth-century Indian internationalists
Rabindranath Tagore and, his friend and admirer, Ananda Kentish
Coomaraswamy (1877–1947) remain crucial to this book because
they both had a stake in the development and propagation of
Indian music, and to some extent they were influenced in this by
the English folk song movement. Though I will examine Tagore's
own Bengali songs, which he felt formed the essence of his being
and the internationalist in him wanted to be known to the world, in
Chapter 4, I will discuss Coomaraswamy's ideas about Indian (folk)
music here, as they directly relate to some of the main issues that
preoccupied proto-ethnomusicologists like Fox Strangways, Bake,
MacCarthy, and Foulds, as well as Hindustani music reformers such
as Sourindro Mohun Tagore, Bhatkhande, Paluskar, and, indeed,
Rabindranath. In addition, Coomaraswamy and Tagore are interesting figures because, as internationalists, they tried to formulate
alternative versions of Indian nationalism, and their cases show that
the history of nationalism cannot be characterized "as merely the
story of unitary, oppositional ideologies competing with universalism" but it must also acknowledge a cosmopolitanism that repeatedly surfaced.[79] This cosmopolitan moment not only demonstrates
"the complex, multidirectional, and hybrid nature of imperialism,"
but, ironically, also shows how the increasing imperial interaction between metropolis and colony led to "a way of thinking that

challenged imperialism more fundamentally than any other nationalist ideology."[80]

Coomaraswamy had associations with the Arts and Crafts Movement, the India Society (he befriended Fox Strangways, Havell, and Rothenstein), as well as Annie Besant and other Theosophists. Like Havell before him, his attention gradually shifted from Indian "arts and crafts" towards "an overriding concern with Hindu India's classical heritage in the arts—a concern both to demonstrate the existence of an ancient, sophisticated heritage based on ideals of Vedanta and yoga and to revive that heritage in the present day."[81] Through his writings and as curator of Indian art in the Museum of Fine Arts in Boston (1917–1947), he played an important role in bringing Asian art, including that of Tagore, to the West. What is commonly neglected, however, is that he was one of the few at the time who tried to explain Indian music to Western audiences and was influenced by the work of Cecil Sharp. He also provided some illustrations for Fox Strangways's *The Music of Hindostan* and commented upon the proofs of the first two chapters. Like Fox Strangways, Coomaraswamy compared Indian music with its Western counterpart but ultimately saw it as distinct because of its "spirituality." Similarly, he advanced the imperial trope of India as Britain's contemporary ancestor in music. As he wrote in *The Dance of Shiva* (1928), Indian music was part of

> the still surviving consciousness of the ancient world, with a range of emotional experience rarely accessible to those who are preoccupied with the activities of over-production, and intimidated by the economic insecurity of a social order based on competition.[82]

In the idiom of comparative musicology, he even argued that south-Indian music was "more akin to ancient Greek music than any other music remaining in the world."[83]

Naturally Coomaraswamy was more defensive about and in search of "authentic" national Indian music than Fox Strangways. For him, Indian music was bound up with national culture in countless ways. Unlike Indian national music reformers, however, he never made a distinction between "art music" and "folk music."[84] Inspired by Sharp, he wrote: "The folk music of the people is still everywhere to be heard, and it is only in a living relation to this that a national school of music can be preserved."[85] Interestingly, he argued that a similar "spiritual" search lay underneath the English folk song movement:

Whatever may be gained by possible combination in the future developments of Indian music, the necessity for this intensely personal and rhapsodical singing—so perfect and so natural an expression of the Indian mind—cannot pass away. It were well indeed if room could be found in the West, which, with all its magnificent choral and orchestral developments, lacks this lyrical and intensely personal and religious element, for individual expression of the same kind. *To some extent, no doubt, the revival of folk-song in England is due to a sense of this need at the present time.*[86]

Just like other Indian national music reformers, Coomaraswamy too believed that Indian music was central to the making of a progressive independent India and, similar to what Sharp and others propagated in England, he found that music education programs had to be developed.[87] This was all the more so because music education was neglected by both the British and the Indian elite, including the enlightened maharajas. He opposed the use of the piano and the harmonium because these instruments afforded the undisciplined and untrained mind the possibility to attempt the work of the true national musician with "the highest ideals of the race consciousness."[88] In 1907, he was particularly irritated when he found out during a visit to the Gandharva Mahavidyalaya in Lahore, the music college established in 1901 by Paluskar for the "revival of ancient Hindu music and its diffusion among the general public," that the majority of its students studied the harmonium because "in three months you can play a tune on it, and earn money at weddings and other entertainments."[89] Simultaneously, Coomaraswamy was a musical modernizer, who quoted MacCarthy, saying that "harmonization, if possible, with due regard to the preservation of the mode, will similarly add to the resources of the Indian musician."[90] In addition, he found that the gramophone, instead of being "an interpreter of human emotion," was useful as a "scientific" instrument for "the recording of songs," "the analysis of music for theoretical purposes," and "the exact study of an elaborate melody."[91]

Coomaraswamy's interest in Indian music was strengthened by his second wife, Alice Richardson, a student of Cecil Sharp, whom he had met at a concert in London in 1910. The following year, the newly married couple lived for a while on a houseboat in Srinagar, Kashmir. There, Alice studied daily for ten weeks under a traditional Muslim teacher (*ustad*), Abdul Rahim, who was employed as a singer at the

Figure I.2   Ratan Devi, undated (Courtesy of the Library of Congress).

Punjabi princely state of Kapurthala. Subsequently, she acquired some fame as a singer of Indian music under the stage name of Ratan Devi (figure I.2) and transcribed and published 30 songs that she had learned from Rahim in *Thirty Songs from the Panjab and Kashmir* (1913), which also included a foreword by Tagore and an introduction by Coomaraswamy. According to Fox Strangways, the book gave "a better idea of the [Indian] song as a whole than any other collection."[92] When Ratan Devi toured Britain and the United States during the following years, her performances, which of course were always in Indian dress to add "authenticity," were praised by many, including Shaw, Tagore, Yeats, and, indeed, Percy Grainger (see Chapter 2). During these concerts, Coomaraswamy explained the character and basic structure of Indian music to Western audiences, whereby he typically emphasized that Indian singing was "not an entertainment but a magical ceremony," and the singer's art was "not one of self-expression, but the means through which a god or goddess influences humanity."[93] Also he argued that Kashmiri folk songs had "certain characteristics in common with European folk songs."[94] Most likely because of Ratan Devi's influence, Coomaraswamy became more liberal and, indeed, critical in his ideas about Indian music. So, despite his overall emphasis on the creation of "Hindu" music and art, he had no problems with the fact that Abdul Rahim, who like most Punjabi Muslims was a descendant of a forcibly converted Hindu, had as much faith in Hindu gods as in Islam and sang with equal earnestness of Krishna and Allah, "exemplifying the complete fusion of Hindu and Muslem [Muslim] tradition characteristic of so many parts of northern India today."[95] He supported his wife's notations of Indian folk music, though he had earlier argued that Indian music could not be written down in staff notation but, to be authentic, had to be transmitted orally from master to pupil.[96] Like Ratan Devi, he was paternalistically critical of Indian "voice production."[97]

Though Coomaraswamy became a staunch defender of "Hindu" culture and music, he definitely too was an internationalist, who struggled with the issues that concerned him on a world scale. As he wrote in *Essays in National Idealism*:

> Nationalism is inseparable from the idea of Internationalism, recognizing the rights and worth of other nations to be even as one's own. For Britain we cannot speak; but for ourselves, the ideal is that of Nationalism and Internationalism. We feel that loyalty for us consists in loyalty to the idea of an Indian nation, politically, economically and intellectually free; that is, we believe in India for Indians; but if we do so, it is not merely because we want our own India for ourselves, but because we believe that every nation has its own part to play in the long tale of human progress, and that nations, which are not free to develop their own individuality and own character, are also unable to make the contribution to the sum of human culture which the world has a right to expect of them.[98]

Simultaneously, he argued: "It is not so much the material, as the moral and spiritual subjection of Indian civilization that in the end impoverishes humanity."[99] Over the years, however, Coomaraswamy increasingly countered the Western concept of history, oriented toward change and progress, with the ideas of Indian traditionality and perennial philosophy. In his review of Sarvepalli Radhakrishnan's *Eastern Religions and Western Thought* (1939), he distanced himself from any efforts at "pacification" in the relationship between East and West and stated the incompatibility of the Hindu tradition with Western thinking:

> The East [...] has still preserved and is still conscious of the metaphysical bases of its life, while the modern West is almost completely ignorant of the traditional metaphysics [...] and is at the same time actively and consciously anti-traditional.[100]

Ultimately, Coomaraswamy denied Western thought any true metaphysical consciousness and dismissed Western scholars as mere fact collectors, ignorant of underlying principles.[101] In his view, Eastern societies were organized to facilitate "spiritual freedom," whereas Western societies obstructed any serious commitment outside the facts of science. Instead of striving for a connection to the West, he argued, India should insist on traditionality, not only for its own sake, but also in the interest of the West. Thus, opposed to the inclusion of Indian art, culture, and society in a supposedly universal process of civilization, he promoted a sense of "eternal" human existence lying beyond the concept of progress.

As is well known, Tagore initially was sympathetic toward Indian nationalists but, over time, similar to Coomaraswamy, he came to believe that they were themselves agents of Westernization, who based their striving for a powerful Indian nation-state on a historical experience that was not their own.[102] Unlike Indian revolutionaries, for whom internationalism was a complete anathema, "a more refined term to prolong the evils of colonialism indefinitely under the guise of a universal humanism,"[103] he found that cultural autonomy was infinitely preferable to political independence. He was much disillusioned with the growing extremism among Indian nationalists during the *swadeshi* movement. When he afterward took a quietist stance toward nationalist politics, his compatriots accused him of apostasy. Following his lecture tour to Japan and United States in

1916–1917, during which he specifically preached against the evils of nationalism, he published his *Nationalism* (1917), which "marked the beginning of a wide-ranging engagement with the question of how different countries and civilizations should relate to one another."[104]

Tagore detested competition with the West: nationalism had to contribute positively to resolve problems worldwide rather than those of a single nation. The "spiritual" East was the necessary complement of the "materialistic" West; nothing was exclusively Western or Eastern anymore. In the view of the universal connectedness of things, he believed that the West had to understand that "the East has her contribution to make to the history of civilization,"[105] especially because the West had missed its own historicizing mission and had brought slavery instead of the envisioned freedom.[106] The future therefore, Tagore emphasized, was "for those who are rich in moral ideals and not in mere things."[107] Instead, he envisaged a scheme of things in which the best and the greatest thoughts and achievements of both the East and the West be offered to the welfare of humanity. It was in this mind-set also that he set up his center for the study of humanity, Visva-Bharati, which may be translated as "India in the World" or alternately as "The World in India." Its Memorandum of Association described its objectives as the bringing together of "thinkers and scholars of both Eastern and Western countries, free from all antagonisms of race, nationality, creed or caste" and the realization "in a common fellowship of study [of] the meeting of East and West." On the whole, Tagore was in search of an alternative nationalism, one that was nonparochial and inclusive. To achieve a balance between the universal and the particular, he chose the difficult middle-path of "neither the colourless vagueness of [universalist] cosmopolitanism, nor the fierce self-idolatry of nation-worship."[108] In his mind, citizens should be united in the nation but with all differences maintained. According to Louise Blakeney Williams, Tagore followed a "cosmopolitan nationalism,"[109] whereby, perhaps under the influence of traditional Indian thinking about the past, a more or less cyclical rather than a progressive view of history helped him "to transcend Western antithetical thinking and anticolonial nationalism."[110] It would incorporate many opposites because he saw "no difference between the best ages of the past and present, East and West" and "no reason why a balance could not be achieved between the modern and the traditional, foreign and native, religion and science, elites and masses, and local and national governments."[111] Ideally, real freedom would be achieved in colony and metropolis alike, as Tagore wrote to Mahatma Gandhi, when India could "prove that she is morally superior to the people who rule her by their right of conquest."[112] Independence, then, would come naturally because Indians could meet the English as their equals, and "all reason for antagonism, and with it all conflict [would] disappear."[113] His ultimate goal was "unity in diversity," whereby people would be unified into one but be allowed to maintain their differences.

Both Coomaraswamy and Tagore referred to the imperial trope of "spiritual" India, as they were conscious of the fact that "the history and contemporary politics of the world became a moral drama in which India had to compete."[114] Their internationalisms nonetheless differed remarkably. Over time, Coomaraswamy became disappointed in Tagore. As his biographer Roger Lipsey wrote: "He thought that the poet did not continue to grow after a certain time, that his literary works were always beautiful, but did not come from a person still in evolution."[115] In comparison to Coomaraswamy, Tagore certainly always remained more ambiguous in his ideas and kept more options open. After all, rather than a systematic political thinker, he was a poet, who solely articulated some of the concerns that existed among politically involved Indians at the time. His interests and sympathies were normally directed to the universal rather than the parochial. Throughout his life, he showed a consistent effort to reconcile East and West, to discover and elaborate common ground, and to intensify toleration and appreciation on both sides of the cultural fence. In contrast, Coomaraswamy's internationalism was narrower and tended to be strongly, even aggressively, traditional. As a perennial philosopher, he argued that the Hindu tradition contained only sublime truths and an irreproachable way of life clumsily distorted by "the modern scholar, whether Western or Westernized, in his profane ignorance [...]."[116] For him, cultural synthesis and the ideal of universal religion simply were no more than naïve capitulations to the Western tradition instead of the Hindu tradition. It was more or less this worldview that eventually attracted Western internationalists, such as James Cousins, MacCarthy, and the French Indologist, musicologist, and Theosophist Alain Daniélou. Indeed, so much so that these Indophiles decided to become Hindus.

I particularly mention Fox Strangways, Margaret Cousins, Coomaraswamy, Ratan Devi, and Tagore because of the interconnectedness between their internationalism and Indian (folk) music research.

To different degrees, their cases make clear both the influence of the English folk song movement on the early history of Indian ethnomusicology as well as the cosmopolitan relationship between British counterculture and Indian (inter) nationalism, especially through the agency of the Theosophical Society, which to some extent also affected the construction of Indian music and dance and its reception in the West as ineradicably "spiritual." Further, among other things, this book shows how the imperial encounter led to certain dominant ideas about Indian music practice. Since the late nineteenth century, some Westerners and a smaller amount of Indians, for instance, saw Western and Indian music as being related through the prisms of evolutionism and Aryanism. In addition, both Westerners and Indians perceived Indian music as "different" because of its *shrutis*, "spirituality," lack of harmony, improvisation, and so on. Consequently, Western modernist composers like John Foulds and comparative musicologists became fascinated with Indian music as part of an imperial counterculture. At the same time, partially in reaction to Western Orientalist writings about Indian music, Indians reempowered some traditional musical concepts. For example, ideas about *shruti* intonation and the relationship between *raga* and mood (*rasa*) as well as the time of the day (*samay*) often gained more authority than before because these were rationalized in the processes of redefinition, institutionalization, and canonization of Indian "classical" music.

All in all, *Music and Empire in Britain and India* investigates how through these dominant musical concepts, meaningful music practices were created that positioned India and the West in relation to each other and that therefore should be seen as imperial rather than properly Western or Indian. In doing so, to be clear, I not only trust Indian agency in the formation of modern Indian music during the imperial encounter but likewise resist the tendency "to read domination and subsumption into any and all musical appropriation" and rather see the musical results as genuine syncretic forms.[117] Though musical boundaries were defined in this intriguing and complicated process, I generally emphasize the intellectual interaction and cross-cultural communication between metropolis and colony. Thus, for example, Western modernist composers in search of an alternative to the existing dominant imperial culture reinvigorated their music tradition by appropriating (ideas about) Indian music. On the other hand, Indians underlined the "difference" between the Hindustani/ Carnatic music traditions and Western music, but simultaneously adhered to Western rational (scientific) ideas about the organization and practice of music. Also Western instruments like the harmonium, violin, and saxophone were transformed into "Indian" instruments. The involvement of Western internationalists and comparative musicologists with "authentic" Indian (folk) music further strengthened Indian "difference" in music. Ultimately, by looking at the meaning and life of some influential musical ideas that were enabled, materially and ideologically, by empire in Britain and India at the same time, this book intends to break down the simple dichotomy between metropolis and colony and contribute to the emerging field of "global intellectual history."[118] Indeed, more than any other subject perhaps, music provides historians and (ethno) musicologists great possibilities to arrive at a better understanding of the imperial encounter in terms of "the interaction between the power of ideas in their own right, on the one hand, and history, tradition and embodied experience, on the other."[119]

Outline of contents

Geographically, this book moves from Britain to India, with an in-between escapade to the imperial settlement colonies through the experiences of the Australian American Percy Grainger. The first three chapters concern the life and work of Cyril Scott, Percy Grainger, and the couple Maud MacCarthy and John Foulds. For different reasons, they all became outsiders to the British music establishment. Their intricate and distinct "imperialisms" show the existence of an alternative ideological cluster of ideas that equally existed in imperial Britain and included for example, internationalism, pacifism, and, indeed, comparative musicological research, as well as postures against empire, Christianity, capitalism, urbanization, and institutionalism. In general, my explorations into their worlds aim to contribute to the discussion about the extent to which British culture was "steeped in empire."[120]

Chapter 1 looks at the impact of Theosophical "spirituality," Indian philosophy, and Orientalism in music on Cyril Scott, who never traveled to the East. During the early decades of the twentieth century, he was known as "the father of modern British music" and was a commercially successful composer. Besides his musical modernism and cosmopolitan radicalism, his exotic interests contributed to the fact that he never belonged to the British music orthodoxy and, indeed, became increasingly reclusive. In addition, Scott was a prolific writer on a wide range of topics and in the chapter, I will particularly take a close look at his two main books on music: *The Philosophy of Modernism: Its Connection to Music* (1917) and *Music: Its Secret Influence Throughout the Ages* (1933). In Chapter 2, I come to the renowned pianist and composer Percy Grainger, who was a prime figure in the English folk song movement and a proto-ethnomusicologist. Like his longtime friend Scott, he never became a member of the British music establishment, partially because of his radical and sometimes anti-imperial ideas. Unlike Cyril, however, he traveled widely through the empire and accordingly the chapter highlights one of the book's central underlying ideas, namely the relationship between European folk music research and comparative musicological research, through a survey of his studies into non-Western music. Alternately, Grainger's primitivism (which he translated in his compositions), racialism/racism (which was common at the time, for example, also among Theosophists), and admiration for Rudyard Kipling's poems shows a different Western internationalism from that of Scott, Foulds, and others. Chapter 3 discusses the life and work of Maud MacCarthy and John Foulds, in particular their Theosophical "spirituality," Indian (folk) music research, and modernist aesthetics. Similar to Scott and Grainger, they too became outsiders to the British music establishment after initial successes in Britain. But, unlike them, they gained theoretical and practical knowledge of Indian (folk) music and eventually also fled to the subcontinent. Specific attention will be given to Foulds's "Indian" compositions, which he created under the influence of his wife, who abandoned her early career as a violinist and traveled the subcontinent for two years to study Indian (folk) music. In addition, I will discuss Foulds's intriguing book on music, *Music To-day: Its Heritage from the Past, and Legacy for the Future* (1934), in which he propagated ideas that to a remarkable extent overlapped with those Scott dealt with in above-mentioned books and that certainly are different from those propagated in the writings of, for example, Vaughan Williams or Edward Elgar (1857–1934).[121]

The focus of the next two "Indian" chapters is on two specific regional genres of north-Indian music that strictly do not fall within the "classical" Hindustani tradition: Bengali *Rabindra Sangit* and Punjabi Sikh sacred music (*kirtan*). So far, the study of these two genres has been neglected because they are concerned with songs rather than extended improvisational music and therefore were seen as uninteresting. Also, of course, Sikh sacred music remains community-bounded music. As in the case of the previous three chapters, the "Indian" chapters therefore concern fringe subjects. The point however is that *Rabindra Sangit* and Sikh *kirtan*, as extreme examples of imperial knowledge formation in terms of "modernist" and "traditional" Indian music making, respectively, show more clearly than in the cases of the "classical" Hindustani and Carnatic music traditions some of the issues involved in the relationship between Indian music and empire, particularly those related to music institutionalization and identity formation. While *Rabindra Sangit* became a crucial identity marker for Bengalis after Tagore's death, *kirtan* lies at the heart of the Sikh tradition. In fact, the Sikh sacred scripture, the Guru Granth Sahib, is the largest collection of sacred hymns in the world and the singing of and listening to *kirtan* is central to community gatherings. Explicitly, the two chapters look at the dilemmas involved in the contemporary discussions around these two genres against the background of the enduring influence of the imperial encounter. Furthermore, Chapter 4 looks into the relationship between Arnold Bake and Rabindranath Tagore in terms of internationalism, cross-cultural communication, and primitivism. Bake learned to sing Bengali folk songs (and Tagore's songs in particular) and successfully performed these around the world. Both he and Rabindranath were dedicated to Indian folk music and "village India," but, at the same time, partially because of Tagore's dedication to internationalism, they had different views on the "authenticity" of Indian folk music. Chapter 5 focuses even more than in the case of Tagore's songs on such issues as "authenticity" in music, the relationships between music and words as well as music and identity politics because, rather than with an "invented tradition," it deals with the real tradition of Sikhism. Approximately, Sikh *kirtan* lies between Hindustani "classical" and folk music but, as part of the so-called Singh Sabha reformation (ca. 1880–1920), it followed an intellectual trajectory of "classicization" that was relatively similar to what Indian national music reformers propagated within the Hindustani and Carnatic traditions. Besides that I discuss the influence of Western Orientalism, Indian musicological research, (staff-) notation, princely patronage, and the introduction of the harmonium in the definition of modern *kirtan*. I especially investigate the relationship between Sikh identity politics and the idea of "authentic" performance against the background of historical change and aesthetics. Finally, in the *Coda*, I reiterate some of the book's most important themes and explore how the imperial sound exercise still continues in these times of "world music."

1
Cyril Scott: "The Father of Modern British Music" and the Occult

Cyril Scott versus the British music establishment

> It is to those who find orthodox religious creeds too illogical or sentimental, and materialism too unsatisfactory and negative, that occult philosophy will prove acceptable, for it renders life vastly more interesting, more intriguing and more romantic. It shows cosmic life to be other than that mechanical "order of things" which the materialist postulates, and it shows personal life as the "adventure magnificent" which does not merely begin with the cradle and end with the grave. Furthermore, it shows the *raison d'être* for all religions worthy of the name, for cults, movements, philosophies, arts and sciences, their evolution and various phases. It explains the apparently unexplainable without making impossible demands upon faith, advocating *reason* as the most reliable stepping-stone to knowledge.
>
> (Cyril Scott, *An Outline of Modern Occultism*, 1935)[1]

Cyril Scott showed early musical talent and, in 1891, at the age of 12, his fairly wealthy parents sent him to the Hoch Conservatory in Frankfurt, Germany, where he studied for 18 months and during a second stint from 1895 to 1898. He became known as a member of the so-called Frankfurt Group of five British composers, including Percy Grainger and Roger Quilter (figure 1.1), who "stood apart in outlook and education from the mainstream of the conservative British musical establishment,"[2] though they were united, not so much by a common musicality, as by a common dislike of the music of Ludwig van Beethoven. All of them were interested in pre-Raphaelite art, which

Figure 1.1   Percy Grainger, Cyril Scott, and Roger Quilter, Harrogate, 1929
(Courtesy of the Percy Grainger Museum, University of Melbourne).

often had Orientalist overtones, and the work of William Morris, the
spiritual leader of the Arts and Crafts Movement. Scott introduced
the others to the work of the Belgian Symbolist and philosopher
Maurice Maeterlinck, whose play *Palléas et Mélisande* (1892) inspired
composers throughout Western Europe, among whom were Claude
Debussy in 1902, Arnold Schoenberg in 1903, and, indeed, earlier in
1900, Scott himself. Also, he made them familiar with the work of
the German poet Stefan George, with whom he had become friends
in Frankfurt (he actually translated a volume of George's poetry into
English in 1910 and wrote a book in German on his life and work in
1952). According to J. W. Burrow, George's world touched, on the one
hand, "the esoteric, ineffable mysteries of the French-bred aesthetics

of the Symbolist movement in poetry and drama" and, on the other, "the more down-to-earth German world of Ariosophic occultism,"[3] being a fusion of Theosophy, including the notion of an ancient Aryan wisdom, and German folklore and mythology.

After his return to Britain, Scott established a considerable name for himself as a virtuosic pianist and modernist composer. In particular, his *First Piano Sonata* (1909), which Grainger ardently performed until the 1950s, was innovative because his attempt to use multi-metricism consistently demonstrated "a rhythmic freedom never seen before in any piano sonata."[4] Among others, he was admired by his friend George Bernard Shaw and Edward Elgar, who was seen by the national music orthodoxy as the quintessential English composer, although there is still much debate about his "imperialism."[5] Generally, Scott became known as "the English Debussy." His friend Eugene Goossens, the famous conductor and composer, even hailed "this exotic personality and lovable but aloof man,"[6] "the father of modern British music." In 1904, Scott signed a contract with Elkin to produce numerous short songs and piano pieces, which were very successful in the emergent mass music market. At the same time, his music was played at the Promenade Concerts (*Second Symphony* in 1903 and the patriotic *Britain's War March* in 1914),[7] as well as conducted or performed by such celebrities as Thomas Beecham, Goossens, Grainger, Fritz Kreisler, Henry Wood, and, during Scott's piano tour through the United States in 1920, Leopold Stokowski. As a cosmopolitan composer, Scott was acquainted with and praised by famous contemporary composers like Gabriel Fauré, Maurice Ravel, Igor Stravinsky, and indeed, Debussy, who wrote the following well-known endorsement:

> Cyril Scott is one of the rarest artists of the present generation. His rhythmical experiments, his technique, even his style of writing, may at first sight appear strange and disconcerting. Inflexible severity, however, compels him to carry out to the full his particular system of aesthetics, and his only. The music unfolds somewhat after the manner of the Javanese rhapsodies which, instead of being confined within traditional forms, are the outcome of imagination displaying itself in innumerable arabesques; and the incessantly changing aspects of the inner melody are intoxication for the ear— are, in fact, irresistible. All those qualities are more than sufficient to justify confidence in this musician, so exceptionally equipped.

From the very beginning, however, there were recurring hesitant reviews of Scott's works in the British press, in which he was depicted as an enfant terrible rather than a musical pioneer. To his own frustration, what he called his "trifles" received most attention in Britain, while his serious music was more appreciated in Germany, and was published with Schott. That said, at the time his *First Symphony* (1899) was premièred in Darmstadt during the South African Boer War period, when the British were very unpopular in Germany, Scott's fellow student in Frankfurt, Henry Balfour Gardiner, overheard one member of the audience say: "They should play that to the Boers, and then they would run to the Equator!" [8] Since the late 1920s, Scott mostly composed larger works. Only a handful of his roughly 215 solo piano pieces and almost 150 songs were written after 1930, a fact that obviously had much to do with the ending of his contract with Elkin. By this time, nonetheless, performing organizations were generally reluctant to program his works, and he almost single-handedly had to bring his music before the public. Though Scott continued composing until his death in 1970, there were few notable performances of his works since the 1940s, and he wrote bitterly about the injustice done to him and his work in his second autobiography, *Bone of Contention* (1969).

All in all, Scott's oeuvre cannot be seen simply in disagreement with what was propagated by the British national music establishment. Although, unlike such contemporaries as Grainger, Gustav Holst, and Ralph Vaughan Williams, he was not involved in the English folk song movement, some of his early music did refer to English, Irish, and Scottish folk music: *Gentle Maiden* (1912) and *Irish Suite* (1917), both for violin and piano, are only two examples. Also he made several (orchestral) arrangements of folk songs, including the *Ballad of Fair Helen of Kirkconnell* (1925), *Lord Randall* (1926), and *Early One Morning* (1931). As remarked above, his music was regularly performed at official celebrations and praised by Elgar. So why did Scott, "the father of modern British music," not make it into the modern British music canon? Was he simply not patriotic enough? Was it his commercialism, musical modernism, or all-roundedness as a composer? To begin with, there was his social background. Akin to the Roman Catholic Elgar, he did not belong to the elitist circle of the British music establishment educated at Oxford, Cambridge, the Royal Academy of Music, or the Royal College of Music. Perhaps of some importance also was the fact that he was a northerner, whereas Elgar, Holst, and Vaughan Williams, for example, came from Gloucestershire and Worcestershire. In addition, Scott never strove to belong to any group or institution and largely kept to his own, although throughout his life he stayed in contact with the members of the Frankfurt Group, especially Grainger. Particularly during the last 30 years of his life, when he lived in the English countryside, he did not cosy up to influential people or socialize at the right parties, and only went up to London when he absolutely had to. At the same time, his complaints about the neglect of his work, which he continued until the end of his life, show that he pined for an appreciative audience. Then again, Scott was not much good at selling himself (unlike Grainger, who was a master at it). His outspoken interest in occultism undeniably played a role as well in his overall decline in popularity. Had he been less "otherworldly," he might have had more drive and ambition to get his work performed.

Scott's occultist beliefs are difficult to summarize because he was anything but dogmatic and often changed his views. Following a Church of England upbringing, he called himself an agnostic for a few years, but in his early 20s his focus turned variously to *Vedanta*, Christian Science, spiritualism, and ultimately, occultism. After attending a lecture by Annie Besant in London in 1903, he became interested in Theosophy and, over the years, he read numerous books by Besant, Helena Blavatsky, C. W. Leadbeater, and other Theosophists. In addition, he developed a general fascination for Hindu philosophy and, among others writings, studied books by Swami Vivekananda, the *Upanishads*, the *Bhagavad Gita,* and Max Müller's *The Sacred Books of the East.*[9] Actually, he became a firm believer in *karma* (fate as the consequence of previous acts) and reincarnation. In 1914, Scott joined the Theosophical Society, though he always remained critical of any sectarianism within the movement.[10] "Just as psycho-analysis has contributed much to explain the *vagaries* of Man's nature," he argued, "Theosophy has contributed even more to explain Man's nature itself."[11] As he explained further:

> Although the spiritualists are proving to the satisfaction of ever-increasing numbers that a human being does not merely consist of a body but also possesses an immortal soul, the Theosophists, or rather the Leaders of the Society, go further, and, as a result of assiduous clairvoyant investigation, have been enabled to give forth specific knowledge regarding the actual constitution of that

soul and its relationship to the body and the higher planes of consciousness.[12]

Over the years, Scott published around 40 books, among which only four are on music, and numerous articles in such disparate fields as occultism, homeopathy, poetry, literary translation, theology, ethics, and music. Most probably he is the only composer who has written two autobiographies, which were published 45 years apart.[13] His occult writings have numerous references to seers, initiates, and Yogis, who he had met, either through their writings or clairvoyance, or turned to for guidance. Appearing under the pseudonym "His Pupil" was the immensely successful "occult" *The Initiate* trilogy (1920, 1927, and 1932) and, under his own name, *An Outline of Modern Occultism* (1935), and its sequel *The Greater Awareness* (1936). Partly because of the teachings of Besant, Master Koot Hoomi (see later) and his pupil Nelsa Chaplin, and other "enlightened souls," Scott came to believe that most of humanity lived in a state of unending childishness, with selfishness, jealousy, and vanity as prime motivating forces. He wrote two books on the subject: *Childishness: A Study in Adult Conduct* (1930) and *Man Is My Theme: A Study of National and Individual Conduct* (1939). Also, he often complained against the moral repressiveness of British Victorian society. Like many of his contemporaries, he was dissatisfied with the organized Christian church. As he wrote in one of his anonymously published books, *The Adept of Galilee* (1920):

> there is no denying that a large proportion of the clergy can barely be regarded as the epitome of spirituality, seeing they are steeped in bigotry and intolerance, and what we may term a certain pious stupidity, utterly at variance with the teachings of Jesus, or any Initiate, who has, or ever will, grace the physical plane.[14]

In congruence with the Theosophical theory that the "spiritual" development of individuals is or can be guided by a secret set of Masters living in Tibet, he presented the idea that Jesus was a Yogi living in the Himalayas. In *An Outline of Modern Occultism*, then, he wrote how Christ would return among men "in an aeroplane from His retreat in Tibet," though the "great glory" would only be perceptible "to those with clairvoyance sight who will be able to see His radiance and the radiance of those angels (*devas*) who will always surround him."[15]

During the early twentieth century, as James Mansell recently emphasized, "music's effects on the human mind, typically associated with emotion rather than intellect, had no scientific explanation and as such were often appropriated as evidence of the occult."[16] Obviously, Scott was much interested and influenced by Theosophical ideas about music such as the "spiritual" importance of vibrations and overtones as well as the belief that links between color, musical tones, and other natural phenomena could be (clairvoyantly/clairaudiently) deciphered and could provide insight into divine manifestations on earth. Overall, he believed in the idea of "the occult power of sound." In his most famous esoteric book on music, *Music: Its Secret Influence throughout the Ages* (1933),[17] he argued that composers like Johann Sebastian Bach, Ludwig van Beethoven, and Richard Wagner had been "mediums" who changed society and guided humanity through their music. The book was inspired by and dedicated to Master Koot Hoomi, whom he described as follows:

> K.H. is of Kashmiri origin, was Pythagoras in one of His previous incarnations, and among His other activities has much to do with music. He is well over a hundred-and-fifty years of age, is over six feet tall, has a fair complexion, hair and beard of a golden brown, and eyes of a wonderful blue. He speaks English perfectly.[18]

Following the idea that Master Koot Hoomi was a reincarnation of Pythagoras, Scott too adhered to the Pythagorean concept of "the music of the spheres," with its analogies between musical consonance and natural phenomena, such as planetary motion,[19] and which he believed ultimately would lead to "the great Cosmic Symphony."[20]

On the whole, it seems that Scott's all too obvious interest in "spirituality" was unacceptable to many within the British music establishment. In her study of the BBC archives, for instance, Diana Swann maintains that, from the 1930s onward, the BBC consistently rejected his music because it did not measure up to their "hidden set of criteria which had to conform to the [musical] Renaissance image, whose characteristics included distrust of any religious or philosophical element that was not based on muscular Christianity or healthy agnosticism."[21] In 1944, Scott briefly gave up composing altogether, only to pick it up again at the behest of Master Koot Hoomi, who was certain that his music would be appreciated again in the future. Religious universalism motivated him to compose his

Hymn of Unity (1947), though without the expectation of its performance during his lifetime because he believed that no British choral society would produce "an English Oratorio which embraced other religions besides the Christian."[22] He wrote the libretto himself, and it not only follows his concept of "unity in diversity," which he repeatedly propagated in his occult writings and in his view was "one of the great ideals of the Masters,"[23] but also was internationalist and perhaps even anti-imperial in its criticism of Western civilization at large:

> Civilization, civilization!—a long and lofty-sounding word it is; but how can there be civilization when there lacketh the essential thing…civility? [...]
> A strange civility to kidnap, plunder, rob, enslave and massacre! And yet the men of Power who ordained these evil things did boast and bellow much about their lofty Culture![24]

Scott had been thinking about "unity in diversity" for a long time. Already in 1932–1933, he composed and wrote the libretto for *Mystic Ode* (originally named *Ode to Unity*), a sort of predecessor to the *Hymn of Unity*. In *Music: Its Secret Influence throughout the Ages*, he expressed, more or less in a Hindu philosophical manner, that the concept was "the keynote to Wagner's music-drama":

> Socialistically speaking, Wagner's music was the prototype of the principle of co-operation in contradistinction to competition; spiritually speaking, it symbolized the mystic truth that each individual soul is unified with the All-soul, the All-pervading Consciousness.[25]

From the perspective of internationalism, Scott's concept of "unity in diversity" undeniably reflected both the fundamental Theosophical creed of a "universal brotherhood of man" as well as Rabindranath Tagore's idealistic worldview, though surprisingly I did not find any reference so far that Scott was familiar with the poet's work. Indeed, the final chorus of *Hymn of Unity* perhaps expressed everything Scott believed in and strove for all his life:

> O LIFE, the One that doth inform the heavens and the earth,
> O LIFE that men do call by divers names,

And cry to Thee as Brahman, Allah, God, or Great
  White Spirit:
O Thou who didst project the World from out a fragment
  of Thyself
Yet dost remain the One Eternal and Supreme,
O Thou whose nature and whose Name is Love,
And by the power of Love dost hold all things together,
And who dost dwell in us, as we in Thee:
Oh grant that we may manifest a greater measure of Thy Love,
And may perceive at last the saving, mystic truth
That with each other we are One, as we are one with Thee!
Oh, may the spirit of that Unity irradiate our hearts
So that the dark and deadly sin of separateness
May vanish like the night when morning wakes,
And that the Age of Brotherhood may dawn and may endure
  for Man.[26]

Cosmopolitan radicalism: Progress and Theosophical spirituality in music

I am aware that in speaking of certain creative musicians as being inspired, although the term may convey something vaguely to religiously minded people, it conveys nothing to the materialist. Yet materialism offers no convincing explanation for that mysterious charm, that elusive *something* which renders a number of works of art immortal. Nor can materialism or even orthodox religion convincingly account for genius. It is only Esotericism which affords a satisfying explanation.

(Cyril Scott, *Music: Its Secret Influence throughout the Ages*, 1933)[27]

Scott did not make his case easier for the British music orthodoxy when he straightforwardly propagated his interest in Theosophy and Indian philosophy in relation to his radical cosmopolitan (read: antinational) ideas about modernist music and aesthetics in such writings as *The Philosophy of Modernism: Its Connection with Music* (1917), which followed upon four lectures that he delivered to the Fabian Society, and the earlier mentioned *Music: Its Secret Influence throughout the Ages*. In these books, he discussed a wide range of issues, including the stylistic changes in modernist music; the conservatism of the British music scene; the pre-Raphaelite movement as a source of inspiration;

his frustration about music critics ("there is only one person who understands a genius, and that person is the genius himself");[28] the magical and healing effects of music; Orientalism in music; "the music of the spheres"; and the relationship between sound and color. In *The Philosophy of Modernism*, Scott specifically argued in relation to progress in music that "the prerequisite to immortality in the world of art is the capacity to create something new, or, in other words, the capacity to invent a style" and that "this capacity to create something new proceeds from a certain divine discontent."[29] At the same time, he emphasized that a new style "must be attained within certain limits only, otherwise it will not be susceptible of comprehension."[30] In his opinion, there were aesthetic limits to progress in music and, accordingly, he made the distinction between the "romanticist," who holds that "in order to create a *beautiful* work of art it is essential to be new" and the "futurist," who holds that "beauty is of no importance whatever."[31] Even so, Scott respected the modernist composer and Theosophist Arnold Schoenberg, whom he labeled a "futurist,"[32] because he was needed:

> For it is an occult musical fact that discord (used in its moral sense) can alone be destroyed *by* discord, the reason for this being that the vibrations of intrinsically beautiful music are too rarified to touch the comparatively coarse vibrations of all that pertains to a much lower plane.[33]

In contrast to Schoenberg, Scott saw in Grainger a great harmonic inventor, who "does not lead us into the excruciating."[34]

Distinctive to Scott's musical style was the imaginative and complex way in which he used chords and harmonies, juxtaposing, as Lisa Hardy put it, "unrelated chords, creating interesting harmonic colour and adding to the sense of tonal ambiguity" (figure 1.2).[35] Like his basically Romantic spirit, it was indispensable to his aesthetic throughout his life, and undoubtedly it was symbiotic with his famed ability to improvise at the piano. To explain the relationship between music and color, he explicitly used the Theosophical idiom. So he referred, for instance, to a table in Madame Blavatsky's *The Secret Doctrine* (1888), wherein each tone corresponds to a color: C-Red; D-Orange; E-Yellow; F-Green; G-Blue; A-Indigo; B-Violet.[36] It comes as no surprise that for Scott the direction of musical modernism aesthetically ended with the Russian master of synaesthesia, Theosophist,

Figure 1.2 Cyril Scott working on a score, Eastbourne, 1952 (Courtesy of the Cyril Scott Estate).

fellow musical modernist, and eventually Anglophile, Alexander Scriabin (1872–1915), rather than with Schoenberg or Stravinsky, who early in his life was interested in Theosophy and was admired by Scott. Following the Theosophical notion of "*Deva*-music" based on "vibration types," to hierarchically classify the aesthetic achievement reached by different composers,[37] Scott called Scriabin "the greatest exponent of *Deva*-music."[38]

Despite his criticism of contemporary British music making, if not society, Scott's thinking followed some of the dominant values and perceptions of British imperial culture. So, the evolutionary ideas of Charles Darwin and Herbert Spencer underlay his notion of progress in music. Also for him, all music represented a stage in an evolutionary process: from "primitive" music (e.g., Western folk music and non-Western music traditions, which increasingly were seen as "pure" music by nationalist musicians worldwide) to contemporary Western classical music. In this context, one can delineate how his thinking was influenced by imperial racialism. For example, Scott's dislike of jazz overtly depended on the trope of the African other as wild, sexual, and uncivilized. In his view, jazz "was definitely 'put through' by the Dark Forces" and followed up by "a very marked decline in sexual morals."[39] In particular, he had problems with the "orgiastic" element inherent in its syncopated rhythm:

> Whereas the old-fashioned melodious dance-music inspired the gentler sentiments, jazz, with its array of harsh, ear-splitting percussion-instruments inflamed, intoxicated and brutalized, thus causing a set-back in Man's nature towards the instincts of his racial childhood. For jazz-music at its height very closely resembled the music of primitive savages.[40]

Yet, Scott too was influenced by the contemporary fashion among Western modernist composers to refer to Black American music in their compositions, as in the case of Erik Satie's "Cakewalk," *Le Piccadilly* (1904),[41] which might have inspired Debussy's "Colliwogg's Cakewalk" from *Children's Corner* (1908). The last movement of his *Tallahassee Suite* (1911) for violin and piano, "Air et Danse Nègre," for instance, consists of a broad diatonic first part (Air) marked *molto espressive* that is clearly reminiscent of a Negro, spiritual in character, and a cheerful, syncopated *alllegro con spirito* second part (Danse Nègre) with ragtime accents. It should be noted, however, that ragtime was different from jazz and generally accepted as civilized music, if only because it was notated and played straight in (semi-) quavers rather than in triplets.

Without ever visiting the subcontinent, Scott's judgment about Indian music and culture was stereotypical racial. From an evolutionary perspective, he described Indian music as lacking variety and being nonprogressive. Besides climatic conditions, he mentioned the "characteristic lethargy" of Indians as a reason for the creation of their "*mantramistic* and trans-inducing" music: "Apart from the warrior caste there are few men of action; the bulk of the people are dreamy, meditative, and given over in excess to the things of the spirit."[42] Here, indeed, much in contrast to his great interest in Indian philosophy, Scott straightforwardly propagated the condescending, false, and essentialist imperial trope of "spiritual" India, which was used by the British to deny Indians the capacity to rule themselves, for, they argued, their "spirituality" made them irrational. At the same time, however, it should be emphasized that his racial notions were in line with Theosophical philosophy, which overall was strongly evolutionary, hierarchical, and racial. Then again, somewhat contradictorily, along the lines of the idea of "the music of the spheres," and including the belief that in the *Vedas* "it is stated that the whole cosmos was brought into manifestation through the agency of sound,"[43] he put forward the binary opposition of "spiritual" India versus the materialist West in terms of note divisions. Thus, he claimed that the "quarter-tone" of Indian music, which he called "the most subtle division of the note," especially affected "the *mental body*, hence the domain of the mind, philosophy, metaphysics," while the half-tone of Western music mainly affected "the sensation-physical body—hence the domain of Matter: mechanics, government of men, practicality."[44]

Since the British music establishment did not acknowledge the originality of his work, Scott increasingly turned away from the public. His inward turn partly also was a negative reaction to the discords of the modern world. So he believed that the "nerve-shattering noise" of mechanized urban society such as "the jarring sounds of motor horns, whistles, grinding brakes and so forth" had "a cumulative and deleterious effect" upon modern man.[45] To counteract this, he continued, "certain composers will be used to evolve a type of music calculated to heal where these discordant noises have destroyed."[46] He increasingly absorbed himself in the writing of occult and other books as well as the systemization of his use of "chords built upon the interval of the fourth,"[47] to the extent of becoming a "mannerism," as he later confessed himself.[48] Actually, these chords are the same as the upper part of Scriabin's famous "mystic chord" (D G C Fis Bes E), which served as the basis of the Russian's final orchestral piece, the Fifth Symphony, *Prometheus: The Poem of Fire* (1910). With the chord, Scriabin aimed to dispend with triadic thinking in favor of a combination of perfect, diminished, and augmented fourths. Moreover, the symphony shows his preoccupation with the Theosophical notion of correspondences between musical tones and color, as he envisaged *Prometheus* as a multimedia event with a score calling for a color organ to project colors on a screen as certain pitches were played. In 1914, Henry Wood gave an acclaimed performance of *Prometheus* in London. Interestingly, it was the organist, composer, music writer, and indeed Scott's uncritical biographer, Arthur Eaglefield Hull,[49] who coined the term "mystic chord" in his biography of Scriabin.

On the whole, Scott began a dialogue with an imagined, ideal audience, beyond the present British nation and more or less endured the eternal fate of so many individual artists before and after this time: a suffering for the sake of a future paradise. Adhering to some kind of musical utopianism, for instance, he wrote:

> For the next decade or so, the prevailing note of serious music will tend to be unemotional and intellectual in character, and although here and there composers far ahead of their time may be "reaching out towards that Beauty and Mystery which are veritably as the garments of God," such composers will not receive their due until a much later date, nay, perhaps only after their death.[50]

Scott's inward turn meant further displacement from a British music establishment that emphasized the significance of the link between music and the national public. As Vaughan Williams put it:

> [It is a fallacy] that the artist invents for himself alone. No man lives or moves or could do so, even if he wanted to, for himself alone. The actual process of artistic invention, whether it be by voice, verse, or brush, presupposes a audience [...] We must cultivate a sense of musical citizenship. Why should not the musician be the servant of the state and build national monuments like the painter, the writer, or the architect?[51]

Following his interest in the hidden, mysterious, and irrational activity of the mind, Scott revolted against musical academicism and, in a closely related manner, emphasized the importance of "spirituality" in the making of progressive music in his writings. His propagation of the critical role of the unconscious in composition, nonetheless, was not unique. Schoenberg, Scriabin, Stravinsky, Vaughan Williams, and other contemporary composers also underlined the need of it in the creation of their music.[52] In any case, Scott's cosmopolitan radicalism and urge for progress as well as utopianism in music was directly related to his Theosophical "spiritual" quest. But how then did his fascination with Theosophy and Indian philosophy relate to his musical style?

Cyril Scott and musical Orientalism

Generally, the decades around the turn of the nineteenth and twentieth centuries were decisive in the history of Western music.

Modernist composers experimented with rhythm and compositional structure. Above all, they liberated themselves from the limitations of the major-minor key system by appropriating different atonal scales (chromatic, pentatonic, modal, whole-tone, and so on). Also they sought exotic inspiration in past European musical practices (in Britain the "Back to Bach movement" was very influential); Mediterranean music; waltz, cabaret, jazz, and other popular musical forms; folk music; and, indeed, non-Western music. In recent decades, "musical exoticism" has emerged as an important field of research.[53] By and large, for early twentieth-century modernist composers like Claude Debussy and Maurice Ravel, an evocation of an exotic "external other" (Orientalism in music in particular) was a sign of radicalism, musical modernism, and cosmopolitanism, while an appeal to an "internal other" (folk music) marked the national music consensus. In this way, nationalism and empire offered an opportunity for aesthetics to triumph as a form of modern exchange-value that "no longer justified only the composer's self-importance but justified everything, from the appropriation of music of other cultures to the leap into atonality."[54]

Clearly, musical Orientalism is a stylistic label that obscures rather than explains. Compositions always have to be analyzed as products of a particular historical moment and a particular place. Until the nineteenth century, exoticism in Western music generally did not have anything to do with non-Western musical traditions, of which transcriptions look and sound like the music of the day.[55] In fact, with concepts like "authenticity" and ethnography still to come, musical Orientalism often reflected a fear of the other's sexuality and barbarism. On the whole, a timeless East was created on the basis of changing Orientalist musical styles that were fashionable at a specific Western time and place. Under labels such as the "Alla Turca style" and "Hindustani Air," the East was represented by bass drones and pedal points, Arabesques, repetitive rhythm, trills, whole tones, augmented seconds and fourths, parallel movements in fourths, fifths and octaves, and so on. During the twentieth century, however, the situation changed somewhat, as a growing number of Western composers gained a more real knowledge of Asian musical traditions through musicological publications, research, and/or gramophone recordings.

The bibliography of Scott's *Music: Its Secret Influence throughout the Ages* includes Arthur Henry Fox Strangways's *The Music of Hindostan,* and obviously he was interested in Indian music. Even so, it seems that he did not use the book's numerous examples of Indian melodies and rhythms in staff notation or feel attracted to Indian music theory for that matter. As I already mentioned, Scott saw the "quartertone" of Indian music as a sign of India's "spirituality" but, despite his reading of Fox Strangways's book, did not make a reference to the mathematical problematic 22 *shrutis*. Conversely, he probably was not glad that Fox Strangways depicted the rhythm, or rather absence of rhythm, in his *First Piano Sonata* negatively in comparison with Stravinsky's in *Petrouchka* (1911).[56] As far as I know, Scott did not write anything about his two "Indian" cycles for piano: *Impressions from the Jungle Book* (1912) and *Indian Suite* (1922). In these cycles and in similar Orientalist works for piano such as *Caprice Chinois* (1919), *Egypt* (1913), *Eastern Dance* (1903), *Song from the East* (1924), *Soirée Japonaise* (1910), *Sphinx* (1908), and, of course, his greatest hit *Lotusland* (1905), which gained wider currency in Fritz Kreisler's transcription for violin and piano, he made use of many modernist musical innovations: exclusion of key signatures, constantly varying rhythms and meters, alternative chords to those founded upon the superposition of unequal thirds, equal treatment of scale notes, longer melodic lines, new compositional forms, and so on. In addition, Scott simply relied on the Orientalist musical practices and tropes of his time. Hence, the title of the *Indian Suite*'s piece "Juggernaut" (a corruption of the Sanskrit *Jagannath* or "Lord of the Universe" and a deity worshipped by Hindus, mainly in Orissa) remains a good example of Orientalist imagination in terms of India's religious barbarism. It points to a Hindu procession held in the east of India (Puri, Orissa), in which an idol on a huge chariot is dragged through the streets by worshippers (the opening of the piece, with its processional drone, is to be played *andante religioso*), and occasionally persons throw themselves before the advancing wheels (the fourth chords of the middle part are to be played *allegretto* and "crisply"). In the same way, the titles of two other pieces in the cycle, "The Snake Charmer" and "Dancing Girls," remain classic Orientalist reflections of the mysterious and exotic East, whereby the irregular and long melody lines of the opening of "The Snake Charmer" can be seen as representing sensual and/or snaky movements.

Another major project among early twentieth-century Western modernist composers was the setting of Eastern poetry, especially Chinese but also Indian (including the poems of Rabindranath

Tagore),[57] Persian, and Japanese. Thus, Scott based the texts for his *Don't Come in Sir, Please!* (1905), *An Eastern Lament* (1909), *Insouciance* (1907), *Vision* (1908), and the five *Songs of Old Cathay* (1906–1919) on translations from Chinese poetry by the well-known Sinologist Herbert Allen Giles. By and large, these songs represent two characteristic Orientalist moods: "slow and melancholic" and "rhythmical," often in a repetitive manner. As to be expected, however, it remains difficult to distinguish Scott's use of modernist musical materials and styles in both his Orientalist piano pieces and songs from those that he used in others. Further, he dedicated *Eastern Lament* to Swami Abhedananda, who was sent to the West by Swami Vivekananda, the founder of the Ramakrishna Mission and "perhaps the most important expounder of the doctrine of 'Hindu spirituality,'"[58] to spread the message of *Vedanta*. In fact, Abhedananda ran the *Vedanta Society* in New York, which according to a British secret report was "a great success, principally with the ladies of the richer class of Americans," and overall was considered a "seditionist" by the British government in India.[59] He published widely on *Vedanta* and, most likely, Scott read some of his books or even visited one of his lectures. Likewise, Scott dedicated the two *Songs from Old Cathay*, "Picnic" (1906) and "Waiting" (1906), to R. R. Vamam Shankar Rav Pandit, about whom I unfortunately could not find anything so far, though I suspect he was a similar figure as Abhedananda.

While it remains difficult to assess how extra-musical influences affected Scott's composing, his musical Orientalism clearly had nothing to do with the reality of Indian music but reflected his superficial awareness of it. Eastern music partially inspired him to write different melodies, chords, and rhythms. In doing so, Scott self-assertively created an aesthetic world apart from the conventions of British national music. Though musical Orientalism only concerned a small part of Scott's oeuvre, his quests for Theosophical "spirituality" and musical modernism were interconnected and for instance led to his three *Piano Sonatas*, from 1909, 1935, and 1956 respectively. In these abstract works, which flow continuously without a cadence from beginning to end, he avoided key signatures and generally used modal and exotic scales rather than pentatonic or whole-tone ones. On the whole, he gave equal importance to the 12 semitones and therefore described his music as "non-tonal."[60] Alternately, his repeated use of fourth chords created a harmonic stasis similar to Scriabin's music. Of course, Scott was not the only modernist British composer with a fascination for Asian philosophies and music. Granville Bantock, for example, was an "ardent lover of the Orient and its philosophies."[61] He wrote some 60 "Chinese" songs and saw in Scott "a man after his own heart."[62] In his musical autobiography, the earlier mentioned Eugene Goossens, another musical modernist with an interest in Eastern instruments and music, wrote amusingly about his visit to the artists' colony Harlech on the Welsh coast in 1918, where he stumbled upon Scott and Bantock "sitting cross-legged, orientalwise" together in the hollow of a dune, practicing "Yogi": Bantock "was seemingly endeavouring to tie knots in the muscles of his abdomen," while Scott "was trying to swallow a length of solid flexible rubber tubing."[63]

Gustav Holst, then, remains the most famous example of an early twentieth-century British modernist composer with a Theosophical background and a fascination for Indian philosophy and music.[64] Since his youth, he had been influenced by Theosophy and, between about 1895 and 1914, he was very much preoccupied with Indian culture and, after being captivated by a work of Max Müller, he began studying Sanskrit, especially its literature, and Hindu philosophy. During this period, he composed some works with Indian themes such as *Indra* (1903), *Sita* (1906), *Savitri* (1908), *Choral Hymns from the Rig Veda* (1912), and *The Cloud Messenger* (1913). Holst remains best known, nonetheless, for his very successful orchestral suite *The Planets* (1917). According to Raymond Head, he had found the inspiration for this work mainly in Alan Leo's *The Art of Synthesis* (1912). Leo was a Theosophist, who had been a member of Blavatsky's close circle in London. In this "innovative astrological book," which also included "an Astro-Theosophical Glossary," each chapter was devoted to a planet and Holst followed this very manner in *The Planets*.[65] The fact that Holst did not drop out of the canon of British national music may be explained, besides the success of *The Planets*, by his membership of the establishment through his education at the Royal College of Music and, above all, his close friendship and musical interaction with Vaughan Williams, with whom he shared a profound interest in English folk music research and, as an editor, worked on *The English Hymnal* (1906). At least since *The Planets*, his work was frequently broadcast by the BBC, and he worked as a music teacher for almost his whole life, including at the Royal College of Music. Moreover, in 1921, he set the patriotic poem *I Vow to Thee, My Country* to the main theme of the "Jupiter" movement of *The Planets* and, though Holst himself came to loathe the tune, for like Scott and John Foulds he was anything but patriotic, it started a life of its own and to this day is performed at Armistice Day and other British national events.

Having said all this, however, I should point out that the inspirations and ideas of Scott, Grainger, and Foulds often overlapped with those of Holst or, indeed, Vaughan Williams. The fault lines between the modernist and establishment music making of Elgar, Charles Hubert Parry, Charles Villiers Stanford, Vaughan Williams, and so on, were not always so clear, and they changed over time. As always, a musical modernist could subsequently become an established figure or, as in cases of Scott and Foulds, be forgotten. As men of their time, all the mentioned composers had more or less a fascination for British folk music, the pre-Raphaelites, the Arts and Crafts Movement, and, indeed, the work of Walt Whitman, who had a lifelong interest in Indian philosophy: Vaughan Williams set his poem "A Passage to India" as part of his *Sea Symphony* (1909), and earlier Holst wrote his *Walt Whitman Overture* in 1899. In addition, Foulds, Holst, and, to a lesser degree, Scott and Vaughan Williams were attracted to socialism and befriended George Bernard Shaw. Conversely, Scott, Grainger, and Holst benefited from the activities of Henry Balfour Gardiner, who used his inherited wealth to help out his musical friends and organize British music concerts. On the whole, he gave young British composers the confidence to think big, act fraternal, and feel independent of the establishment patronage of the choral festivals, the Philharmonic Society, the Covent Garden, and so on. In 1912–1913, Gardiner featured four of Holst's pieces at his famous concert series in London and, indeed, in 1918, he made possible the first incomplete performance of *The Planets* at the Queen's Hall, London. While Scott and Foulds much admired this modernist work,[66] Grainger was struck by it but, like Gardiner, thought that "the see-sawing back & forth on two chords was a bad habit."[67]

Holst died in 1934, the same year that Elgar did. It seems unlikely, however, that had he lived as long as Scott did, his music would have been forgotten. *The Planets* had become too much part of the canon, and there always would be his friendship with Vaughan Williams. True, Holst sought inspiration in Theosophy, Sanskrit literature, and later in astrology, and all this led to his musical modernism. Like Scott, he was a believer in *karma* but, on the whole, he did not propagate his exotic interests as openly as Scott, Bantock, or, indeed, Foulds, the only one among these composers, as I will discuss later, who gained some insight in the theory and practice of Indian music, and appropriated this knowledge into some of his compositions. At the same time, as Raymond Head emphasized, Holst had all reason to be careful because, in 1917, Alan Leo was prosecuted under "the infamous Vagrancy Act that could declare all astrologers, palmists, clairvoyants and mediums common thieves and vagabonds."[68] Hence, during the early incomplete performances of *The Planets*, Holst stated that he wished the work "to be judged as music (although) the poetical basis is concerned with the study of the planets" (note that astrology is not mentioned here), while at its first full performance in 1920 the program note simply gave "an outline of themes and orchestrations."[69] Lastly, maybe unexpected in the light of their shared "spiritual" interests, it needs to be mentioned that Holst's musical style was closer to that of Grainger and Foulds than of Scott. While the first three more or less shared a desire for directness of expression, although Percy was far more extroverted, Scott created music of a different kind altogether.

Conclusion

Before the First World War, Scott undeniably was a key figure "in helping Britain to break away from musical conservatism and the prevailing Germanic influences."[70] Like that of the members of the pre-Raphaelite and Arts and Crafts Movements, however, his cosmopolitan radicalism in music in many ways was one that looked back as much as it looked forward and overall had Romantic overtones. Moreover, it often looked to the East. As a composer, he wished to circumvent the dominant conventions of British music and culture, and in doing so make a name for himself, but simultaneously he believed that there were aesthetic limits to modernist music making. He found inspiration in his study of Theosophy and Indian philosophy. This not only gave him confidence to pursue unfamiliar musical ideas but also directed his "spirituality," utopianism, universalism, criticism toward Christianity, and modern Western civilization. Because of his fascination for occultism and the East, Scott logically became an outsider to the British music establishment. Instead, he found some connection with similar countercultural musicians such as Bantock, Grainger, and Goossens, though he always remained a loner. Another reason for the fact that "the father of modern British music" did not make it into the British music canon might have been related to the fact that the cultural preoccupations within British society during the 1930s became very different from those that had bred his musical style. Accordingly, his work met with aesthetic confusion and was superseded both by other musical modernisms as well as British national music.

Scott was affected, albeit rather erratically, by the imperial encounter in different ways. First, his Theosophical "spirituality" and musical Orientalism was part of an interdependent musical and social modernism that generally verged toward internationalism and comparative religion, as exemplified by his idea of "unity in diversity." Second, his judgments of jazz and Indian music make clear that he was much influenced by evolutionist and racial thinking. Besides the fact that his fascination with the East was a reflection of Victorian doubt and apprehension, it shows how the empire led to a radical Western elitist "inner critique" and how the modern self is subjective and rational, but not necessarily secular.[71] Under the inspiration of the heroism, adventure, and innocence of Rudyard Kipling's *Jungle Book* (1894), he further composed his *Impressions from the Jungle Book* perhaps for the same reason as for which his best friend, Percy Grainger, wrote his Kipling settings (1898–1947), namely as "a protest against civilization." In the next chapter about Grainger, Scott will regularly turn up again. The differences between their personalities are remarkable. While Scott was a quiet and reclusive personality, Grainger was extrovert and outgoing, and all this is reflected in their music. Also, Grainger was less elitist and more radical in his ideas, musical or otherwise. He definitely did not look down upon "primitive" music from an evolutionary perspective. On the contrary, as one of the leading members of the English folk song movement, he embraced all the world's folk music. Similar to Scott's occultism, however, his primitivism in music was yet another feature of empire.

2
Percy Grainger: Kipling, Racialism, and All the World's Folk Music

Cosmopolitanism, primitivism, and modernist musical aesthetics

Today, Percy Grainger is often celebrated as a proto-ethnomusicologist because of his original ideas about and transcriptions of British and Danish folk songs as well as non-Western music. Recently, Graham Freeman investigated the impact of his complex modernist musical aesthetic (read: his conception of "free music") upon his English folk song collecting.[1] Among other things, this chapter complements Freeman's argument by showing that Grainger's proto-ethnomusicological research at large was influenced by primitivism. In doing so, it highlights the relationship between his study of European folk songs and non-Western music research. On the whole, it argues that his "world music" research and musical modernism were closely interconnected, and to a great extent part of a cosmopolitan but imperial counterculture.

Following his early youth in Australia, Grainger's interest in folk music was aroused during his student days at the Hoch Conservatory in Frankfurt (1895–1901), particularly after his composition teacher Karl Klimsch showed him a copy of *Songs from the North* (1884), a collection of Scottish folk songs, of which Grainger made 14 settings. In 1901, he moved to London, where he established himself as a pianist and teacher, and published his first folk song settings. His interest in folk music was boosted after he heard a lecture by Lucy Broadwood of the Folk Song Society. Between 1905 and 1909, as a member of the society, he collected and transcribed well over 300 British folk songs. He was one of the first in Britain to use the Edison

Bell cylinder phonograph as a collecting tool. Also, he instigated the issue of the first nine commercial English folk song recordings on gramophone. In 1914, Grainger migrated to the United States, where not only did his fame as a pianist and composer reach its peak, but also he was recognized as the ethnomusicologist who promoted the idea of an international musical society "for the purpose of making all the world's music known to all the world."[2] Unlike Cecil Sharp, however, he never looked for British folk songs in America but, on the contrary, showed an interest in American Indian and Black American folk songs, as well as the music of George Gershwin and jazz.

As a modernist composer, in Frankfurt, Grainger had already experimented with rhythm, compositional structure, atonal scales, and so on. As he wrote in a letter to Klimsch in 1902:

My task has not been to conform to existing formal conventionalities—still less to create new ones—but rather to clear away all structural & formal limitations (regularity of bars, beats & phrases, themes, motives, sections) barring the way to the realization of my style ideals.[3]

In the same letter, he mentioned that he felt particularly attracted to explore the possibility of intervals smaller than the semitone:

What is particularly sympathetic to me is that the human voice (like whistling, & stringed instruments) has all possibilities of pitch, is not bound to certain notes only (like woodwind, piano, organ) but can (at least, theoretically) make twenty & more divisions to the half-tone, & can *slide at will from note to note*. This sliding-*portamento* (although condemned by singing teachers as "bad style," which it undoubtedly is when only the result of faulty technique & uncertainty of pitch) I much desire in the performance of my vocal works (especially those non-textual) & wish the notes of melodies to glide one into the other in curving lines.[4]

It should be clear that equal temperament became the standard tuning in the West only during the nineteenth century, and that many musicians and musicologists still felt that it was undesirable. Not so surprisingly, in 1903, Grainger studied briefly with Ferruccio Busoni in Berlin. Apart from the Italian's pianism, he was influenced by his radical philosophy as well, as noted down in his iconoclastic *Sketch of a New Esthetic of Music* (1907), that "music was born free; and to win freedom its destiny," and his idea that in the future music "may be restored to its primitive, natural essence" through a division of the octave into more than the traditional 12 tones.[5] Even so, rather than to Busoni, he attributed his inspiration for "micro-tonality" to his knowledge of non-Western music. In 1915, for example, he wrote:

> It is, of course, widely known that many races use quarter-tones and other divisions of the scale smaller than those hitherto in vogue in Europe, and Ferruccio Busoni's illuminating pamphlet "A New Esthetic of Music" contains some very clear-sighted suggestions for the use of third-tones and other close intervals—suggestions which I fondly hope the near future may see carried into practice.
>
> My own experience with such small intervals has been in the "waiatas" [songs] and chants of the Maoris of New Zealand.[6]

Thus, Grainger's interest in folk music and musical modernism intermingled since his student days. It created a cosmopolitan intellectual outlook that particularly came to the fore when, as an Australian "colonial" outsider with an early experience of non-Western music, about which more later, he began to collect British folk songs.

Grainger and the performance of folk song

Grainger's reputation as an original thinker about the performance and study of "primitive" music in Britain and elsewhere is largely based on two of his articles: "Collecting with the Phonograph" (1908) and "The Impress of Personality in Unwritten Music" (1915). In the first, he noted down the results of his British folk music research. On his insistence, it included a number of songs in full, exactly as phonographed (including the extremely popular *Bold William Taylor* [figure 2.1]), rather than a representative tune plus some variations, as was usual. Of course, he still relied on conventional staff notation, but he aimed to give a more detailed representation of the way a song was sung by adding numerous performance directions in notation and words. In general, Grainger strongly favored the use of the gramophone and the phonograph over the "inaccurate" and "clumsy" use

Figure 2.1 Percy Grainger's transcription of *Bold William Taylor*, 1908 (Courtesy of the Percy Grainger Estate).

of human ears and staff notation. He found that the greatest advantage of these instruments was:

> that they record not merely the tunes and words of fine folksongs, but give an enduring picture of the live art and *traditions* of peasant and sailor singing and fiddling; together with a record of dialects of different districts, and of such entertaining accessories as the vocal quality, singing-habits, and other personal characteristics of singers. And a knowledge of such points is every bit as

indispensable to good renderings of folk-music as is experience of the traditions of cultured music to its proper interpretation.[7]

Percy's ideas were seen as controversial by other folk song collectors like Sharp and Ralph Vaughan Williams, who also would make use of the phonograph but saw more limitations in the instrument's usefulness than Grainger. Sharp thought that "singers produced stiff, rehearsed versions when they sat down in front of the machine, and much preferred to write down their spontaneous performances by ear."[8] He accepted the importance of Grainger's detailed verse-by-verse transcriptions, but asked himself whether it was worth doing it. Vaughan Williams found Percy's transcriptions the work of a madman and a "waste of time" because folk singers always introduced alterations in every performance.[9] Grainger's ideas were all the more controversial because, in contrast to what most of his fellow folk song collectors assumed, he emphasized that folk music rarely could be analyzed in terms of Greek modes and, moreover, because he never had a nationalist agenda and refused to produce "simplified" folk song arrangements for the education of the British nation. Indeed, though he respected Sharp as a collector, he generally was dismissive about his harmonic treatment of folk songs.[10] Instead, it was his ethic to represent through staff notation, as far as this was possible, the original performance of a folk song, to provide the coming generations of composers and students, who would not enjoy a first-hand experience of "primitive" music, "with the best *second-hand* material" he could.[11] Subsequently, he turned folk music into art music in his own compositions, by giving great attention to technical artistry, to produce music that was in accordance with his aesthetic. A good example is the piano score of *The Sussex Mummers' Christmas Carol* (1911), based upon a tune collected by Lucy Broadwood in 1888 (figure 2.2). As Wilfrid Mellers argued, if one meticulously follows Grainger's instructions "as to voice-leading, dynamic range, and pedalling, one will learn much about the relationship between oral and literate traditions."[12] In result, his folk settings influenced succeeding generations of British composers, including Benjamin Britten, who recognized him as his master in this regard and dedicated his orchestral *Suite on English Folksongs, "A Time There Was"* (1974), "lovingly and reverently" to Percy's memory.

In "The Impress of Personality in Unwritten Music," Grainger emphasized that "primitive" music was too complex for modern Western ears attuned to the well-tempered harmonic system. He argued that its "lack of harmonic consciousness" presented the

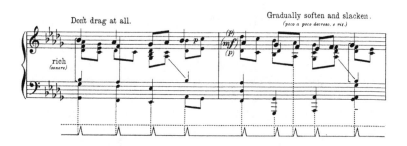

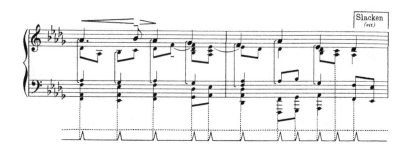

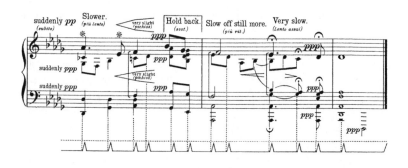

Figure 2.2   Percy Grainger, *Sussex Mummer's Christmas Carol*, 1911, ending (Courtesy Schott Music).

possibility for the complete reproduction of "natural" autonomy in musical form, free of the "tyranny of the composer." Overall, he approached tradition as dynamic rather than static and never separated music from its social context. As H. G. Wells whimsically remarked after he had accompanied Grainger on a "folk-song hunt" in Gloucestershire: "You are trying to do a more difficult thing than record folk-songs; you are trying to record life."[13] In opposition to the idea of folk music being "communal" music, as propagated by Sharp and Vaughan Williams among others, he underlined that the oral transmission of folk music led to a great degree of individuality and creativity in performance:

> The primitive musician unhesitatingly alters the traditional material he has inherited from thousands of unknown talents and geniuses before him to suit his own voice or instruments, or to make it conform to his purely personal taste for rhythm and general style. There is no written original to confront him with, no universally accepted standard to criticize him by. He is at once an executive and creative artist [...].[14]

Grainger believed that irregularities, variations between verses, essential stylistic accents, dynamics, and ornamentation were inherent to folk songs, and he aimed to translate all these aspects in his folk song transcriptions, which no one repeated. While other collectors generally made "the idea of the song a sort of fetish," as Graham Freeman rightly emphasized, Grainger instead valued "the performance, not the song itself."[15] His notations were "imperfect transcriptions of a perfect original."[16] Thus he was antipathetic toward Vaughan Williams, who, he felt, abused folk songs by separating the words from the melody. At the same time, it is useful to remember, as John Blacking did in relation to Grainger's "exceptionally accurate score" of *Bold William Taylor*, that his transcriptions do "not convey the reality of performance to someone who is not acquainted with the *sounds* of the music."[17]

Over the years, some of Grainger's folk song settings became immensely popular and were incorporated in the British national and imperial music canon, as they were broadcast by the BBC and performed at Empire Day, imperial exhibitions, and other official occasions. Nonetheless, he deliberately intended some of his music to be subversive to Western civilization and generally was critical of empire.[18] Like Vaughan Williams and other British composers, he rejected the reigning Austro-German hegemony in music. Yet, in the end, he probably remains the only modernist composer, in Britain and elsewhere, who never actually used the associated musical forms (sonata, symphony, and so on). Simultaneously, he was much disappointed that the British music establishment largely ignored him as a modernist composer, though of course his migration to the United States and the fact that he became a celebrity as one of the world's prime pianists also played a role here. But who would think that he wrestled with such problems as polytonality, complex rhythms, postimpressionist harmony, and aleatory music, after hearing his greatest hit, *Country Gardens* (1919), which earned him a little fortune? In the next sections, I shall consider Grainger's life and work explicitly in the light of (British) imperial culture. I will show how his "blue-eyed" Nordic patriotism and racialism contradicts with his openness toward non-Western music traditions. But first, I want to explore why Grainger, the critic of empire, was so much influenced by Rudyard Kipling (1865–1936), "the laureate of empire," that he eventually became the record holder of the settings of his poems.

Grainger and Kipling: Popular culture, morality, and empire

In 1897, Grainger's father felt that his son was "getting too Teutonic" in Frankfurt and sent him a copy of William Henry Fitchett's *Deeds That Won the Empire* (1896) as well as several Kipling books "to tickle up the British lion in him."[19] Ever since, Grainger believed that his compositions were based on "patriotism & racial consciousness."[20] In 1916, then, Cyril Scott, wrote about him:

> At sixteen he had, in fact, developed a style, and that style was the outcome of a discovery, and a literary discovery, not a musical one; for he had discovered Rudyard Kipling, and from that writer he imbibed an essence and translated it into music. [...] and in finding Kipling he found also *himself*.[21]

By this time, Kipling had become the most popular writer in English, and in George Orwell's words "the prophet of imperialism in its expansionist phase." Yet, Kipling's "imperialism" was ambivalent and problematic.[22] He was an allegorist and not apologist of empire, who made Mowgli and Kim, the protagonists of the *Jungle Books* (1894–1895) and *Kim* (1901), fraternally serve imperial rule. He was a paternalist but not a racist. Though he wholly supported the British civilizing mission, Kipling never meant to replace local cultures with that of Western civilization. In his mind, Britons simply were more capable than indigenous people in creating a modern society. Most of all, he was dedicated to the gospel of work. He admired the men who did their duty and obeyed "the Law" over those who lived "without the Law," being his largely intuitive and nonsystematic philosophy that permeates the *Jungle Books* in particular. Alternately, Grainger was not only a fanatic believer in the virtues of hard work but specifically also saw connections between work, race, and nationality. So, for example, he found that Americans did not work hard enough in comparison to the Nordic Europeans. In 1920, he even argued that the races that did not work would become extinct, as had the "artistic South Sea Islanders," whereas, he continued, "the enslaving of the Negro has really been his safeguarding."[23]

In 1959, Grainger wrote in a letter to Ronald Stevenson that to him Kipling, whom he met one or two times, was "something like an Australian" because he was born in India.[24] In any case, they both were "colonials" and therefore always remained outsiders to British society. This all the more so because they regularly traveled for extended periods to Australia, New Zealand, and South Africa, and lived in the United States. Throughout their lives, they cherished warm feelings for the countries of their birth. For Kipling, India remained a realm of exotic imagination, unspoiled nature and, as exemplified in *Kim*, of "spirituality." Grainger especially found inspiration in the Australian landscape and people, despite his criticisms of Australians, especially the women.[25] For instance, he wrote in the program note of *Colonial Song* (1914) that he composed the piece as an imagined folk song, born out of a longing for authentic origins (figure 2.3). Most of all, he felt attracted to the New World's self-reliant frontier mentality, as epitomized for him in the works of Mark Twain and Walt Whitman (in 1897, Scott presented him a copy of *Leaves of Grass*) as well as the music of Stephen Foster, and actually believed that it was his "joyous duty" to play his part in

> the creation of music that should reflect the easy-going, happy-go-lucky yet robust hopefulness and the undisciplined individualistic energy of the athletic out-of-doors Anglo-Saxon newer nations.[26]

Both Grainger and Kipling admired the vitality that flourished outside the cramped domestic experience of the English middle classes

| SENTIMENTALS |

Nº 1. COLONIAL SONG

| Originally composed for 2 voices (soprano and tenor), harp and full orchestra. |
| Composed as Yule-gift for mother, 1911 | Scored as Yule-gift for mother, 1912 | Rescored, early 1914 |

Short Program Note

In this piece the composer has wished to express feelings aroused by thoughts of the scenery and people of his native land, Australia. It is dedicated to the composer's mother.

Long Program Note

No traditional tunes of any kind are made use of in this piece, in which I have wished to express feelings aroused by thoughts of the scenery and people of my native land, (Australia), and also to voice a certain kind of emotion that seems to me not untypical of native-born Colonials in general.

Perhaps it is not unnatural that people living more or less lonelily in vast virgin countries and struggling against natural and climatic hardships (rather than against the more actively and dramatically exciting counter wills of their fellow men, as in more thickly populated lands) should run largely to that patiently yearning, inactive sentimental wistfulness that we find so touchingly expressed in much American art; for instance in Mark Twain's "Huckleberry Finn," and in Stephen C. Foster's adorable songs "My Old Kentucky Home," "Old Folks at Home," etc.

I have also noticed curious, almost Italian-like, musical tendencies in brass band performances and ways of singing in Australia (such as a preference for richness and intensity of tone and soulful breadth of phrasing over more subtly and sensitively varied delicacies of expression), which are also reflected here.

Percy Aldridge Grainger

Piano Solo

Figure 2.3 Percy Grainger, *Colonial Song*, 1914, program note (Courtesy of Schott Music).

in the life of the mariner, the settler, the soldier, the colonial official, and so on. As Cyril Scott put it:

Grainger, then, unblushingly likes vulgarity, and I wish to emphasise the fact, because when the obvious and the vulgar appear in his music at times, it is *not* because nothing better "occurs to him" (to use a foreign idiom) but because, as with Kipling, the vulgar evidently means to him a certain strength.[27]

Accordingly, Grainger made settings of "military" and "sailor" writings from Kipling's *Barrack-Room Ballads* (1892) and *The Seven Seas* (1896). In particular, he was drawn to Kipling's poems because of his belief that the latter showed "the tragedy, not the splendours of imperialism" (*The Widow's Party*, 1939, program note). In 1929, he made a hymnlike tune of *Recessional*, a setting that definitely remains different from anything else in his output but surprisingly is not mentioned by his biographers John Bird and Wilfrid Mellers.[28] The famous poem was published in *The Times* of July 17, 1897, on the occasion of Queen Victoria's Diamond Jubilee and it elicited "great praise from critics and public alike for its note of humility amidst the swagger of the celebration."[29] In *Recessional*, Kipling seemed to voice both the hopes and the fears of his own generation by calling "his fellow-imperialists to a sense of responsibility and pride, reminding them of the mutability of all things, and the dangers of pride."[30] By being caught up in the pomp and circumstance of imperial tributes, he made clear that the British could "forget the need for God, the need to behave responsibly, the need to be humble."[31] Though others might be "without the Law" and therefore did not have its demands, in Kipling's view, the British certainly were not, as it was "the pre-eminent duty of a chosen people not to forget God or neglect his laws."[32]

In 1941, in a letter to Henry Balfour Gardiner, Grainger actually referred to himself as "Kipling-in-tones."[33] Obviously, Grainger and Kipling were cosmopolitans rather than masculine Christian empire builders. They wanted to tell others about the debilitating effects of modern urban life on human character and what was happening in the world of empire at large. Kipling in particular was cynical about the delusion of the British intelligentsia who, according to him, believed they were practicing a new, totally altruistic morality, while in fact were pursuing an egoistic hedonism of the most savage kind. His hatred of the imperialism of the Boer War period was directed exclusively against white men: Afrikaners, Germans, Americans, and "Little Englanders." Undeniably, Grainger and Kipling were fascinated by the world of empire because it provided them possibilities to escape the stifling embrace of Western civilized places and values. Grainger composed his *Jungle Book* cycle, on which he worked between 1898 and 1947, specifically as "a protest against civilization" and wrote romantically in the introduction to one of the movements of the cycle, *The Inuit*, about his longing for the innocent "noble savage":

> The urge behind this poem is the very strongest & most pronounced root emotion of my life: the love of savagery, the belief that savages are sweeter & more peaceable & artistic than civilized people, the belief that primitiveness is purity & civilisation filthy corruption, the agony of seeing civilisation advance & pass its blighting hand over the wild.[34]

It remains surprising that Grainger, who greatly enjoyed Kipling's Indian stories and felt attracted to his ambiguous feelings toward patriotism and empire, wrote derogatorily about *Kim* that it simply was the novel that gained Kipling status "just as any silly composer does in writing a symphony."[35] Then again, he thought that Kipling was "a great genius in concentrating on the heroic (that is, the Scandinavian) elements in the British world" but lamented the fact that "he didn't have the insight or courage to separate the superior from the inferior elements in British life."[36] "The only hope for the English-speaking world," he wrote, "is to realise the tragedy of their own mixed blood & to cleanse their own races by studying the inferiority of the dark-eyed, dark-haired elements & the superiority of the fair types."[37] Compared to Kipling, Grainger certainly had very peculiar racial ideas.

Grainger's Nordicism: Music, racialism, and empire

Toward the end of the nineteenth century, Kipling's friend and empire builder in South Africa Cecil Rhodes remarked: "The British are the finest race in the world, and the more of the world they inhabit, the better it will be for mankind."[38] Since the emergence of the science of evolutionism, white European imperialists envisaged their empires in racial terms of superiority and inferiority. They placed themselves at the top of a scale of civilization and achievement, while they ranked all other nonwhite races in descending order beneath them. In this context, the creation of a national music in the United States during the early decades of the twentieth century was directly linked up with the issue of race as the country "was in the midst of a great debate about immigration, in which race was the central issue, and eugenics one of the proposed solutions."[39] In 1931, the American composer, writer on music, and professor at Columbia University, Daniel Gregory Mason, wrote:

> [O]ur whole contemporary aesthetic attitude toward instrumental music, especially in New York, is dominated by Jewish tastes and standards, with their Oriental extravagance, their sensuous brilliancy and intellectual facility and superficiality, their general tendency to exaggeration and disproportion.[40]

In contrast to "Jewish tastes and standards," he continued, the music of contemporary British composers such as Edward Elgar, Grainger, and Vaughan Williams epitomized "the deeply passionate yet outwardly reticent English character, and by extension the same Anglo-Saxon traits that had determined the Yankee—and by extension American—temperament."[41] For the creation of a national music, therefore, Mason emphasized, a reconnection with America's historic Anglo-Saxon "racial" roots in music was necessary. In 1921, in fact, Mason had written a positive review of a concert by Cyril Scott of his own compositions in New York: "It was frankly sensuous, it was music for the fun of it, it was not only not thoughtful but it did not want to be, it despised thoughtfulness."[42]

Between 1916 and 1918, Cecil Sharp had already begun the rediscovery of the American colonial musical heritage. He and his collaborator Maud Karpeles did fieldwork in the southern Appalachian mountains, believing that by preserving the remnants of old "English" folk song they were doing the groundwork for a proper educational program for Anglo-Saxon Americans, "so that they may as quickly as possible enter into their racial inheritance."[43] Sharp also did establish American branches of the English Folk Dance Society and gave lectures on folk music that drew large audiences. As Mark Slobin recently emphasized, however, in his Appalachian "English" folk song research, Sharp "scrupulously ignored any ties to the black musics also indigenous to the region."[44] Grainger had always admired Sharp's work and, in 1920, Percy actually offered to finance the publication of his American work, a payment as it were for his arrangements of several English tunes collected by Sharp, including *Country Gardens*. The latter refused the offer, but after his death Karpeles accepted it and edited *English Folk Songs from the Southern Appalachians* (1932).

In *Music in My Time* (1938), Gregory Mason expressed his gratefulness to Grainger for propagating his music during a period when few others cared for it. In their correspondence, nonetheless, Grainger was solely interested in Mason's music and not in his ideas about music and race. This remains unexpected, since race was for Grainger what religion was "to *other* fools."[45] He developed a complex theory of the superiority of what he called the "blue-eyed" people, the Anglo-Saxons and Nordic races, and their music, though he excluded the Germans, whose musical "tyranny" he found unacceptable. At an early stage, he read books by Otto Weininger and, Richard Wagner's son-in-law, Houston Stewart Chamberlain, authors who according to John Bird were "proto-Nazis of a particularly noxious variety."[46] In the United States, he found inspiration for his racial ideas in the works of American Nordicists such as Madison Grant and Lothrop Stoddard. He felt particularly attracted to Grant's *The Passing of the Great Race or The Racial Basis of European History* (1916) and it was from him that he adopted the term "Nordic." In his Yale University lecture of March 6, 1921, "Nordic Characteristics in Music," however, Grainger rejected Grant's faith in the "magic of 'blood'" arguing that he looked at racial characteristics in music from "an utterly cosmopolitan angle": "I believe that Jews, Negroes and plenty of other non-Nordic races could and would, if presented with Nordic surroundings and conditions, acquire all Nordic traits."[47] Then again, in spite of his Nordicism, Grainger was as easily dedicated to a "war" against German culture and music. Also, he had Jewish friends, and he performed and transcribed the music of George Gershwin, though he had strong anti-Semitic views. Likewise, he openly supported Black Americans in their opposition to segregation, participated in concerts for negro charities for free, and generally developed a great interest in Black American music, which he believed was closely connected to Anglo-Saxon music, despite what he called its "tribal" influences. When Grainger taught at New York University (1931–1932), he actually invited Duke Ellington and his band to come to one of his lectures to illustrate some of his music theories.

During the early 1930s, then, Grainger developed a bizarre and exotic racial theory that included all music traditions in the world. Basically, he divided the world into two musical spheres: the "Mongolian-Nordic" and the "Muhammedan" (by which he meant Mediterranean) musical traditions. The former geographically encompassed Nordic Europe and its colonies, Russia and China, Japan, Thailand, Java, and so on, and had as its main musical characteristics "long notes, or at least clearly-defined intervals; gapped scales; solemnity or spirituality of mood; and a tendency towards underlying harmonic thought."[48] This in contrast with "the nervous, passionate, excitable tunes [...] consisting largely of quickly changing notes that scamper about like the flitting of insects" of the Muhammedan tradition.[49] These two traditions, Grainger continued, were reflected in facial stereotypes: the Mongolian "high cheekbones, small, upturned noses, and calm, smooth looks" versus the Muhammedan "larger, more prominent and more hawk-like noses, smaller cheekbones and a more aggressive facial expression."[50] In his view, the Nordics were originally individualistic rural folk, inclined to musical and social freedoms, and hence to strongly individual and wide-ranging melodic utterance. Those from the South, often urban folk, were prone to be collectivists, more fettered by social and religious restrictions, and inclined to communal music making, which naturally curbed the freedom of melody. Over time, the Nordics sought "art" and replaced their individualistic melodies by complex polyphonies, while the Southerners sought "civilization" by curbing complexities either through greater coordination of the notes of different lines into a few predictable harmonic progressions or through the distractions of soloistic display. In other words, according to Grainger, Nordic music was "more scientific, more highly complicated and organized, more restrained, more tender and tolerant than any other known music and civilization."[51] Surprisingly in the light of his racialism and interest in Maori culture in particular, he did not make any Orientalist connection between the Maori race and Aryanism.[52] In fact, despite his admiration of Hitler and reading of books written by "proto-Nazis," he seems to have paid scant attention to Aryan race theory.

After living a "slave-life," as he saw it, as one of the world's celebrated pianists for 60 years, Grainger believed that a return to the all-roundedness of "traditional Scandinavian or outback colonial communities" was "the only antidote to modern-day 'experts' and provided the basis for a return of dignity and happiness to the individual man."[53] Needless to say, his Nordicism was unscholarly. As Malcolm Gillies and David Pear have argued, "his first fifty years show a move from being a naïve, even playful, racialist to becoming an increasingly intolerant racist" and "this racial-to-racist transformation was maintained in the remaining three decades of his life."[54] As so often with Grainger, one wonders to what extent he launched ideas simply to shock and provoke. In 1933, for instance, he wrote anything but dogmatically:

> All these unscientific thoughts about geographical and racial origins of Asiatic and European music seem to me quite harmless, as long as we entertain them with inquiring and elastic minds and do not claim any scientific authority for our guess-work. Some day theories may be proved or disproved by researches of comparative musicology, a much-needed society for the prosecution of which in America has been started by the composer Charles Seeger, and others.[55]

In any case, his Nordicism was much in contradiction with his genuine interest in exotic non-Western musical traditions and his overall fascination with "primitive" music in metropolis and colony.

Mapping all the world's folk music

> The worth-whileness of all races & all cultures is proved by all the world's music, & to delay needlessly a drenching of ourselves in all this glorious "exotic" music is simply (in my opinion) to criminally postpone the dawn of inter-racial worldwide understanding & brotherhood.
>
> (Percy Grainger, Letter to Bernard Heinze, December 3, 1947)[56]

During the imperial encounter, the world was mapped with folk music and imagined from a Western perspective. With childhood memories of Maori chants as well as the music that he had heard in Melbourne's Chinatown and Japanese bazaar, Grainger developed an early interest in non-Western music and, for example, composed *Eastern Intermezzo* in 1899. Above all, Asian music stimulated his love for tuned percussion, of which he began to incorporate a great amount in his compositions. This especially after he heard the sound of a Balinese *gamelan* at the Paris World Exhibition of 1900, and it will be recalled that after a similar *gamelan* experience at the World Exhibition of 1889, Claude Debussy composed his *Pagodes* (1903). In fact, in 1905, Percy not only gave the first British performance of this piece but he later also made an arrangement for "*gamelan*-like" tuned orchestral percussion and keyboard instruments to give it back "to the sound-type from which it originally emerged."[57] Intermittently between 1910 and 1914, Grainger studied the collection of Javanese instruments at Leiden University's Ethnological Museum in the Netherlands. In the early 1930s, he transcribed Javanese and Balinese music from the first world music anthology series on record, *Music of the Orient* (1931), compiled by Erich Moritz von Hornbostel, one of the leading figures in German comparative musicology. Also he performed the American composer and proto-ethnomusicologist Henry Eichheim's *Oriental Impressions* (1918–22), a suite of seven pieces based on melodies that he had gathered in Japan, Korea, China, and Thailand.[58]

Grainger was more or less up to date with the burgeoning field of comparative musicology. He knew the work of Alexander John Ellis[59] and, after Sharp's suggestion, was familiar with the writings of Charles Samuel Myers.[60] He was especially interested of course in people who were mapping the world's folk music. In 1909, during one of his concert tours of Australasia, he got hold of seven cylinders recorded by Alfred J. Knocks (1851–1925) during the time of the New Zealand International Exhibition held in Christchurch in 1906–1907: five with Rarotongan music from the Polynesian Cook Islands and two with Maori music.[61] Knocks was "a licensed interpreter and native agent of Okaki, New Zealand," and, as he wrote to Grainger, he "came into contact with the native race, their customs and usages, and always made it a point to learn anything that was of interest from them."[62] Fortunately, Grainger copied Knocks's recordings at the time because the original copies now are lost. Also he attempted to notate the music but, of course, as Paul Jackson recently emphasized, these notations

> [...] do not *represent* the music in a meaningful way and, for all of Grainger's care in the matter, must be viewed in a similar light to his seminal transcriptions of English folk songs: as aids in the apprehension of otherwise lost examples of orally transmitted music.[63]

Likewise, it is useful to keep in mind that because Grainger knew Rarotongan music only from Knocks's recordings (though he did hear live examples and made recordings of Maori music), his transcriptions are "already at a further state of remove from the original performances."[64] In addition, Grainger met the British biologist and ethnographer Walter Baldwin Spencer, who wrote *The Native Tribes of Central Australia* (1899) and other works in Australian ethnography, and, together with F. J. Gillen, made the first field wax cylinder recordings of Australian Aboriginal songs in 1901–1902, of which Percy made three transcriptions.[65] On the whole, Grainger subscribed to the diffusionist theory of comparative musicology, which stimulated comparisons of seemingly disparate cultures and times in search of common origins. So, for instance, he did find a "spiritual alikeness" between the Russian American organist and musicologist Josef Yasser's transcription of a "typical Chinese melody," of which he made a pentatonic chinoiserie piano piece to be played on the black keys, *Beautiful Fresh Flower* (1935), and Edvard Grieg's C-minor sonata for violin and piano.[66] Likewise, he saw parallels in terms of "going-onness" and "long flow form" between the music of Bach and the dance-songs of the Faeroe Islanders as well as the Rarotongans' improvised choral polyphony.[67]

While India lay at the heart of the British Empire and the country's music offered many possibilities for Western modernist composers, surprisingly Grainger seems to have known nothing about Hindustani or Carnatic music. He transcribed one Indian tune from Hornbostel's *Music of the Orient* and further only referred to Indian music superficially in passing. For example, he believed that "the origins of the coloratura singing in Italian operas" were to be found in Indian music, assuming that "these traditions of florid Asiatic singing" most probably had entered Europe "with the Moors in Spain."[68] Also, after hearing an Indian wind instrument, he thought that the "perfectly-toned woodwind" was to be found in the East.[69] Though it is not clear to me whether Grainger was familiar with Ratan Devi's *Thirty Songs from the Panjab and Kashmir*, he praised a concert of Indian folk songs by her in his article "The World Music of To-morrow" for *Etude* in 1916:

> Here is a consummate artist rendering consummate music—and "absolute" music. Here are delicacies and refinements of vocal technic utterly undreamt of by European art-singers, though not equally unknown to European folk-singers. Our art-singers should go and listen. Our composers will hardly need telling. Those of us who love subtle harmonic effects find them in plenty in the blend of her wondrously controlled voice with the vibrant buzzing drone of the "tambura" [*tanpura*: Indian lute], the indescribably satisfying native plucked instrument with which she accompanies her Indian "professional" songs. Those of us who are especially responsive to the fragrant freshness of unaccompanied unison are ravished by her Kashmiri folksongs. How can it be that such pure

and irresistible artistic delights as these have been withheld from us for so long? Perhaps the difficulties and limitations of musical notations and the lack of familiarity with them on the part of our travelling classes is accountable for much of our amazing ignorance of exotic musics, and apathy towards them.[70]

As far as I know, Grainger never mentioned Fox Strangways's *The Music of Hindostan* in his writings. This is surprising because Fox Strangways was a fellow member of the Folk Song Society with a similar interest in "primitive" music and was the biographer of Cecil Sharp. Likewise, as in Scott's case, I did not find any reference in his writings to the songs of Rabindranath Tagore.

Conversely, the relationship and comparison between Grainger and the American proto-ethnomusicologist Natalia Curtis Burlin should be noted in relation to Grainger's mapping of all the world's folk music. Curtis recorded songs of the North American Hopi Indians and in 1907 wrote her groundbreaking and popular *The Indians' Book*, a collection of songs and stories, illustrated with handwritten transcriptions as well as with artwork and photography. Later, she studied Black American as well as African music and culture. Grainger regularly performed her music and explained the importance of her folk music research. Overall, he praised her "human sympathy with all primitive art."[71] Specifically, he was delighted with her four-volume collection of Black American music, *Negro Folk-Songs* (1918–1919). Curtis too had some lessons with Busoni, who based his *Indian Fantasy* (1913) for piano and orchestra on some of her collected melodies. Like Curtis, Grainger feared that non-Western music traditions would die out in the face of Western civilization and progress:

> We see on all hands the victorious on-march of our ruthless Western civilisation (so destructively intolerant in its colonial phase) and the distressing spectacle of the gentle but complex native arts wilting before its irresistible simplicity.[72]

He explicitly wondered when the "Anglo-Saxon iconoclasm" that sought to change Hopi ways would end.[73] The primitivism of Curtis and Grainger had an anthropological dimension, and they "went native" to different degrees. So, for example, Curtis adopted native dress and the Hopi name "Tawi-Man" (Song-Maid), while Grainger collected Australasian artefacts, wore grass skirts, and learned to make up intricate decorative beadwork. Simultaneously, it should be emphasized that like Curtis and other proto-ethnomusicologists, Grainger was repeatedly influenced by imperialist racial stereotypes in his descriptions of non-Western musicians as pure, simple, child-like, and in the possession of inborn rather than learned musical talents. Also imperial and paternalistic remains the fact that Curtis and Grainger at all times staged their "primitive" musicians for their recordings and indeed photographs, which generally show them heroically at the center of the occasion.

By and large, Grainger opposed the teleological idea of music history that music moved from "primitive" and simple to civilized and complex. On the contrary, he believed that "all races are genuinely musical, at all times and places, and that each phase of human existence brings forth its own perfect musical expression."[74] One could even argue that he was a visionary, who heralded the contemporary era of "world music," for example, when he wrote in 1933:

> I firmly believe that music will someday become a "universal language." But it will not become so as long as our musical vision is limited to the output of 4 European countries between 1700 and 1900. The first step in the right direction is to view the music of all peoples and periods without prejudice of any kind, and to strive to put the world's known and available best music INTO CIRCULATION. Only then shall we be justified in calling music a "universal language."[75]

At the same time, as I said earlier, Grainger's position was imperial and closely connected to his racial worldview. In "The Impress of Personality in Unwritten Music" for instance, he argued that what defines European music history was the development of harmonic thinking, for which Nordics had a "natural" tendency, and that with this development, which he insisted made it superior ("this most transcendental and soul-reaching of all our means"), there had been an atrophy in melodic thinking and, hence, "primitive" music was to be called upon as a corrective resource.[76] Though Percy saw ("natural") value in non-Western music traditions, he considered Western civilization's superiority to be ultimately unquestionable for Westerners and non-Westerners alike, irrespective of his jibes about its "ruthless" and "victorious" on-march, and the destructive intolerance characterizing its colonial phase. This explains also why he did not see any loss of "authentic" music in the appropriation of Christian hymnology by the Rarotongans in their chorals along the lines of their own "individualistic dictates of Unwritten Music."[77] On the contrary, he saw it is a model for the integration of a European sense of form with folk "authenticity," a musical style that could be surpassed only by his utopian "free music."

A "Noble Savage" in modernist music

In his quest for "free music," Grainger experimented all through his composing career with new piano techniques, musical instruments, poly-rhythms, poly-tonalities, clashing harmonies, irregular rhythms, and so on. Also, he was always in search of new musical forms and composed for flexible groupings of instruments, unusual combinations of instruments, and so on. Though most of these experiments are part of the modern history of Western "classical" music, one could equally argue that he was twentieth century modernist music's "noble savage."[78] According to Ronald Stevenson: "Grainger had absorbed so much folk-music that he was a folk-musician" and at the piano "articulated as a folk-musician does."[79] As Percy himself wrote: "My music should be fiercely & wildly performed, rather than in a staid & modest manner."[80] It does not come as a surprise that in 1940 Grainger employed the American modernist composer Henry Cowell, the presumed inventor of tone clusters with a similar fascination for non-Western music traditions. After Cowell was arrested as a homosexual and received the maximum sentence of 15 years, it was Grainger who in 1939 wrote successfully to the prison board at San Quentin, California, that he would offer him a job as a live-in research assistant if he were granted parole. Cowell had studied comparative musicology in Berlin with von Hornbostel and teachers from India and Java. In his article "Towards Neo-Primitivism" for *Modern Music* (1933), he specifically projected a new twentieth-century music that did not imitate non-Western music but drew "on those materials common to the music of all the peoples of the world."[81] The two met for the first time in 1933, when Grainger was teaching at New York University, and Cowell, together with Charles Seeger (who also befriended Percy), a few blocks away at the New School. Throughout that decade they exchanged many ideas but unfortunately they did not come to a close musical collaboration. In fact, though they kept in contact almost until Grainger's death in 1961, as Suzanne

Robinson recently emphasized, Cowell played down Grainger's influence on his work, perhaps because he was embarrassed "to be associated with an eccentric who was known to dress like a vagrant and support vegetarianism."[82]

For Grainger, civilization stood in opposition to art. While civilization followed creative simplicity in the face of social complexity, he argued that true art (read: *his* art and "free music" in particular) sought complexity. In his mind, it was the modernist composer's goal "to bring music more and more into line with the irregularities and complexities of nature and away from the straight lines and simplicities imposed by man."[83] As he wrote in 1938:

> Out in nature we hear all kinds of lovely and touching "free" (non-harmonic) combinations of tones; yet we are unable to take up these beauties and expressiveness into the art of music because of our archaic notions of harmony.[84]

Of course, Grainger's conceptualization of nature contradicted not only with his conscious and rational composition of "free music" but also with his overall scientific study of "primitive" music. For example, he failed to see that the careful repetition of irregular rhythms by "primitive" musicians, which he himself indeed saw as inherent to their music and notated, was a cultural and institutionalized action that was not intended to reflect nature and did not bring them any closer to nature.

The combination of Grainger's alternative intellectual outlook and involvement with "primitive" music proved crucial to the development of his compositions. Inspired by the polyphony of the Rarotongan chorals, for example, he explored the phenomenon of stratified polyphony in the context of the aleatory musical structure in *Random Round* (1912), a work embodying a conception of "communal improvisation" that allowed the performers unprecedented control over its structure.[85] Each subsection of the composition begins with a stroke on a Javanese gong and then builds up from between ten and twenty melodic variants, whereby choice of variant and tempo are left to the performer's discretion. Similarly, Grainger argued that his setting of a Faeroe island folk song, *Let's Dance Gay in Green Meadow* (1905 for chorus; 1932 for three players on one harmonium!; 1943 for four hands on one piano), was rhythmically at one with the "orgiastic" dancing and singing habits of the Faeroes, generating "group frenzy of a religious, erotic or war-like character" (program note). This unusual, rather austere, and "primitive" work, deriving from the metrics of Icelandic folk verse, is constantly in seven-bar phrases, which sometimes overlap. Grainger explained that he used repetitive rhythms and dissonant harmonies, functioning as a quasi-percussive accompaniment to dancing feet, to capture the "tireless keeping-on-ness" of the Faeroe Island narrative songs, which may run into 200 or more verses. Grainger's most extensive work, *The Warriors* (1916), on which he worked more or less during the same period that Gustav Holst did on *The Planets*, then, follows his vision of a meeting of warriors of all times and races for an orgy of warlike games. Its orchestral version includes a large percussion section and three (or nine!) grand pianos. While the pianists are required to play inside the pianos with marimba sticks, six off-stage brass players perform at a totally different speed from the rest of the orchestra, for all of which two extra conductors might be needed.

Interestingly, in "Democracy in Music" (1931), Grainger linked a "polyphonic" approach to the composition and practice of music to his political ideal of democracy:

> [...] not all forms of music are "democratic." True folk-song [...] is individualistic rather than democratic. Top-melody, accompanied by subservient unmelodic chords & basses, cannot be called democratic; nor can soloistic display-music [...]. Such musics are closer to musical feudalism, aristocracy or high-priest-craft than to democracy. But all true many-voiced (polyphonic) music [...] may be said to be musically democratic. Such music is not only richer & more subtle in a purely musical sense than all other existing music, but also satisfies the spiritual, religious, ethical & emotional cravings of modern humanity as does no other.[86]

For Grainger, all Nordic music, even when it was not technically polyphonic, was generated from an underlying framework of "polyphonic thought." At once, however, he made clear that his polyphonic and democratic world was open to other races as long as they attained the "Nordic" traits. When this would happen, he believed, a truly internationalist world would emerge in which the Nordic

> shall abandon his quest for slaves to do the rough work for him [...] shall do his rough work for himself [...] shall build up

communities of *racial equalities*, consisting of Nordics and *any other races* that measure up to Nordic requirements.[87]

Irrefutably, Grainger's ideal of Nordic polyphonic democracy was straight in line with the Western civilizing mission or, better in his case, Kipling's "The White Man's Burden":

> Our Nordic gift to the world is the gift of *freedom*. And we Nordics, who fail in almost every other virtue of life as compared with other traces, *dare not fail* in the matter of freedom.[88]

Even so, in comparison with Edward Said's notion of polyphony as "a metaphor for humanist emancipation," as Rokus de Groot recently put it,[89] Grainger's ethical ideal was less utopian because, due to his adherence to primitivism, he included conflict and violence as inherent to human relationships in his thinking and compositions.

Conclusion

Grainger's internationalist worldview was anything but morally or politically consistent. He was not only a Nordicist and racialist but also claimed to be a socialist,[90] pacifist, and anti-imperialist, who found much inspiration in the writings of both Kipling and George Bernard Shaw. His fascination with non-Western music was cosmopolitan but simultaneously often exotic, paternalistic, and racial. No doubt, Grainger's self-perception as a "colonial" outsider and experiences of non-European music and cultures affected his aesthetic and worldview. His Australian childhood gave him an early experience of Maori, Chinese, and Japanese music, as well as a different natural landscape. Perhaps it also saved him from the predominant influence of church and orchestral music that was so common among British composers. To a great deal, his primitivism, which included the idea of an idealized Australian bush, was a therapeutic means of coping with life in an increasingly urban, industrial, and modern world. In any case, Grainger translated his love for nature and primitivism in his detailed folk song settings, *Jungle Book* cycle and modernist compositions such as *The Warriors*. Indubitably, he had sincere scholarly aspirations in his studies of "primitive" music in metropolis and colony, and his research was unusual among Western composers at the time. In his ideas about transcription, the uniqueness of the moment of music performance and the worth of "primitive" music worldwide, which are commonly accepted today in the study of "world music," he was ahead of his times. Like Fox Strangways, Grainger was much influenced by the English folk song movement in his research of non-Western music traditions and overall in favor of humanizing the musical "primitive." Ultimately, however, he appropriated "primitive" music traditions as a resource for the development of his own modernist musical aesthetic, but at least he himself was aware of this:

> The fact can hardly be too often emphasized that it is largely the "hyper-modern" men who prove to be the most susceptible to the lure of "primitive" music, which not only confronts them with a simplicity (in certain directions) refreshing to them by reason of the sharp contrast it affords to art music, but which also contains certain elements of extreme complexity particularly as regards rhythms and dynamics, to which the modernist may turn to *increase* the range of his ornate compositional resources; the artist with the healthiest appetite for complexity can generally be relied upon to possess the strongest craving for simplicity also.[91]

Both Grainger's primitivism and Cyril Scott's occultism were countercultural but imperial forms of thinking. In different ways, they revolted against the repressiveness of Victorian morality as well as the growing rationalization and institutionalization of society and music. They were against many modern developments and in search of alternative lifestyles. Well before his time, Grainger warned against the dangers of population growth, pollution, and, like Scott, meat eating. Though their music and worldviews differed remarkably, they greatly respected each other's personality and work throughout their lives. Grainger was not only a propagator of Scott's work but at different times also helped him out financially, and indeed repeatedly was irritated by Scott's inability to promote his own music. Conversely, Scott may have been able, as his son Desmond recently suggested, to look beyond the numerous contradictions that Grainger presented to the world and recognize "the deeply spiritual man" in him.[92] This then would be in congruence with the fact that Percy's interest in all the world's folk music followed an urge to find out whether or not this music, at least for himself, carried "any spiritual message,"[93] as well as with his belief that the interest in non-Western music among modernist composers was "the inborn desire for more cosmic musical experiences."[94] But there were tensions as well. As already said, Grainger was an ardent champion of Scott's *First Piano Sonata*, the work that Fox Strangways wrote so negatively about in *The Music of Hindostan*. Percy had a vested interest in its success because he believed that the metric freedom of the work was his Australian invention, and Scott had asked him permission to use the technique. Over the years, he often wrote frustratingly, and even somewhat accusingly, to Scott about the fact that he never received recognition for being the first to employ these rhythms, before Scott and Stravinsky did.[95] Also, Grainger never understood Scott's interest in Theosophy and Indian philosophy. As he wrote in 1954: "That a sweet & well-meaning genius like Cyril Scott should be taken in by the Yogi business is utterly beyond my grasp."[96]

As far as I know, Grainger did not know John Foulds, the main protagonist of the next chapter, or his music. Even so, Foulds can be taken as someone in whom some of the most important interests of Grainger and Scott were combined. So, for example, his position within the British music establishment was more or less comparable to that of Scott, as they both had great musical successes followed by failure, which in part perhaps was the result of their intense fascination for Theosophy. Moreover, Foulds's absorption into Indian culture and music led to a level of knowledge that would have made Grainger jealous. Before I turn to Foulds, however, I will first discuss the activities of his second wife, Maud MacCarthy, a Theosophist, internationalist, and musician, who at the time was considered an authority on south-Indian music.

3
John Foulds and Maud MacCarthy: Internationalism, Theosophy, and Indian Music

Maud MacCarthy: From Ireland to India through music and Theosophy

Maud MacCarthy was born in 1882 in Clonmel, County Tipperary, Ireland. Her father Dr. Charles William MacCarthy made a name for himself as a physician, surgeon, painter, sculptor, and musician. Her mother was MacCarthy's second wife, the contralto, Marion Cuddihy. Because of Charles's ill health, the family moved to Australia in 1885, where Maud spent her early childhood. She later wrote about her Irish Roman Catholic parents that they were talented amateur musicians "gifted with inborn psychism."[1] In Australia, Charles composed several comic operas and patriotic war songs like *Our Boys, You Bet!: Recruiting Song* (ca. 1915), *Oh Mother, Asthore!: A Soldier's Parting* (1916), and *The Boys of the Dardanelles* (ca. 1915). His best-known piece remains *The Lyceum Valse* (1895) for piano, "dedicated with much affection to his little daughter Maud MacCarthy," who is pictured on the sheet music's cover with her violin. He also lectured and wrote on music. A child prodigy on the violin, Maud practiced "for some six hours a day for fourteen years" and had no time to read or to go to school.[2] Yet, she had "visions," "wonderful dreams," and "natural psychic experiences," and overall was "thrilled" by religion: "not a religion, not any study of books" but a longing "for alignment with Cosmic Consciousness."[3] During her youth, she also became familiar with the *Bhagavad Gita* and Theosophy, about which over the years she became "more convinced than ever of its underlying truth."[4]

In 1891, Maud began her studies at the Royal College of Music in London. Later, she successfully performed as a soloist in Britain and toured the United States, as first ever female soloist with the Boston and Chicago Symphony Orchestras, for example. Actually, in 1906, she did two concerts with Percy Grainger: one at the London's Queen Hall and one at Leeds Town Hall, where they performed Johannes Brahms's *A Major Violin Sonata* (Opus 100).[5] A year later, at the age of 22, however, she startled the musical world and made it into the newspaper headlines when she decided "to renounce success and fame, and devote the rest of her life to the study of Theosophy" and in doing so fulfilled a "mystic prophecy."[6] As she explained to *The Times*:

> I am not setting up as a teacher of Theosophy. At this stage I am a student and nothing else. But I have never found anything so completely satisfying. Of course, you can't convince people by arguing with them. There must be a personal experience. Every step of progress I have made in art both intellectually and emotionally I owe to theosophy. These things have always had an attraction for me from my earliest youth—as a child I was precociously religious; I have always felt that the work of my life—my whole life—must be something different from the practice of my art alone.[7]

At the same time, Malcolm MacDonald emphasized in his seminal work on John Foulds that MacCarthy also had to abandon her career as a concert violinist because of neuritis.[8] As she described herself: "rheumatic and neurotic conditions of the arms and hands" curtailed her career as a soloist but allowed her to continue to lead orchestras.[9] Though Maud's own account for her withdrawal and her subsequent life interests makes one think that her fascination for Theosophy was more important than her neuritis, most likely the two reasons combined resulted in her metamorphosis.

MacCarthy became a follower of the then newly appointed president of the Theosophical Society, Annie Besant, for whom she already for some time had "a profound reverence." Until then however she had met Besant only briefly for three times, of which the longest meeting "lasted only half an hour" and took place after she quit her violin career.[10] Even so, something happened between the two because Besant invited her to come to India. Here, besides her great interest in Theosophy, the fact that MacCarthy was an outspoken feminist might have played a role. In 1908, the two toured together in India, where MacCarthy collected and transcribed Indian folk songs: "a vast field almost unexplored," as she later wrote, and "the soul of Indian music."[11] Among other places, she studied Indian music in Benares (Varanasi). Altogether Maud stayed for about a year in the subcontinent. Eventually, she knew most about Carnatic music and sang the ornamentation integral to *ragas*, including the 22 *shrutis*, for which she found the term "quarter-tones" a "misnomer," because "thirds of tones are found, and perhaps fifths also."[12] She also learned to play the *tabla* and the *veena* (south-Indian lute). Her lecture-recitals received positive reviews in the Indian newspapers. Between 1907 and 1914, she also was a founder-member of the Theosophical Arts Circle and wrote for their journal, *Orpheus*.

Upon her return to Britain, she began to deliver lecture-recitals on Indian music, for example at the Universities of Oxford, Birmingham, and Glasgow. On January 16, 1912, she gave a presentation called "Some Indian Conceptions of Music" at the (now Royal) Musical Association in London, which was published in the society's proceedings under her first married name Maud Mann. For her, Indian music was part of a lived-in world and accordingly for its real study, she told the audience:

> We must look for our materials in an analysis of existing records according to Indian methods, in the beautiful utterances of a few rare living artists; above all, in the traditional beliefs about music which linger with passionate persistence in the very heart of the people, which influence all worthy modern developments, and which find occasional outlet in the all-night musical ecstasies of devotees in the temples or on the roadways, and in the inexpressibly lovely songs of the folk which, by their rhythmitonal complexity, far in advance of ours—that is a point to note—suggest the remains of a noble art, rather than the spontaneous expression of untutored natures. If we heard these artists, these devotees, and these folk of India, and heard them at their best, we must be convinced that the East can speak to us in music, as it has spoken in philosophy, in poetry, and in religion. But they are difficult to hear. Only real sympathy will unlock the barriers between the musicians of the West and the East.[13]

MacCarthy pointed out that the traditional Indian beliefs about music were not "mere fanciful dreams" and that Indians *ragas* transcended being "a mere arrangement of notes."[14] Overall, she propagated the radical standpoint at the time that "the study of the Indian view-point may be of artistic value to Western musicians."[15] Speaking the terminology of comparative musicology and Aryanism, she observed that the similarities to be found between Indian and Western music pointed to the common origins of a single Indo-European Aryan culture. So, for example, she saw identical "basic Aryan conceptions of rhythm" in the phrasing of the opening theme of the Adagio from Ludwig van Beethoven's *Violin and Piano Sonata* (Opus 30) No. 1 and an Indian *tala*.[16] For MacCarthy, Western music needed to be reconnected not with its national folk traditions but with the music of India:

> Many of the *ragas* and *talas* have an indefinable but appreciable power, *entity*, even to Western ears. They sound, indeed, more "modern" than anything of that "school" which one has heard in the West, and one feels, moreover, that, handled by Western musicians, they could not possibly sound alien. And this last would only be natural, since the basis of our own culture is mainly Aryan.[17]

In 1912, Rabindranath Tagore declared that MacCarthy, who sang the poet's songs in public and also corresponded with him, was "so eminently fitted to introduce Indian music to a Western audience."[18] Around this very same time, she talked with Gustav Holst about Indian *ragas* and most likely was an influence on him. To be clear, however, he made no systematic use of *ragas* in his music, though there are suggestions of particular *ragas* and some of his song accompaniments are *tanpura*-like. In addition, Maud made an impression on Arthur Henry Fox Strangways, who attended and very much liked one (or more) of her lectures and later also used her "Some Indian Conceptions of Music" for *The Music of Hindostan*. In 1915, MacCarthy fell in love with John Foulds. Despite strong opposition from family and friends, both left their respective partners and lived together from 1918 onward. They had two children and finally married in 1932. Maud became Foulds's muse. She not only reinforced his already existing fascination with occultism but also aroused in him an interest in Indian music and initiated him in the study of *tabla*. She stimulated him to move in new creative directions and provided him with "a metaphysical basis for his work."[19] Indeed, one of the goals of this chapter is to do justice to the influences of both MacCarthy and Theosophy on the life and work of Foulds. Conversely, one can easily understand why Foulds was attracted to her idealistic internationalist view on music. As she wrote in the preface of the re-publication by the Theosophical Society of her lecture for the Musical Association:

> In all modern musical creations of any importance there is [...] a tendency towards change and exchange: change of subject and of materials and methods; and exchange of ideas and of theories between cultures hitherto considered irreconcilable. Thus, under the impetus of common ideals, the boundaries of nations (and, slowly, of races) are being overpassed; and its seems as if in the blending of East and West, ancient and modern, esoteric and exotic, and in the flights of imagination which result therefrom, we could already hear the first faint notes promising the music of a glad new day.[20]

In contrast, interestingly, Fox Strangways was not so much attracted by MacCarthy's musical internationalism, as becomes clear from the detailed notes that he had taken during one of her lectures and included in a letter to her:

> *Didn't* understand altogether *what* rapprochement she desired between East and West. Surely we *don't* want to model *our* music on *theirs*; and must suppose that they have no intention of modelling or modifying *theirs* in *our* direction. And what are they to do about instruments? If the fiddle (and co) come unglued, and the piano is anathema, there remains the wind: ours is constructed for the concert room wh. [*sic*] they don't want, theirs for the hillside which they do.[21]

The re-publication of MacCarthy's lecture for the Musical Association ended with the announcement of her then-forthcoming book, *A Garland of Indian Song*, which unfortunately was never published. It would have consisted of some 50 songs in different Indian languages with English translations and notated in Western staff notation with the characteristics of the *talas* and microtones preserved as far as possible. According to the announcement, the book would have afforded the Western musician a way "to study and apply for himself the fundamental principles of Indian music, if not perfectly, at least to a degree which has been unattainable under the old method of record."[22]

In hindsight, MacCarthy more or less remains a key figure in the history of the relationship between Indian music and the West. On the one hand, because she learned Indian music in practice and, on the other, because she explained it to Western audiences from an internationalist cross-cultural perspective, and in doing so had an influence on Holst, Fox Strangways, and Foulds. Also it should be noted that she belonged to a group of women who wrote about and gained some practice of Indian (folk) music. Besides Margaret Cousins and Ratan Devi, Anne Campbell Wilson is another example. She was married to the British civil servant, James Wilson, and lived for many years in Punjab, where she developed an interest in local folk music. Subsequently, she studied Hindustani "classical" music with "chance instructors" and, especially, with the earlier mentioned Hindu national music reformer Vishnu Digambar Paluskar, at the Lahore Gandharva Mahavidyala. The results of her studies she noted down in *A Short Account of the Hindu System of Music* (1904).[23] Because of their practical knowledge of Indian music, these women should be contrasted with those of the more Orientalist variety who had already played a role in the Western encounter with Indian music, from eighteenth-century notations of "Hindustani Airs" to Amy Woodforde-Finden's 1902 setting of "Four Indian Love Lyrics" from *The Garden of Kama* by Laurence Hope (a pseudonym of Adele Florence Cory).[24]

In 1935, MacCarthy returned to India, together with Foulds and their two children, as well as the East End London laborer William Coote, who was illiterate but supposedly had amazing mental powers, including an unprompted knowledge of Sanskrit. She simply called him "The Boy" and she wanted him to work with "the Brothers," a group of learned devotees of occult wisdom.[25] While Foulds worked at the All India Radio (AIR) in Delhi, about which more later, MacCarthy founded both an *ashram* (religious hermitage) to promulgate the teachings of "the Brothers" and a fabric factory in Kashmir. Also she did some freelance journalism and wrote mystic poetry under the name of Tandra Devi. Actually, the earlier mentioned Irish internationalist and Theosophist James Cousins wrote the preface to her *Poems* (1937). Following his successful activities at the AIR, Foulds was transferred to take charge of the newly opened Calcutta station. Yet, a few days after his arrival there, he contracted cholera and died unexpectedly on April 25, 1939. In 1943, Maud married "The Boy," and after she outlived him as well, she became a Hindu, took *sannyas* (renunciation of worldly life), and renamed herself Swami Omananda Puri. About her marriage with Foulds, MacCarthy wrote in her esoteric autobiography *The Boy and the Brothers* (1959):

> He was a great artist, whose output in serious musical composition was unfortunately small, but of superlative quality [...] We were entirely at one on inner things, and he was truly dedicated to his art. His life was tragically wasted, however, for we were so dreadfully poor that most of his work had to be of the pot-boiler sort.[26]

The fate of internationalism: Foulds and the failure of *A World Requiem*

John Foulds was born in Manchester as the son of a bassoonist in the Hallé Orchestra. His parents belonged to the Plymouth Brethren, and he found the narrowly religious atmosphere at their Mancunian home oppressive and constricting. Without much formal schooling, he was taught music from an early age by his father, whom he joined at the age of 20 in the Hallé Orchestra as a cellist under Hans Richter, who also launched him as a conductor and programmed Foulds's *Cello Concerto* (1908–1909) in his farewell concert in 1911. Perhaps Foulds performed Cyril Scott's *Heroic Suite* (1900) when it was premièred by the Hallé Orchestra under Richter on December 12. 1901. Already from childhood, Foulds composed abundantly and, following the performance of his *Epithalamium* (1906) at the 1906 Promenade Concerts, he dedicated himself completely to composing. He soon achieved success as a composer of light orchestral and salon music, which included some pieces in the Scottish-Celtic folk idiom. His greatest hit *Keltic Lament* (1911), which was performed at the 1911 Promenade Concerts, is only one example. Moreover, he managed to establish a reputation in Britain and Europe as a critical progressive composer. Over the years, he counted Darius Milhaud, Igor Stravinsky, Edgard Varèse, and other musical modernists among his contacts. Together, Foulds and MacCarthy belonged to the world of British internationalists. They were acquainted with George Bernard Shaw and W. B. Yeats. Actually, they made theater music for Shaw's *Saint Joan* (1924), Yeats's *At the Hawk's Well* (1917), and a production of Tagore's *Sacrifice* (1920) by Kedar Nath Das Gupta's Union of East and West, a multiracial organization promoting cultural exchange between Britain and India. Under the inspiration of the Arts and Crafts

Movement, MacCarthy wrote *The Temple of Labour: Four Lectures on the Plan Beautiful in Relation to Modern Industrialism* (1926).

Between 1918 and 1921, in the aftermath of the carnage of the First World War, the couple worked wholeheartedly on Foulds's *A World Requiem* (1921), conceived as "a tribute to the memory of the Dead—a message of consolation to the bereaved of all countries." The work was dedicated to Maud, who had compiled the eclectic internationalist and pacifist text, which included passages from the Bible, John Bunyan's *Pilgrim's Progress,* and the sixteenth-century Hindu *Bhakti* poet Kabir. Being heavily inspired by Theosophical thought, the work appealed to "the indestructible spiritual unity of mankind."[27] Its subtitle, "A Cenotaph in Sound," not only "referred to Theosophy's belief that musical sound could alter the physical and spiritual state of the listener,"[28] but also emphasized that Foulds offered his composition as a musical equivalent to Whitehall's iconic Cenotaph, which was designed by his friend Edwin Lutyens, the architect of New Delhi, whose Theosophist wife, Emily, was a student of Foulds. As James Mansell put it:

> Foulds imagined a war requiem that was simultaneously modernist and spiritually cathartic. The idea of refashioning a cenotaph in sound, an empty tomb from the physical vibrations of music, drew upon an ancient occult tradition revived by Theosophy in which music, above all other forms of human expression, was thought to connect mankind with the natural workings and divine inspiration of the universe.[29]

The *Requiem* was endorsed unanimously by the Committee of Management of the British Music Society, an organization founded in 1918 by the earlier mentioned biographer of Cyril Scott, Arthur Eaglefield Hull, "to champion the cause of British composers and performers at home and abroad." Besides Eaglefield Hull, the committee included some well-known names in the world of British music such as Arnold Bax, Adrian Boult, and Eugene Goossens.

Following the recommendation of the British Music Society, the *Requiem* was accepted by the Royal British Legion for performance on November 11, 1923 at the Royal Albert Hall on its first Festival of Remembrance, better known as Armistice Night. Foulds conducted a chorus and an orchestra of around 1,250 performers to an auditorium packed to capacity and under the eye of the Prince of Wales. The demand for tickets had broken all previous Albert Hall records, and this success led to three consecutive annual performances, though in 1925 at the Queen's Hall. To be clear, Foulds and MacCarthy set up the Festival of Remembrance at their own expense and never made any money out of the performances, as all profit was donated to the British Legion. MacCarthy not only led the orchestra in the performances but also played the violin herself, accompanying the solo soprano in the "Song of the Blest," which replaced the "Hymn of the Redeemed."[30] Though the *Requiem* was successful with the general public as well as with intellectuals and musicians such as George Bernard Shaw and Cyril Scott, it was criticized by the press for being too humanist rather than muscular Christian and patriotic, and the British Legion withdrew its patronage for the work in 1927. MacCarthy was convinced that there was a conspiracy against Foulds among influential people in the British Legion, the *Daily Express,* that took over the promotion of the Festival of Remembrance in a different format, and the BBC. If so, this most likely was related, as both Rachel Cowgill and James Mansell recently argued, to the *Requiem*'s propagation of Theosophical "spirituality," which was troublesome to the Anglican Church.[31] In any case, the following somewhat defensive program note was added for the performance in 1925:

> It should not be thought, however, that the composer demands of his hearers an initiation into some esoteric, Gnostic, or theosophical system for the full appreciation of the "Requiem." Nothing could be further from the truth.[32]

Instead of Foulds's internationalism, the *Daily Express* wanted music for Armistice Night that was "compatible with national pride and the necessity of war."[33] In fact, during the 1930s and 1940s, the annual event was provisionally renamed "A Festival of Empire and Remembrance."

Some critics were perplexed by the *Requiem*'s lack of musical material.[34] Yet, Foulds purposely adhered to "simplicity" in composing it: on the one hand, because, he sought to attain "the correct vibration types" rather than "formally pleasing harmonies, melodies, and rhythms";[35] and, on the other, because, in consonance with the Theosophical Society's overall social political stand, he wanted his healing and "spiritual" message to reach a large audience.[36]

As it was stated in the 1926 program note, the work's "universal appeal demands that its broad basis and central themes be of the most utmost simplicity, even at the risk of seeming, to more musical tutored minds, too obvious in statement."[37] It also demanded that the *Requiem* be addressed "to the spiritual rather than to the emotional in man" and that therefore "much of the music may seem to be remote, bleak, lacking the human touch and the personal appeal."[38] Evidently, the Fouldses were great believers in the Pythagorean concept of "the music of the spheres" and were familiar with the classical mythology of Orpheus and his musical powers. As MacCarthy wrote in her posthumously published second book on the teachings and message of "the Brothers," *Towards the Mysteries* (1968):

> Pythagoras was a great initiate in the ancient Mysteries, as well as a devotee of sound. The teachings which were imparted to me under Mystery conditions from 1906 onwards, are—in my humble opinion—from him and his; otherwise there could be no explanation fitting the facts.
>
>   This event, *and the techniques of magical sound which were given out, and fully tested by John Foulds and me,* justify my claim—apart from the evidence of many ancient thinkers—that there *is* an Orphic Mystery of Sound.[39]

In fact, after Foulds met MacCarthy, he increasingly began to declare that (parts of) his compositions, including parts of the *Requiem*, were the result of clairaudience.

From the very beginning, the BBC excluded Foulds's *Requiem* as appropriate broadcast repertoire for Armistice Day. In 1923, the corporation chose to broadcast an alternative concert to the *Requiem*, which included a rendition of *God Save the King* and two pieces, *Imperial March* (1897) and *Land of Hope and Glory* (1902), by Edward Elgar. A year later, it did the same, preferring instead two works by British composers who were killed in action: George Butterworth's *A Shropshire Lad* (1911) and Ernest Farrar's *English Pastoral Impressions* (1915). Most likely, the exclusion of the *Requiem* from the radio had to do with the influence of the BBC's first director-general, John Reith, who dominated the corporation until 1938. In the words of John MacKenzie: "Reith had an almost mystical approach to the [British] Empire, which he regarded as the most successful example of internationalism and peaceful coexistence in modern times."[40] It was under his leadership that the BBC promoted "a blend of nationalism, monarchism, Protestantism, duty, and moral discipline, by no means considered incompatible with its simultaneous adherence to principles of impartiality and objectivity in public service broadcasting."[41] Eventually, Elgar's *The Spirit of England* (1917) on the war poems by Laurence Binyon would become the sound of Armistice Day, while "Nimrod" from his *Enigma Variations* (1899) was performed for the first time at the Cenotaph in 1946.[42]

Foulds believed that the failure of his *Requiem* to establish itself in the British music canon was a crucial setback in his career as a serious composer and helped to validate his reputation as simply a composer of light music. Subsequently, he spent the years 1927–1930 in Paris, the center of modernist music at the time. There, he worked as an arranger, accompanist for silent films, copyist, and overall went through a period of profound creativity, while Maud lectured on Indian music and, for example, performed with the troupe of Uday Shankar, the Indian dancer and brother of Ravi Shankar, in "Dances et Chants de l'Orient."[43] After their return to London, Foulds had fallen by the wayside as a modernist composer. In 1933, he actually complained in a letter to Adrian Boult, the conductor of the BBC Symphony Orchestra, that the BBC continually broadcast his light music but did not dare to touch his more serious works.[44]

Foulds's *Music To-day*: Modernist music, internationalism, and Theosophical spirituality

Real music is not national—not even international—but *supranational*. I believe that the power of music to heal, to soothe, to stimulate and recreate, is just the same in Timbuctoo as in Kamtchatka, and was the same in the time of Orpheus as it is today.

Anyone who believes that the phrase "the music of the spheres" is not simply an idle phrase but means something definite, will find no difficulty in accepting this idea, that real music is not an affair of Time and Space, but a series of vibrations coming we know not whence, going we know whither, but some of which we humans are *permitted*, as it were, to overhear from time to time [...]

We incline to forget that music is a force in Nature as is Light, or Heat, or Electricity, and like these great natural forces, real music has nothing essentially national about it at all.

(John Foulds, "Is the Gulf between Eastern and Western Music Unbridgeable?" A talk broadcast on All India Radio, Delhi Station, March 6, 1937)[45]

At several places in his main piece of writing, *Music To-day: Its Heritage from the Past, and Legacy for the Future* (1934), Foulds referred to Cyril Scott and his earlier mentioned books on music: *The Philosophy of Modernism* and *Music: Its Secret Influence throughout the Ages*. In the latter work, Scott had hailed Foulds's *A World Requiem* as a great achievement, and one can easily imagine how its appeal to the unity of mankind was attractive to him. Actually, he compared the work with Alexander Scriabin's *Prometheus: The Poem of Fire* (1910) but simultaneously made clear that Foulds's attempt to reach a similar high aesthetic stage in music through the employment of quarter-tones was unsuccessful and solely "gave rise to the idea that the orchestra was playing out of tune."[46] Foulds, who was another admirer of Scriabin, replied that if he reached out at all for such an aesthetic, quarter-tones definitely were not central to the composition.[47] In spite of his criticism, nonetheless, he still respected Scott and mentioned him as a leading contemporary British composer. On the whole, Foulds's case remains much comparable to that of Scott. Also, his oeuvre to a large extent fitted in with what was expected by the British music establishment: music in both Scottish-Celtic and English pastoral veins; regular performances at official celebrations; praise by established British composers, including Elgar; friends with Ralph Vaughan Williams; and so on. Likewise, Foulds did not receive his education nor worked at one of the established British music institutions and became a successful multitalented composer with esoteric interests.

Despite their similar choice of topics, Foulds's writing style is much more outspoken and political than Scott's. So, for example, he wrote about Arnold Schoenberg, whose music he found "a mere intellectual device," without any "magical spell":[48]

The value of Schönberg's contribution to the progress of music is that in the making it he has helped to hew out a new road. That he has become absorbed in his engineering to such an extent as to have forgotten whither his road leads; (so utterly obsessed indeed as to be indifferent to its leading anywhere at all), is all that need be said in depreciation of this sturdy iconoclast.

[…]

Now in the case of Schönberg we have a specific instance of a composer elevating reason above imagination; allowing the machine to usurp instead of sub-serving the higher function. [...] Despite all of which, he may be considered the most stimulating figure in the musical world to-day.[49]

Foulds disliked jazz even more than Scott and was disgusted when Duke Ellington appeared at the Albert Hall in London. He found the syncopated rhythm of jazz simply banal but recognized the importance of the genre's use of improvisation.[50] At the same time, he felt inspired by Negro spirituals and accordingly wrote some pieces in this vein, for example *The Florida Spiritual* (1924) for orchestra and the more extensive *Fantasie of Negro Spirituals* (1932) for orchestra with improvised chorus. Predictably, despite their interest in many kinds of music, including Black American music, Scott and Foulds were much more inclined toward Asian music traditions for inspiration because these were in line with their Theosophical worldviews. Furthermore, Foulds's turn to India was related to the Theosophical idea of the racial unity of the Indo-European tradition. In his view, India was not only the source of the Aryan race and languages but also of its music, and he emphasized the influences of Indian music on Spanish, Hungarian, and Russian folk music.[51]

In the postscript of *Music To-day*, Foulds acknowledged his debt to MacCarthy for his knowledge of occultism and Indian music. The book largely is a justification of modernist music and its connection to the occult, which he saw as a scientifically verifiable set of natural laws waiting to be discovered. As he wrote: "Human progress takes the form of concentrating upon, and rendering overt, the workings of natural law which were formally occult."[52] Unsurprisingly, Foulds's language often was esoteric, as in the following excerpt, wherein he resolutely promoted progress in music:

The vast majority of us are so obsessed by the emotions that a recent pronouncement that no new possibilities in music remain to be exploited has gone almost unchallenged. No new possibilities! Think of that. Consider [...] that the upper levels of the Mental plane (the Causal world), the glories of the whole of the Intuitional world (the Buddhic) and the wonders of the Spiritual (Atmic) realm remain practically unexplored by composers, or, more precisely, not conveyed to us in their music. Having realized this, what will be our reaction to such statements as these; that we have reached a terminal point; that to progress further is a manifest impossibility?

It will surely be abundantly clear [...] that no additions to our technical equipment—no quarter-tonal, no modal systems, no additions of new *timbres* to our orchestral resources, in short, no technical means whatever—will in themselves aid us in our efforts to widen the field of musical appeal. What is needed is the spirit of the intrepid explorer; his contacting instrument the human consciousness; his driving power the Will, and his recording instrument the brain. Once able consciously to contact and freely roam the hitherto neglected higher-mental, intuitional and spiritual realms, once able to realize these extremely rarified vibrations in his brain, assuredly all the technical devices we have so far evolved *and many new ones* will be needed by the composer adequately to transcribe for us the records of his pilgrimage.[53]

Like Scott, he dealt with the relationship between music and color, and also mentioned Blavatsky's table from *The Secret Doctrine*.[54] As an extension of Scott's *Music: Its Secret Influence throughout the Ages*, as it were, he discussed some leading contemporary composers in the light of "*Deva*-music" based on "vibration types."

Following the negligence of his larger serious works by the British musical orthodoxy, Foulds wrote bitterly about the British "habit of discounting in advance any work by a composer who is not content to purvey stereotyped emotional stimulant *via* the old-established melodic and harmonic routes."[55] In accordance with "the main evolutionary trend of the art," he felt a historical destiny for his music whereby, he argued, the use of atonal music was crucial because it "entirely lost its nationalist character."[56] In consequence, he made a straightforward attack on the making of a national music based upon folk music:

There are a number of persons in the musical world who look for the salvation of a country's music to the intensification of its national characteristics, and would base a new national music upon its old folk-songs. Frankly, I am not of these. The time is past and will not return. Interest in folk-music from an archaeological and ethnological point of view, and the greatest delight in its characteristic and perennial beauty, will, let us hope, never die.

But for present-day composers and protagonists to concentrate upon such, or any other narrow nationalistic phenomena, goes clean against the main evolutionary trend of the art. Only out of a new realization of world-wide emotional-mental solidarity—even sodality—can the real music of the future be born.[57]

Or elsewhere:

It is all very well for Vaughan Williams to scoff at those musicians who profess in their art what he calls a "backboneless cosmopolitanism," and to instance Wagner's Meistersinger as his greatest work because it was his most German one in its philosophy. [...] No "backboneless cosmopolitanism" for me, but also, and equally emphatically, no "little Englander" music either. English music in the main has been of little or no effect abroad because—as E. J. Dent says somewhere or other—"it has been the wrong kind of English music because it was composed for purely English audiences."[58]

Though Foulds accepted the advantages of technology and eagerly wanted his works to be broadcast by the BBC, he was overall critical of contemporary mass culture with its commercialization of music, in particular of the translation of music through the "mechanized music" of the gramophone and radio, which with its distortion of dynamics and timbre was against "the ensouling of music."[59] He explicitly lamented that the importance of "spirituality" in the making of music was completely ignored at British music schools and conservatories in favor of technique.[60] In contrast, he propagated a "world-wide emotional-mental solidarity" in the making of a progressive music for the future, which included an appropriation of Indian music. Indubitably, his Theosophical "spirituality" and internationalism, as well as his appropriation of modernist musical techniques such as quarter-tones, glossolalia (open vowel sounds conveying mystical ecstasy), and, as I will discuss below, Indian-inspired modes, made him an unorthodox British composer.

Indian music and internationalism: The universality of modes and quarter-tones

By and large, Foulds advocated a more genuine contact with Asian music traditions and was irritated with what he termed "Orientalities"

in Western music, such as that found in Scott's Orientalist compositions. His first India-inspired composition, *Gandharva-Music*
for piano,[61] which was published by the Theosophical publishing
house in London and reached its definite form only in 1926, then,
is Orientalist music of an altogether different modernist kind. This
unusual abstract work was dedicated to the founder of the Parisian
"Les Amis des Arts Esotériques," G. Constant Lounsbery, and alleg-
edly heard clairaudiently and afterward partly notated. It consists of
a continuous unbarred and unaccented ripple of notes over a six-note
basso ostinato, repeated sixty-five times. The piece barely rises above
an almost inaudible volume and foreshadows the work of minimalist composers (figure 3.1). His goal was to capture the actual sound
of the Gandharvas or the angels (*devas*) with superb musical skills
of Hindu mythology, whereby he emphasized that *Gandharva-Music*
was "transcribed approximately for Pianoforte" but he originally had
heard the music in "natural intonation, not tempered" and in a tone
color close to that of the flute (program note). Here, Foulds distanced
himself from musical Romanticism and, instead, aimed to uncover
"the workings of natural law":

> It should not be listened to as we listen to the music to which we
> are accustomed, for it does not represent human emotion, but is
> part of the music inherent in things themselves. (Ibid.)

Interestingly, Foulds wrote that "all the music he has ever heard
clairaudiently, was in natural intonation, not tempered" (Ibid.).
This might indicate that his countercultural internationalism, as
in Grainger's case, also stood for a search for other than half-tone
intervals, respectively, in Indian and Maori music. Most probably,
MacCarthy's ideas had been influential here as well. Before she met
Foulds, she already made clear that the best Western musicians
worked in "just intonation," which she argued was "common to all
Aryan peoples."[62] In addition, she took a firm stand in the contemporary discussion about *shruti* intonation, whereby she emphasized
that to the performer it was of no importance whether or not there
actually existed 22 *shrutis*, though she herself found out through
her notations of Indian songs that they all work.[63] In her opinion,
the *shrutis* did not belong "to modes or *ragas* proper" but solely were
"graces" or "microtonal shades" that could be added to the seven-
tone scales and, "after a little ear-training," could be "distinguished
as notes subsidiary to the mode."[64] They did not depend "upon a

Figure 3.1 John Foulds, *Gandharva Music*, 1926 (Courtesy Theosophical Publishing House).

fixed 'law' of the theorist, but upon the capacity of the individual musician to hear and reproduce them."[65] As to be expected, she loathed the modern Indian music schools, where "the pupils are carefully trained out of their capacities for natural intonation, and their tonal ideas are stifled by tempered pitch on screeching harmoniums."[66]

Like many musical modernists, Foulds was much attracted to composing in nondiatonic modes and already before the First World War he was experimenting with music in the Greek modes.[67] Following this interest, as well as his fascination with Indian *ragas* and an admiration for Ferruccio Busoni's modal compositional ideas, as written in *Sketch for a New Aesthetic of Music* (1907), he realized that in addition to the diatonic major and minor scales, the 12 chromatic notes of the well-tempered system could yield no less than 111 further 7-note scales. In particular, he was interested in the scales that corresponded to the 72 modes of the south-Indian *melakarta raga* scheme, as originally devised in the seventeenth, century by Venkatamakhi. In congruence with Western harmonic thinking, however, he preferred to work with those scales in which the fifth from the keynote remained perfect, so as to preserve a tonic-dominant relationship. Accordingly, he codified 90 modes, of which the first 72, with two small exceptions, correspond exactly to the *melakarta* scheme (i.e., they accommodate the interval-structure of the Indian scales to their nearest well-tempered equivalent on the piano) and the remaining 18 are logical derivations (the table of 90 modes is printed in *Music To-day*). Each of these modes, Foulds argued, expressed "certain states of consciousness, certain ranges of vibration, which are incommunicable by any other means at present known to us."[68] Along the lines of MacCarthy's idea that the harmonization of *ragas* would open "a vast field to the musician of the future" in East and West,[69] he made use of some of these modes in several innovative compositions such as the *Essays in the Modes* (1928) for piano, the first movement of the *Dynamic Triptych* (1929), and the third "mantra" of the orchestral *Three Mantras* (1919–1930), originally planned as part of a large Sanskrit opera to be called *Avatara*.

Through his appropriation of what he labeled "Aryan" modes, Foulds set himself a task no less rigorous than that of Schoenberg's 12-tone serial technique or Ferruccio Busoni's ideas about modal composition. His use of Aryan modes aimed to be an alternative, as it were, to both the tonal music in major and minor scales, which it replaced, and Schoenberg's "obsessive" serialism, which he found representative of the crisis in Western music. In strictness, nonetheless, Foulds's approach to composing in modes was more like that of Schoenberg than Busoni, whom he greatly admired and himself in fact often turned to the East for inspiration. For, unlike what Busoni proposed, each of Foulds's above-mentioned works stays within its mode and does not modulate (change of key) or introduce unrelated notes. As he explained: "Once the vibration of any particular mode is really established, the introduction of any note which is foreign to it produces an almost unbearably discordant effect."[70] Thus, he followed the orthodox Indian musician's attitude to *raga* in feeling that "the power of mode resides in its utter purity."[71] At the same time, however, Foulds based harmonies on the specific modes. Though reassuringly these were to be played on the equal-tempered pitches of the piano, like in the case of *Gandharva-Music*, he expressed his inconvenience in relation to the use of the piano in *Essays in the Modes* and emphasized that in accordance with Indian traditional practice, his modes should be studied through singing.

Another example of Foulds's innovative appropriation of Indian music remains his use of Indian microtonality in the concerto *Lyra Celtica* (mid-1920s) for solo female voice without words and orchestra. He obviously wrote the piece for MacCarthy because she was one of the very few Westerners who could sing Indian microtones and assumingly was his teacher too in this field. In terms of his use of modernist musical techniques, Foulds's employment of Indian microtonality seems to be the logical follow-up of his use of quarter-tones, which he claimed to have pioneered in his music since 1898 and subsequently used for example in the second movement of his *Cello Sonata* (1907; revised for publication in 1927), the second movement of *Dynamic Triptych,* and the second movement of his string quartet, *Quartetto Intimo* (1931). In contrast to Percy Grainger, however, he saw his use of quarter-tones not as an influence of non-Western music, or like Scott as a sign of India's "spirituality," but as a natural development of the Western diatonic scale:

> It must be understood that the quarter-tone as here used has nothing whatever to do with those "microtones" with which Eastern musicians are wont to embellish their modal melodies. It is an indigenous growth, natural offspring of the Bach equal-tempered scale.[72]

In any case, it should be clear that Foulds's *Gandharva-Music, Essays in the Modes, Lyra Celtica,* and other compositions do not sound Indian at all because his goal was not to copy Indian music but to absorb its underlying thought processes and perhaps spirit.

Recently, James Mansell argued that Foulds "used quarter-tones in a similar way to the use of micro-tones in Indian music" already early in his career, to demonstrate "the shared musical heritage of

European and Indian music,"[73] and that the fascination of Foulds and MacCarthy with intervals between semi-tones particularly should be read against the background of both their Theosophical thought, central to which was the "Aryan" unity of India and Europe, and "modernist internationalism."[74] As MacCarthy wrote:

> [...] our field of harmony is far from exhausted [...] the writer of modern "programme" music [...] is reaching out towards musical forms which may lead him suddenly into the archaic theosophical tradition of the Aryan race; [...] if we can teach much to India, India may, in turn, teach us how to teach; [...] there may be more things in music than we or our Eastern brothers have dreamed of—things which will only come to birth when the peoples of East and West search for them together; and that our orchestras, to be complete, may still need the tones of the *vina* and *tabla*, and our hearts, to be full, the melodies of the East.[75]

It seems plausible to argue that what Foulds knew about and heard of Indian music confirmed the feelings and thoughts that he had, at least subconsciously, already for a long time about music. Instead of a study of Indian music, his table of 90 modes therefore perhaps was an attempt to present scientific evidence for "the music of the spheres." Then again, in considering them "representative of a universal history of world music" and the means for the creation of a truly modern music,[76] he followed a cyclic view of music history that was more or less similar to Rabindranath Tagore's internationalist view on history as mentioned in the Introduction. As he wrote in *Music To-day*: "It may appear a backward step. But all progress is cyclic; look back but far enough and you perceive the vantage-ground whence the next forward-step may be taken."[77] In 1916, in fact, Foulds had already mentioned this very same idea in the Theosophical magazine *The Herald of the Star*. At that time, however, he also argued that "the ancient tradition" was best preserved and alive in India, "the seat and root of so many of our Western art tendencies" and the country where Pythagoras supposedly had traveled and derived his knowledge for the Greek modes from.[78]

Foulds in India

In 1935, Foulds and MacCarthy fled to India. Though Foulds's Indian period only lasted for a mere four years and the sources are few, he would have some most interesting musical experiments and even some influence on the development of modern Indian music. Still on the way to India, he finished the *Indian Suite* (1935) on the basis of Indian melodies collected by Maud and *The Song of Ram Dass* (1935), a miniature for small orchestra, which follows one of her improvisations "in Indian style." The opening of the *Indian Suite*, "Bhavanutha," a joyful song to the Hindu God Ram, attributed to the south-Indian saint, musician, and composer, Tyagaraja, was one of the first transcriptions that MacCarthy showed Foulds after they met. On the whole, he aimed to paraphrase the tunes of the *Indian Suite* by using Western instruments and musical technique "as to convey to the listener something of the *effect* which these beautiful and characteristic melodies have made one him."[79] As he wrote:

> The whole suite therefore reflects the happy, joyous gaiety and, at the same time, the severity of the Hindu art. What the Western world commonly supposes to be *the* "oriental" type—the languorous, the magical, the more erotic (due to Persian influence)—is not represented at all in this work.[80]

Unlike Foulds's earlier mentioned compositions, the *Indian Suite* is more akin to a folk song suite and largely an Orientalist piece of work, though he does make some use of the *talas* implicit in the themes themselves and derives the harmony exclusively from the pitches of the melodies.

In India, Foulds taught composition and piano, gave some public lectures, and wrote for local newspapers and journals. Furthermore, he worked together with musicians playing traditional string instruments and generally experienced the reality of Indian classical *ragas* and folk music. In 1937, Foulds agreed to become director of European music at New Delhi's AIR-station, despite his earlier mentioned criticism of the translation of music through the radio. There, he not only became very active as commentator (on February 15, 1939, he even provided the commentary to the first All India Cattle Show!), solo performer, accompanist, and conductor but also attempted a musical syncretism between East and West through the formation of an Indo-European orchestra, incorporating indigenous instruments. In point of fact, Foulds's orchestra was in line with AIR's civilizing mission of "cultivating good taste" in music. The first controller of broadcasting, Lionel Fielden, complained that Indian music was too limited a field for broadcasting and therefore had to be reformed to create sufficient variety "to command the continu-ous attention of a large public."[81] Foulds was employed to compose pieces, teach musicians to read staff notation, and experiment with a new Indian music.

During 1935–1936, Foulds devoted much time to the study of the folk music of Punjab and Kashmir. Accordingly, he made arrange-ments for his Indo-European orchestra, based upon his transcriptions of north-Indian folk songs (*Kashmiri Boat Song, Kashmiri Wedding Procession, Pahari Hill Tune,* and so on). Apparently, the last work he was working on before his death was *Dance-Tunes from Punjab* for piano. Also during his last years he was busy with his *Symphony of East and West,* of which unfortunately the score no longer exists. What he was looking for was not so much a blend between Western and Indian instruments but a way of using Indian instruments in an orchestral manner. Above all, he wished to avoid the constant unison that seemed to be the only way of playing together. Foulds saw no future for the orchestra, however, when Indians continued to neglect both the condition of their instruments and the quality of tone in their playing or singing.[82] Similar to other contemporary Westerners with an interest in Indian music and Indian music reformers like Tagore and Ananda Coomaraswamy, he complained about the sing-ers' voice technique, or what MacCarthy described as "the ugly mod-ern Indian convention of singing through the nose."[83] Amusingly, when he taught Indian musicians to read Western staff notation, his by no means illiterate musicians, who were used to the Urdu (*nast-aliq*) script written from right to left, often played wrong notes. Also, some of the musicians later confessed "that they knew the music by heart and only pretended to look at the score really!"[84] Although the AIR National Orchestra (Vadya Vrinda) was not set up until 1952 under the direction of Ravi Shankar (1920–2012), it followed Foulds's experiments in combining European and Indian instruments, use of notation (though this was not uniform), orchestration of *ragas* in new ways, mixing of ensemble playing with solos and so on. Though Shankar of course had been equally influenced by the Maihar Band established by his guru, Ustad Allauddin Khan, perhaps Foulds had some influence here.

No matter what, Foulds definitely played a role in the banning of the use of the harmonium by AIR. The harmonium was widely dissem-inated by the British, especially the missionaries, and became a cru-cial accompanying instrument in all north-Indian music traditions, including the native Christian one and in Sikh sacred music. This because it was cheap, portable, not easily damaged in transport, and, unlike the piano, held its tune regardless of heat and humidity. Like folk song collectors in Britain and comparative musicologists around the world, MacCarthy and Foulds adhered to the idea that "authentic" Indian (folk) music had to be saved from extinction and, ironically, Western influence. They both loathed the harmonium because, as Foulds put it, its rigidly well-tempered scale straitjacketed Indian music's flexible intonation (microtones, glissandos, and so on) and so ruined the Indians' ear for pitch.[85] Following Foulds's article "Harmomnium" in *The Indian Listener* of July 7, 1938, which was translated into Urdu, Hindi, Gujarati, and Marathi, Fielden forbid the use of the instrument for broadcasting, only to be back in unrestricted use by 1980, after a partial lifting of the ban 1972. In contrast, the Western violin was accepted without discussion in Carnatic music. This was not only because it could mimic the voice, the basis of all Indian music, but also because the emerging Indian middle class (like the European one) took the violin as a serious Western classical instrument, and gave it more status than the harmonium.[86] It certainly remains ironic that Hindustani music revivalists eagerly adopted an imported keyboard instrument with a tempered scale as suitable accompaniment to the voice (in 1874, Sourindro Mohun Tagore wrote a harmonium manual in Bengali). Whatever the pros and cons, however, the harmonium, though long forgotten in the West, is still widely used, and the AIR ban therefore seemed to have had little effect. On the contrary, the instrument is fully indigenized in South Asia and has developed in unique ways, for example, through the additions of drone stops and a scale-change mechanism.

Of course, Foulds's adherence to "authenticity" in Indian music was inconsistent with the performances of his Indo-European orchestra on the radio or, for example, on March 28, 1938, at the Regal Theatre in New Delhi before a large audience, which included the viceroy. Also his teaching of ensemble playing and staff notation to Indians was paternalistic in the sense that he wanted to transform them, as it were, into Western musicians. He had a great willingness to learn from Indian musicians but simultaneously believed that Indian music was in need of Western music. As he made clear during one of the 12 radio talks entitled "Orpheus Abroad," which he gave on AIR between March and May 1937: on the one hand, Western musicians could learn from Indian music "lessons of melodic purity and rhythmic emancipation, new methods of tuning, the expressive use of micro-intervals, new timbres, and the value of meditation, timelessness, and spontaneous improvisation"; on the other hand, Indian music "if it was to develop rather than ossify or merely be corrupted, could capitalize upon its melodic riches by learning the Western arts of polyphony and ensemble playing."[87] In making this statement, then, for Foulds, Western music with its idea of (harmonic) development was the ultimate reference point. In comparison to what he did with his own orchestra, he certainly did not think much of Indian efforts in combining Indian and Western music that followed the impact of Western music through radio, films, and the gramophone. As he wrote to the editor of *The Musical Times* in 1938:

> Indian professional musicians are importing just these methods to be up to date and are plastering Occidental harmonies, jazz rhythms, and mongrel orchestrations upon a basis of their own beautiful melodic, subtly rhythmic and exotic instrumental art.[88]

Finally, it remains typical that in his search for "authenticity," Foulds never referred, either for study or inspiration, to the gramophone recordings of Indian music, which by that time were abundantly available.

Conclusion

While Maud MacCarthy undeniably influenced John Foulds's interest in Indian music and Theosophy, he clearly had his own agenda and overall created his "Indian" compositions "more despite MacCarthy than because of her."[89] In fact, she disliked not only some of his best works such as the *Mantras* and *Dynamic Triptych* but also his *Music To-day* because in her view he distorted her writings in the process.[90] Alternately, it should be clear that the Fouldses much adhered to Theosophical thoughts but neither of them ever was a very active member of the Theosophical Society for any length of time. Malcolm MacDonald seems right to assume that, like many other (pseudo-) Theosophists, they distanced themselves from the mainstream when Besant proclaimed Jiddu Krishnamurti to be the new World Teacher in 1925.[91] In fact, Scott's Introduction to David Anrias's *Through the Eyes of the Masters* (1932) can be read as a rebuttal of Krishnamurti's well-known speech at the annual Star Camp in

Ommen, the Netherlands, on August 3, 1929, when he dissolved The Order of the Star of the East in front of Besant, who had founded it to support his role as World Teacher, and took a firm stand against the Theosophical notion of "spiritual" evolution and the possible, organized help one could get from souls significantly more advanced on the path than oneself.[92] Further, it is not clear to what extent the Fouldses supported the Indian nationalist movement, as Western Theosophists living in India often did, though one suspects that in comparison to Foulds, MacCarthy, who met the future leaders of India and Pakistan, respectively, Jawaharlal Nehru and Mohammed Ali Jinnah, had views that were more in line with those of, for example, Besant and the Cousins.

For their times, MacCarthy and Foulds gained a significant understanding of Indian music and aesthetics. Yet, as is to be expected, they also adhered to such imperial tropes as staff notation, paternalism, and "authenticity." In their Indian music research, they were influenced by a wide configuration of ideas, ranging from comparative musicology to Aryanism. Predominantly, their commitment to Indian (folk) music concerned a "spiritual" search. For Foulds, this search primarily was related to a self-consciously modernist musical aesthetic, whereby, as for Cyril Scott and Gustav Holst, "music was not simply an art form or a mode of representation, but an objective physical phenomenon with an active occult agency in social, psychological, and spiritual life."[93] For MacCarthy, it was related more generally to an internationalist counterculture and, indeed, increasingly her own version of occultism. Both aimed to overcome the "difference" of Indian music and reached out for musical universalism. The fact that they were musicians in the first place undeniably helped their attempts at cross-cultural communication. Like Fox Strangways, they reached a respectable understanding of Indian (folk) music but their activities were too disparate to label them founders of the discipline of Indian ethnomusicology, though in hindsight they deserve some credit as proto-ethnomusicologists. Regardless, their cases show the relationship between the English folk song movement and comparative musicology: from MacCarthy's collecting of Indian folk songs to Foulds's arrangements of them and from Foulds's early compositions in a Scottish-Celtic idiom to his folk song hunt in north-Western India. Then again, it seems that Foulds and MacCarthy had a more practical knowledge of Indian music than Fox Strangways, Margaret Cousins, or Anne Campbell Wilson and, hence, perhaps their case can be better compared with that of Arnold Bake. Though the Dutchman was politically anything but an internationalist, because of his knowledge and practice of Indian (folk) music and culture, he became one of the close Western acquaintances of the quintessential Indian internationalist, Rabindranath Tagore, who in the making of his own songs partially was influenced by the English folk song movement.

4
Rabindranath Tagore and Arnold Bake: Modernist Aesthetics and Cross-Cultural Communication in Bengali Folk Music

The poet, the singer, and the songs

In 2009, Reba Som wrote a biography of Rabindranath Tagore with music as the key theme to understand the man and his work.[1] The fact that such a book was published only at this time remains remarkable because Tagore composed over 2,000 Bengali songs, known as *Rabindra Sangit* (literally, Rabindra Music). As he wrote in *The Religion of Man* (1931), he believed that music, "the most abstract of all the arts, just as mathematics is in the region of science," was the purest and most unimpeded form of creative expression in existence.[2] His celebrated *Gitanjali* (1912) was a collection of mostly songs, which he set to music, and he overall felt "that his greatest gift was for music, and it was this that he should try to communicate to the outside world."[3] Also he repeatedly used musical metaphors in his writings, and there is a connection between his music and his painting. Music, in other words, formed the very essence of Tagore's artistic being. The goal of this chapter is twofold. First, it examines Tagore's musical oeuvre from the perspectives of modernist aesthetics and cross-cultural communication, whereby it specifically investigates his appropriation of Bengali folk music and ideas, especially of the so-called Bauls, in the light of primitivism. Second, it takes a close look at Rabindranath's relationship with the early twentieth-century Dutch pioneer in South Asian ethnomusicology Arnold Bake, who successfully performed Tagore's songs in India and the West, and notated a number of them in *Twenty-Six Songs of Rabindranath Tagore* (1935). Their relationship shows how folk music research was a concurrent phenomenon in Europe and India, and in this context I will take a close look at Bake's analysis of Tagore's songs. Indeed, the fact that Bake is scarcely mentioned in the works on Tagore, including Som's book, and the poet's (auto) biographical writings, remains surprising because, more than anyone else, the Dutchman did all he could to make *Rabindra Sangit* known to the world. Besides the overall neglect of Tagore's music in historiography, one explanation for this might be that there exists no abundant correspondence between the poet and Bake, comparable to, for example, William Rothenstein or his early biographer Edward Thompson.[4]

According to Tagore's student and the doyen of *Rabindra Sangit* Santidev Ghosh (1910–1999), the poet never made any derogatory remark about Bake's interpretations of his songs, "in spite of variations in pronunciation and voice,"[5] of which the Dutchman of course was fully aware himself.[6] On the contrary, Rabindranath always praised the Dutchman's baritone and was especially grateful to him for his efforts in familiarizing European and American audiences with his songs. In 1933, in fact, Bake wrote that Tagore had told him: "While you have got your voice to earn money, I have got my pen."[7] The fact that Bake gained Tagore's complete trust in the performance and notation of his songs remains particularly intriguing because Rabindranath at that time believed that even Bengalis had not reached a full understanding of their beauty and significance. As he spoke candidly during a conversation with Edward Thompson in 1926:

> I often feel that, if all my poetry is forgotten, my songs will live with my countrymen, and have a permanent place. I have very deep delight in them. But—[very sadly] it is nonsense to say that music is a universal language. I should like my music to find acceptance, but I know this cannot be, at least not till the West has had time to study and learn to appreciate our music. All the same, I know the artistic value of my songs. They have great beauty. Though they will not be known outside my province, and much of my work will be gradually lost, I leave them as a legacy. *My own countrymen do not understand.* But they will.[8]

So why did Tagore, who throughout his life wrestled with questions about the universality and translatability of his music, have faith in Bake, a Westerner with a wholesome knowledge of Bengali music, language and culture?

Over time, *Rabindra Sangit* became the Bengali identity marker par excellence, a sort of collective inwardness into Bengaliness, in Indian West Bengal, Bangladesh, and the Bengali diaspora. Simultaneously, there have been discussions about the "authentic" performance of Tagore's songs, whereby it is ultimately assumed that non-Bengalis will never be able to understand and sing them. Many Bengalis around the world probably are surprised to hear therefore about Tagore's support for Bake's singing and notating of his songs. In this chapter, I will argue that the discussions about the "authentic" interpretation of *Rabindra Sangit* contradict Tagore's modernist aesthetics and cross-cultural communication in "primitive" music, and instead have more to do with processes of Bengali identity formation and music institutionalization. Before that, however, I will discuss how, as a definite result of the imperial encounter, Tagore created an aesthetically unique musical oeuvre and, second, look into Bake's life and work, including his relationship with Tagore.

Rabindra Sangit: The making of modernist Bengali folk music

As is well known, Rabindranath Tagore grew up in a large aristocratic Hindu family that owned estates mostly in what today is Bangladesh and was connected to the British East India Company since it settled in Calcutta in 1690. Tagore's grandfather Dwarkanath was the first big local and successful entrepreneur of British India, who socialized with Queen Victoria and other notables on his trips to Europe. Moreover, he was an eager student and performer of Western music, who in 1845 actually impressed the young Max Müller in Paris with his piano playing and singing of Italian and French songs. Generally, he earned himself a reputation as a patron of the arts and learning in Britain and India. In his grandfather's footsteps, then, Rabindranath heard and performed Western classical music, besides Indian music, of course, already from an early age. At the Jorasanko family home in Calcutta, a hive of cultural and intellectual activity, he was captivated by the illustrated 1846 edition of Thomas Moore's *Irish Melodies*, heard the music of Frédéric Chopin and other Western composers, and sang Ludwig van Beethoven's *Adelaïde*. He absorbed the piano playing of his elder brother Jyotirindranath, who was very active in the Calcutta music and theater scenes, and who became his mentor.

When Tagore went to London for the first time for his studies (1878–1880), he was often welcomed at musical soirées to perform Indian and British (folk) songs. Emotionally and aesthetically, Western music altogether moved him into a different realm. So, for instance, he was impressed by the ease with which many British folk songs "conveyed emotions such as laughter or merriment, which was unknown in the Indian musical repertoire."[9] Upon his return in Calcutta, he wrote several Bengali songs inspired by folk songs (*Auld Lang Syne, Ye Banks and Braes,* and so on) and he actually used some of them in his musical plays, *Valmiki Pratibha* or The Genius of Valmiki (1881) and *Kalmgrigaya* or The Fatal Hunt (1882), which generally were inspired by Western opera and stage production. Interestingly, in the latter play he used *The Vicar of Bray*, of which the melody is from an eighteenth-century song *Country Gardens*, indeed the same song that Cecil Sharp collected and Percy Grainger later arranged into his greatest hit! In 1961, in fact, Arnold Bake made an interesting study of Tagore's transformation of the English folk song *Drink to Me Only with Thine Eyes* into a Bengali song based upon his poem *Kotobaro Bhebechinu*, as sung to him by Rabindranath's niece, Indira Devi, when she was well over 80. He shows how in Tagore's song the relationship between words and melody becomes radically different: "There is not one bar in it which could not have come into being in an original Bengali tune and yet it carries the memory of its English ancestor so clearly that it cannot be missed."[10] During later visits to Britain, Tagore continued his studies in Western music and regularly sang, for example, Charles Gounod's *Serenade, If,* and *Ave Maria* in public.

In 1843, Rabindranath's father, Debendranath, took control of the influential Hindu reform movement, the Brahmo Samaj, which was intended to complete the work of the pioneer reformer Rammohun Roy. As Brahmos became involved in the Indian nationalist movement, they began to compose and publish patriotic literature and songs, whereby they adopted the practice of Christian congregational singing, often with the harmonium as an accompanying instrument. Rabindranath began to compose patriotic songs when he was 16. He wrote the music for Bankim Chandra Chattopadhyaya's *Bande Mataram*, which later became the national song (not anthem) of India, and he sang it for the first time at the 1896 session of the Indian National Congress. Among other Brahmo composers, he would contribute numerous patriotic songs, particularly between 1905 and 1907, at the time of the *swadeshi* campaign. Yet, while Tagore's songs continued to inspire patriotism, as Bake rightly emphasized, they were never narrow mindedly nationalist.[11]

Since his stay at Shelidah (1890–1901) on the bank of the river Padma in East Bengal, where he managed the family estates, Tagore increasingly showed his "spiritual" bond with rural Bengal in his writings and songs. He became fascinated with Bengali devotional *kirtan* and folk music, especially the literature and songs of love, mysticism, and universal brotherhood of the Bauls. These wandering minstrels and mystics recruited from both the Bengali Hindu and Muslim communities rejected "the orthopraxis and orthodoxies of both religious traditions, including the worship of images and transcendent deities, the authority of scripture and indeed any other knowledge which is not one's own."[12] In 1883, Tagore had already written a review of a collection of Baul songs in which he asked for "renewed acquaintance and identity with the 'uneducated, authentic heart' of Bengal, and specifically, the language and literature of the villages."[13] He emphasized that Baul poems were important because of their universal appeal, and he rebuked those elitist Bengalis who used English themes and idioms in their writings, or others who tried to counteract British influences "by 'purifying' Bengali with stilted Sanskritisms."[14] It was only from 1914 onward, nonetheless, after his disillusionment with the Indian nationalist movement, that partly under the influence of Kshiti Mohan Sen (1880–1960), who taught Sanskrit and Hindu culture at Santiniketan, he began to study Baul music and words seriously. This also, as Reba Som put it, because he hoped that

> the simple lyrics and profound wisdom of folk songs in general and Baul songs in particular, could be a unifying element among the Bengali population threatened by religious strife and political challenge.[15]

Tagore's growing fascination with bucolic Bengal and appropriation of Baul songs was not unique. Already for some time, members of the elite (*bhadralok*) of Calcutta were in search of their historical and geographical roots in the villages of "Golden Bengal" as part of a growing patriotic regional consciousness. For here was a critique of traditional Hindu practices from within ancient Bengali society itself, which was very much like the attacks formulated by the British and "had thrown the Bengali intelligentsia on the defensive."[16] Their study of vernacular Bengali literature followed upon the earlier craze for India's classical (read: Sanskrit) heritage and undeniably was a form of "internal Orientalism." It was especially through the writings of Tagore and Kshiti Mohan Sen, however, that the popularity of the Bauls and their songs as an object of "culture" reached its peak. For elitist Bengalis, the romantic image of the wandering, unattached, and unworldly Baul became the embodiment of ancient indigenous wisdom and became visually represented until today by Tagore's role as a Baul in his musical play *Phalguni* (1916). Because of the writings of Tagore and Sen, Bauls also began to be mentioned extensively in official colonial sources such as the Gazetteers and the Census during the late 1920s.

On the whole, Tagore's songs remain atypical compositions because of their combination of elements of Hindustani classical music (*khayal*, though not its improvisations, which he never liked, and especially *dhrupad*), Bengali *kirtan* and Baul songs, British folk songs, and much else. While this eclecticism meant that he never became a master of any instrumental or vocal style, and he therefore always remained a fringe figure within Hindustani music, it encouraged him to become an experimentalist. Specifically, Rabindranath's absorption in Bengali folk music as a source of inspiration was a reaction against both Indian classical music and Western music. On the one hand, he reacted against the strict rules of Indian classical music. On the other, under the influence of Western classical compositions and British folk songs, he sought the universal in music by comparing folk songs from different countries.[17] Similar to Indian national music reformers in the Hindustani and Carnatic music traditions, Tagore was much attracted to the idea of modernizing Indian music making. For example, he established a Department of Music at Visva-Bharati, supported the subject of music in the curriculum of the National University in Madras, and was favorable to the notating of his songs in Western staff notation. In his criticism of classical Indian music making, however, Tagore definitely went further than Indian national music reformers. In particular, he complained that Indian singers neglected their instrument and stage presentation: "India goes to the extreme of almost holding with contempt any finesse in singing, and our master singers never take the least trouble to make their voice and manner attractive."[18] On the contrary, he was much impressed by the voice quality of Bake and other Western singers like the Swedish soprano Christine Nilsson, the English contralto Clara Butt, and the earlier mentioned Ratan Devi, about whom he wrote: "There was not a sign of effort in her beautiful voice, and not the least suggestion of the uncouthness we are accustomed to in our singers."[19] Also he was stirred by the fact that Western musicians, unlike their Indian counterparts, tuned up before they entered the stage. As William Radice emphasized, Tagore made it clear in several of his writings that he believed that in the sphere of music, at least, "Bengal really did need a strong dose of Western influence—not in order to denationalize her music, but to make Bengalis appreciate and nurture it better."[20]

Tagore's urge to modernize Indian music was most apparent in his musical innovations (read: modernist aesthetic). In general, he questioned conventions in Indian classical music practice that were solely authorized by tradition. Thus, he regularized the rhythm in his melodies, leaving out "detailed florid ornamentation and the rhythmical ambiguity which is so much part of a classical vocal performance."[21] Much to the satisfaction of Maud MacCarthy,[22] he also created several new *talas* and was never a purist in his use of *ragas*: his song *Krishnakali* (1931), for example, changes *raga* from verse to verse. Then again, according to Pradip Kumar Sengupta, he felt that Indian classical musicians gave too much importance to the first beat (*sam*) and, its counterbalance, the "empty" unstressed beat (*khali*) within each and every rhythmic cycle, and he wanted to free the *tala* system of such "rigid obligatoriness."[23] On a more abstract level, Sengupta continued, he argued that *ragas* should be classified "not arbitrarily, nor according to the *vadi-samvadi* notes,"[24] but purely "according to the *rasas* which the *ragas* are expected to invoke."[25] Rather than traditional musical theories, it was the emotional mood or "flavour" (*rasa*) reflecting the totality of the performance that mattered. Like many Western musicologists, Tagore had difficulty in defining Indian *ragas*. For example, Fox Strangways cryptically wrote that a *raga* received its *rasa* "not so much from its being what it is, as from its being something else, closely allied to it, which is present all the time in the musician's consciousness."[26] Tagore's viewpoint certainly was different from Vishnu Narayan Bhatkhande's *that* system of *raga* classification.[27] But how did Tagore decide whether someone's interpretation of his songs captured the right *rasa* or not?

By and large, Tagore's adherence to Baul music and the world of Bengali tribals represented his primitivism or Romantic longing for premodern innocence in the face of contemporary politics. As Bengali (Baul) folk songs were adhered to by members of all communities, it was directly related also to his criticism of Indian nationalism. In response, Indian nationalists and internationalists such as Ananda Coomaraswamy became increasingly disappointed in Tagore and began to depict him as an irresponsible apolitical poet. Significantly, through his primitivism, Tagore also questioned the Western idea of history and its underlying idea of linear time concurrent to the ideology of progress.[28] According to his view of cyclical history, which I already mentioned in the Introduction, the contradistinction between the times of the "primitive" and the "historical" was itself "the source of creative and practical temporality."[29] To a great extent, Tagore followed the traditional Indian concept of the past in which time is reversible, as there is, as Ashis Nandy put it, "no real disjunction between the past and the present," though the past is always open, whereas the future "is so only to the extent that it is a rediscovery or renewal."[30] Be that as it may, Tagore's idea of history ultimately was as abstract as that of the *rasa* of his songs: as time moved beyond the present and the past, for him the most important thing it seems solely was an understanding, as it were, of its *rasa(s)*. At the same time, however, this "theorizer par excellence of creative and non-linear temporality," as Prathama Banerjee labeled him,[31] was not a traditionalist. On the contrary, for example, he believed that "improvement" was needed for Indian society and especially for those living in poverty.

In sum, Tagore's songs were the result of an imperial intellectual formation, which included patriotism, primitivism, "internal Orientalism," and modernist aesthetics. They are all the more interesting because of the poet's interest in British folk songs and Western classical song at large. Obviously, both Fox Strangways and Bake were attracted to Tagore's songs because their form, rhythm, and melody were relatively simple in comparison to the endless improvisations of Indian classical singers, and they therefore could be studied more easily and comparatively as "primitive" folk music. Furthermore, Bake shared with Tagore the modernist nostalgia for "village India" and believed that Bengali folk culture and music embodied the "soul of the people" unhampered by modern civilization.

Bake and Tagore: A perfect encounter in music?

During the period that Bake studied Arabic and Sanskrit at Leiden University, he seriously considered a career as a professional Western classical singer. He sang European folk songs as well and developed an early and genuine interest in folk music research. He was familiar with the writings and fieldwork of Cecil Sharp, Lucy Broadwood, and other English folk song collectors, though I so far did not find any reference to Percy Grainger in his writings. Together with Sharp's collaborator and biographer, Maud Karpeles, in fact, he eventually prepared a *Manual for Folk Music Collectors* (1951) at the request of the International Folk Music Council.[32] In comparison to Fox Strangways, Grainger, MacCarthy, and John Foulds, Bake undeniably was more academically inclined. Over the years, he became a key figure to the establishment of Indian ethnomusicology as an academic discipline, whereby he certainly had a wide scope of interest. Overall, he believed that the study of "primitive" folk music was as important as that of the classical Hindustani and Carnatic music traditions. This especially because in his view the "primitive" and classical musical forms continually interacted with each other, and neither could be properly understood without the other. In 1923, after the advice of his teachers to combine his interests in Sanskrit and music, Bake continued his studies at Utrecht University. For his thesis, he chose to translate a part of the very same Sanskrit music theory treatise that triggered Fox Strangways's interest in Indian music, *Sangit Darpan*, simply because there were many copies available in Europe.[33] Following Tagore's visit to the Netherlands in 1920, Arnold had become much charmed by two of the poet's songs, sung to him by an acquaintance of a friend, and of which he later "rediscovered" notations in Fox Strangways's *The Music of Hindostan*.[34] Assumingly, it was because of these interests and experiences that he decided to complete his thesis at Tagore's Visva-Bharati in Santiniketan.

During the years 1925–1929 and 1931–1934, Arnold and his wife lived and traveled in India, always with Santiniketan as a base. There, he studied Hindustani music with Bhim Rao Shastri, Sanskrit and Hindu culture with Kshiti Mohan Sen, and especially Tagore's songs with the poet's grandnephew Dinendranath Tagore (1882–1935), on whose memory Rabindranath relied almost completely and from whom he sometimes had to learn his own songs anew. Also Bake learned to sing Bengali *kirtan* (devotional singing). He gave numerous lecture-recitals of European and Bengali folk songs in India (almost 70 in 1932 only) and the West, including a lecture-recital tour of 7 months through the United States, from New York to Honolulu, in 1935–1936. Before he joined the School of African and Oriental Studies in London as a lecturer in Sanskrit and Indian Music in 1948, Arnold and his wife spent nearly ten years in India (1937–1946), during which time they regularly stayed at Santiniketan again. In the footsteps of Foulds, he temporarily worked as music adviser to All India Radio in Delhi and as director of European music at the Calcutta broadcasting station. Altogether, Bake spent nearly 20 years in British India, wherein he toured the subcontinent, including Ceylon, Ladakh, and Nepal, while studying and performing its music, and making extensive recordings, films, and photographs. During the last years of his life, he was working on a book on Indian music for Oxford University Press. Had he been able to complete it before his death, he most probably would have been more famous today. In any case, the assessment in *The Times* of October 9, 1963, was clear: "No other Western scholar has ever rivalled Arnold Bake's profound knowledge of Indian music."[35]

Bake's numerous writings on Indian music reflect his background in Indology, comparative musicology, and European folk music research. He too often used the theory of comparable Greek modes in India and Europe in his analysis of Indian (folk) music and generally explained the relation between European and Indian music against the background of their common Indo-Aryan history.[36] Unlike Grainger, he did not see Western music as superior to Indian music because of its development of harmony. Like Fox Strangways, he did not approach Indian music from an evolutionary perspective as "primitive."[37] On the contrary, he saw European and Indian music as separate from each other. While in Western music, "the ideal of harmony is unity in diversity: the binding together of entirely different strains of music into unity," he argued, "the ideal of the purely melodical Indian music is diversity in unity: diverse voices and instruments join eventually in the same melody."[38] Similar to Bhatkhande, Arnold generally rejected the direct relevance of ancient Sanskrit music theories for contemporary music making. In fact, while working together with Fox Strangways on the further translation of *Sangit Darpan*, he repeatedly complained about the musicological worth of the text.[39] In line with later research, Bake underlined the importance of microtones in the performance of *ragas* in terms of aesthetic embellishments but because of the flexibility of intonation "rejected the convention of applying *shruti* as a fixed pitch."[40] As he wrote in *Bijdrage tot de Kennis der Voor-Indische Muziek* (1930):

So much is certain that in India a scale of *shrutis* never has been sung or played in the way we play our modern chromatic scale, each succeeding note being on the *shruti* just above the previous one. *Shrutis* do exist in practise and certainly are used in ornamentation, when the voice sweeps up or down, sounding the interval of one *shruti* above or below the note which is being ornamented. There is, however, no doubt, that the *shruti* has mainly theoretical value.[41]

During his early career, Bake cared much for "authenticity" in Indian music, and he paternalistically raged against the use of the Western harmonium, popular Indian film music, and the brass bands employed by the Indian princes, the traditional patrons of the arts. All these modern developments, Bake argued, corrupted Indian musical taste, which "like the whole of Indian culture, rests on the foundation of the village community with its vast store of religious and artistic tradition."[42] Alike what Tagore and many Bengalis thought at the time, for him too, Indian folk music was the "soul of the people" and, moreover, the salvation of Indian music because it had a "spirituality" that "Europe does not know or has lost, a folk-life filled with a deep and living mysticism."[43] Similar to other folk music researchers simultaneously in metropolis and colony, Bake thought folk music was "a dying art." Telling in this context is the following observation that he made during his first field trip to Punjab in 1926:

> I know that there is a group of ballad singers in Chamba, a little hill-state in the Punjab, who wander about with their various instruments singing the deeds of heroes of times long past, and also commemorating important facts of the present. One of their modern ballads even sings the praises of the opening of a new post office in Chamba-town, thus unconsciously acclaiming, in this beautiful and necessary institution, one of the very causes of their own imminent death![44]

Later in his life, nonetheless, Bake developed a more positive view about change and continuity in Indian music. In "Synthesis of Indian and Western Music" for *The Illustrated Weekly of India* (1961), for example, he emphasized that change and interaction were inherent to music history and that thoughts about musical decline generally concerned emotional involvement. In comparison to what happened in Western music history, he argued that there always would be continuity in Indian music as well. Thus, on the one hand, he depicted an end of the modal system in Indian music's confrontation with the West, especially through the introduction of the harmonium. Yet, on the other, he had much faith in the internal dynamics of Indian society and culture:

> Music is created by the genius of a living human being, not by setting rule against rule. Everything depends on the strength of the forces on both sides. Changes are inescapable, but, as with culture in general, it depends on the strength of the individual who makes them just how Indian the result will be.
>
> [...] In 50 years, Indian music will be very different from what we call classical Indian music now, but it will be Indian, if the Indian identity of the composers is strong enough. Synthesis there will be, but only the genius of the composer will know how this synthesis, impossible on paper, will come about and live, bringing new beauty. [45]

Bake believed that Tagore's songs were "unthinkable without the Bengali folk-songs, very much in the same way as the music of several modern European composers is unthinkable without the background of the folk-songs of their respective countries."[46] The idea that "half of Rabindranath's life-work" would be lost for posterity after his death, made him transcribe some of Tagore's songs, as sung by Dinendranath, into Western staff notation. In 1920, his teacher Bhim Rao Shastri had published some of Tagore's songs in his *Sangit Gitanjali*, using Bhatkhande's system of notation.[47] According to Bake, however, this system, as well as the Bengali system of notation used by Dinendranath and others at Santiniketan, was "a recent and incomplete one" and "little more than a memorandum" for those who were "already familiar with the melody," while by means of letters it solely conveyed "the mere skeleton of a song" and left out "ornamentations and details."[48] Bake's project resulted into *Twenty-Six Songs of Rabindranath Tagore* (1935), which of course was favorably reviewed by Fox Strangways.[49] For the book, Bake transcribed: six songs from *Gitanjali*; twelve songs that Tagore composed during his travels in Europe in 1926; three Baul songs of which the poet only altered the words but did not touch the music and which Bake included so that Tagore's songs could be compared with the "authentic" ones; and, finally, five songs which he published in an appendix because these had not been revised by Dinendranath. Surprisingly, though Tagore authorized and gave much help to the publication of Bake's book, he did not write a foreword similar to what he did to Ratan Devi's *Thirty Songs from the Panjab and Kashmir*. Was it because Bake never asked him, while Ratan Devi or, more likely, Coomaraswamy did? Or did he perhaps not wish to get too much involved in a project that concerned his own music? With the book, however, Bake did not achieve his goal of turning out Indian folk song arrangements in accordance with "modern taste" and of "educational and moral value."[50] A goal, indeed, that was similar to what Cecil Sharp, Ralph Vaughan Williams, and other folk song collectors aimed at to improve the national spirit.

Unlike many Western internationalists, and especially those of the Theosophical variety, Bake did not place "spiritual" India above Europe, but nevertheless was very much against placing Europe above India.[51] While he was familiar with internationalist literature and met quite a few internationalists at Santiniketan and elsewhere, he was self-conscious and critical but certainly not politically radical. In general, he distrusted the Theosophists. As John Brough put it: "Being a scholar, not a convert, Bake was hardly the man to see profit in exploring the tenuous atmosphere of mysticism."[52] Even so, like Tagore, he relied much on their network during his tours, and he also stayed a few times at the movement's headquarters in Adyar. Always in the company of his wife, who also was his accompanist on the piano, Bake very much remained on his own. He was solely interested in what intrigued him, namely, the study of Indian (folk) music and culture, and never had an urge to belong to any group, though he was always eager to meet people. In his numerous letters, he often comments critically but humorously, from a distance, as it were, about events and personalities such as: the "over-extensive" bureaucracy at Santiniketan; the "unsympathetic and treacherous" Mahatma Gandhi; the "splendid isolation" of the British and their "racism," especially among the women; the "unscientific" work of the French Indologist, musicologist, and Theosophist Alain Daniélou, who later in his life became a Hindu and about whom more later; and the "intelligent but dangerous" Annie Besant.

Tagore named Bake "Aruni" (Son of Dawn) and undeniably had warm feelings for him. At Santiniketan, they often shared the intimacy of singing in chorus during their meetings. Also they traveled together, for example, in 1926 to the All India Music Conference in

Lucknow and, a year later, to the Dutch East Indies, a trip for which Arnold acted as mediator and that was part of Tagore's unsuccessful larger project of regenerating an "Asian spiritual civilization," which also took him to China and Japan.[53] As a matter of fact, Bake found it tragic to see Tagore suffer from his travels around the world to collect money for Santiniketan, because it made it impossible for him to follow his real nature of being a poet and writer.[54] Still, in 1929, he wrote that he did not feel much for Tagore. He thought that he was incredible weak, unpredictable, and vain, though he found the latter unsurprising in the light of all the attention he received from the world. Concurrently, he believed that as an artist he was a genius with an astonishing broad vision. Indeed, he asked himself, "Maybe one should not become too familiar with great artists?"[55] Having said this, Bake's initial negative reaction to Tagore might have been related to the fact that toward the end of their first period at Santiniketan, the Bakes experienced a campaign of slander against them. At the time, they evidently were much bothered with it, as Arnold considered giving up working on Tagore's music. They found it especially disturbing that Tagore was not present at their departure and never mentioned anything about what happened, let alone offered his apologies.[56] Yet, as Krishna Dutta and Andrew Robinson put it, Santiniketan "was always rife with rumour" and sometimes Rabindranath "took note of it, sometimes he did not."[57] In any case, it seems that the relationship between Bake and Tagore generally always remained somewhat formal. But what does one expect in the light of, for example, their individual self-sufficiency; Tagore's status as a "spiritual" world teacher; their age difference (when they met for the first time, Bake was 26 and Tagore 65); and their constant traveling? In hindsight, it seems as if Bake only really began to appreciate Tagore after his death. In 1953, for example, he wrote full of admiration for him as "an imperious and often impatient seeker after perfection and after the essence of beauty, the divine spark."[58] All in all, unlike William Rothenstein, Edward Thompson, and, indeed, William Butler Yeats,[59] Bake never distanced himself from Tagore out of disappointment with him or because of enduring irritations or disagreements. Hence, at least from the Dutchman's perspective, the relationship between Bake and Tagore more or less seems to have been a "perfect encounter," and perhaps this was so because their cross-cultural communication concerned music rather than words.

The authenticity and translatability of *Rabindra Sangit*

In Bake's view, Rabindranath was especially attracted to Baul music because of its essential relationship between words and melody, which he thought was lost in contemporary classical Indian music but still available in Bengali folk music. He wanted to bring back the meaning and importance of words into his compositions, "away from the flourishes and ornaments for their own sake and the urge to stun the audience with their sheer virtuosity."[60] After realizing the completeness of European classical compositions and folk songs, Bake continued, Tagore became "the first composer in India to regard his songs as inviolable entities":[61]

> Tagore's attitude towards his compositions was much more akin to that of a Western composer. The tune as given is the one that was intended for those words. His ornaments were brought in where *he* wanted them and where they, as he felt, heightened the inner meaning of the words. By changing them or leaving them out, or worse, adding new ones indiscriminately, the very purpose of the melody, to carry the words above the sphere of every day life, was defeated. The consequence is that we have here a body of song with regard to which one can speak of an "authentic" version. That this authentic version is the way in which Dinendranath gave them stands to reason.[62]

Unquestionably, Bake approached Tagore's songs as "a sort of fetish" and thus, as I discussed in the chapter on Percy Grainger, in a similar manner to what European folk song collectors did. Likewise, his attraction to Tagore's songs as well as his soft and controlled singing style are not surprising in the light of his criticism of Indian classical voice technique, and, closely related, the long performances and improvisations common to Indian classical music.[63]

Yet, did Tagore himself see his own songs as "inviolable entities" and is the idea of their "authentic" version not strange when he almost completely relied on the memories of Dinendranath and others? As the poet wrote in 1928:

> My own testimony with regard to my compositions is always untrustworthy. My songs, for example: I'm always thinking up tunes for them. I sing the tunes to whoever happens to be at hand.

Thereafter, responsibility for the tunes rests entirely with my pupils. If later I try to sing them, they are quite ready to say that I've got them wrong. I frequently have to accept correction from them at this.[64]

After his death in 1941, Tagore was canonized as Bengal's greatest creative artist, whereby two of his songs also were immortalized as the national anthems of India (*Jana Gana Mana*) and Bangladesh (*Amar Shonar Bangla*). For many Bengalis in West Bengal, Bangladesh, and the Bengali diaspora, Hindus and Muslims alike, singing or listening to *Rabindra Sangit* has taken, as Reba Som put it, "the role of a personal religion."[65] Accordingly, the "authentic" performance of *Rabindra Sangit* became an issue for debate under the supervision of the Visva-Bharati Music Board, the copyright holder of Tagore's songs between 1941 and 2001, whereby ironically several recordings of Dinendranath also were forbidden to be released.[66] The point however is that except when sung by the master himself, Tagore's songs of course never were "authentic" but always interpretations. In addition, there are numerous examples that show that Tagore had a very liberal attitude toward the interpretations of his own songs. As in Bake's case, for instance, he continuously supported Bhim Rao Shastri to sing his songs as well as teach them, though the Maharastrian's Bengali pronunciation was not always correct.[67] Conversely, Tagore held musical experiments throughout his life. In 1904, he allowed the Portuguese bandmaster Roberto Lobo and his Eden Garden Orchestra to play arrangements of some of his songs at a family wedding.[68] Likewise, he did not mind the use of chords for accompaniment, as long as these were played on the piano rather than the harmonium, which was an instrument that he loathed and actually banned at Visva-Bharati. In fact, he requested Alain Daniélou, who visited Santiniketan in 1932 and several times afterward,[69] to make arrangements of several of his songs for voice and piano, and translate the Bengali lyrics into English and French, so that his music and words would receive recognition in the West. As Daniélou wrote in the foreword of his *Trois Mélodies de Rabindranath Tagore* (1961): "Given his ideas on the need to establish greater understanding between peoples, he much desired that his songs should be known outside India and sung by other singers too." Despite the fact that the Frenchman for a long time was a member of the Visva-Bharati Music Board, however, that very same body did not give permission for the publication of his 18 transcriptions of Tagore's songs, *Poem-Songs:*

As for now, despite Tagore's own ambiguous but overall open internationalist attitude toward the interpretation of his own songs, there
are two dominant positions in relation to the performance of *Rabindra
Sangit*. On the one hand, for example, the renowned Tagore scholar
Uma Das Gupta is very positive about the latest appropriations of
Tagore's songs by Bengali pop groups, which she sees as a testimony
to their enduring popularity:

With the copyright now gone his songs are seen to have touched
the lives and imagination of a much wider circle which also
includes "pop" singers and their various "bands." This has been a
revelation as his songs have hitherto invariably been presented in
a sedate and serene style. The new singers remain loyal of course to
the poet's words but are setting them to the popular music of their
taste. Rabindranath had predicted that his songs will live after
him. "You cannot find the poet in his biography," he wrote in one
of his poems, "you can find him in his songs." It is encouraging
that the connoisseurs have spread out beyond the classic mode,
that they are being creative with his songs.[86]

On the other hand, there is the standpoint of another well-known
Tagore scholar, William Radice, which indeed is rather in line with
Bake's position and the British civilizing mission at large, that past
and present appropriations of Tagore's songs (he gives the examples
of the currently popular *Rabindra Sangit* singers Srikanto Acharya
and Lopamudra Mitra) often do great injustice to the intimate and
ineducible interrelationship between words, melody, and rhythm,
which, he believes, is characteristic to them and "unique in the history of music and poetry the world over."[87] In order to reach the high
standards that Tagore himself wanted and for a better appreciation of
his songs in the West, he argues, *Rabindra Sangit* therefore desperately
needs: "the kind of care, scholarship, insight, training, and respect
for the composer's intentions that we take for granted in the worldwide performance of Western classical music."[88] But again, did Tagore
ever want his songs to become classical music? Is Radice not paternalistically enforcing his own elitist Western classical musical aesthetic
here? Is it not more plausible that Tagore, the musical modernizer,
modernist aesthetic, and internationalist, would have found innu-
merable possibilities in these times of "world music" to write songs
that would be in harmony with the times but still evoke the right *rasa*?

Rabindranath Tagore (2005), until the copyright was lifted, after which
indeed the songs were recorded in cooperation with Visva-Bharati.[70]

In 1941, Tagore wrote to Santidev Ghosh, "The treasure of my
songs is within you. It will be your duty to disseminate these songs
correctly."[71] In his book on *Rabindra Sangit*, Ghosh explains how discussions about the "authentic" performance of Tagore's songs are
futile because when the poet would have found the topic important,
"he would certainly have written something about it," but he did
not leave behind "any direction or order about the right to sing his
songs."[72] On the contrary, "he encouraged all to sing, without making any assessment" because he trusted that "the good singers would
come up by their own merit and would survive, while the bad ones
would by themselves be extinct."[73] Having said this, Rabindranath
no doubt felt sad to hear a song interpreted in such way that he could
not recognize it as his own anymore. In 1926, for instance, he ordered
record companies to stop selling their early recordings of artists
who interpreted his songs as they liked themselves and afterwards:
"It was decided with the companies that whenever one would sing,
one would have to properly learn the tune of the song and then one
would sing."[74] Later, in conversation with Albert Einstein in 1930, he
theoretically made clear also the possibility of the (limited) exercise
of "free will" in the performance of his compositions.[75]

Throughout his life, Tagore wrestled with the questions of music's
universality and, closely related, the translatability of his writings and
music. He always felt reluctant to publish books with words of songs for
lack of soul, movement, and color.[76] In 1936, H. G. Wells told Tagore:
"Music is of all things in the world the most international."[77] Initially,
the poet argued to the contrary that his songs probably would remain
unintelligible for Westerners, even if he could provide them in staff
notation. Wells's reply that "the West may get used to your music,"
however, convinced him of the fact that "perhaps closer acquaintance
with them may gradually lead to their appreciation in the West."[78] Did
Bake's successful performances in the West perhaps play a role to this
change in attitude? Whatever the case may be, already for some decades
the poet had open-minded ideas about the translation of his writings
and music. In 1913, for instance, he made the following remark about
Ratan Devi's singing of Indian folk songs in English translation:

Sometimes the meaning of a poem is better understood in a translation, not necessary because it is more beautiful than the original,

but as in the new setting the poem has to undergo a trial, it shines more brilliantly if it comes out triumphant. So it seemed to me that Ratan Devi's singing our songs gained something in feeling and truth. Listening to her I felt more clearly than ever that our music is the music of the cosmic emotion.[79]

Likewise, he came to enjoy translating his verses from Bengali into English, though he often admitted his insecurity in writing in English. As he wrote in 1918 to J. D. Anderson, lecturer in Bengali at the University of Cambridge:

It was the want of mastery in your language that originally prevented me from trying English metres in my translations. But now I have grown reconciled to my limitations through which I have come to know the wonderful power of English prose. The clearness, strength and the suggestive music of well-balanced English sentences make it a delightful task for me to mould my Bengali poems into English prose form. I think one should frankly give up the attempt at reproducing in a translation the lyrical suggestions of the original verse and substitute in their place some new quality inherent in the new vehicle of expression. *In English prose there is a magic which seems to transmute my Bengali verses into something which is original again in a different manner.* Therefore it not only satisfies but gives me delight to assist my poems in their English rebirth though I am far from being confident in the success of my task.[80]

Thus, in his English translation style, Rabindranath found a perfect vehicle for worldwide transmission, one that suited his internationalist outlook and was as durable and "authentic" as his writings in Bengali, and actually can be read as a sort of commentary on his Bengali works.

Unquestionably, Tagore had a strong urge to speak for and to all human kind, and not just to his fellow Bengalis. His support to the projects of Bake and Daniélou shows that he wanted his songs to be known to the world and was committed to cross-cultural communication. His open-minded attitude towards the "authenticity" and translation of his writings and songs therefore should be placed in the context of his universal humanism and internationalism. At the same time, significantly, Tagore's position of being both a

traditionalist Bengali and an internationalist is reflected i In them, he not only was the nearest to the people an Bengal but also was able to escape any literary and musi tions, and to express himself aesthetically as a modernis chose between traditionalism and universalism because that one could be cosmopolitan only with a profound kr one's own tradition:

I have come to feel that the mind, which has been the atmosphere of a profound knowledge of its own c of the perfect thoughts that have been produced in t ready to accept and assimilate the cultures that come countries.[81]

Intriguing from the perspective of empire and the intellec of (inter) nationalism in particular, then, Tagore's positic similar to the visions of the relationship between identity, and internationalism of both Bake and Ralph Vaughan W for example, Bake wrote:

Nothing can give more satisfaction and happiness than of what is so deeply related with our own soul [...] be real internationalists without contributing to the which is most really ourself. Of that real self the music out of the soil is a vital expression.[82]

Likewise, Vaughan Williams believed that the love of one one's language, one's customs, and one's religion were e the "spiritual health" of an internationalist world where "every nation would be different and all at peace."[83] It v "to be self-consciously cosmopolitan as self-consciously nat wrote, because a composer could not be universal "withc having been local."[84] Overall, Vaughan Williams thought tl ical internationalism" was compatible with "cultural patric that the two in fact were necessary complements:

I believe that all that is of value in our spiritual and cu springs from our own soil; but this life cannot develop ar except in an atmosphere of friendship and sympathy v nations.[85]

Were his songs meant to be bound by time and place or to convey his universal message forever in whatever interpretation or location? Be it as it may, the positions of Uma Das Gupta and William Radice, as well as the history of Tagore's songs in general, show that the study of and debate about the performance of *Rabindra Sangit* remains very much a part of Bengali identity politics and, closely related, rather dominated by the imperial tropes of "authenticity," "spirituality," and the "classical" (in terms of Western song) in music.

Conclusion

With his background in European folk music research, Bake's pre-occupation with the "authenticity" of Indian folk music, if not its national "spirituality," leaned much toward the side of Indian nationalists in music. In contrast, Tagore's appropriation of Bengali folk music into his songs was internationalist. Bake's research most clearly shows the link between the European folk song movement and the early twentieth-century development of the discipline of Indian ethnomusicology. Undeniably, he adhered to a Romantic worldview. During his research trips throughout the subcontinent, his focus was always on folk music, rather than the music of the cities, because it supposedly was untouched by Western influences. At the same time, however, it should be clear that he knew and admired many "classical" Indian musicians. During his years on the subcontinent, Bake never referred to commercial recordings of Indian "classical" music but, as a "salvage" ethnomusicologist, he made numerous recordings of Indian folk music. Unlike Grainger and Tagore, he was not a primitivist but above all a scholar whose internationalism primarily related to his music research. Later, at the School of African and Oriental Studies, he would illustrate his lectures with gramophone recordings. Conversely, like Fox Strangways, MacCarthy, Foulds, and other Westerners, Bake obviously was much seduced by the image of Tagore as a world teacher. Also one can easily understand why, as folk song researchers, they were so much attracted to his songs. In his analysis of them, however, Bake fetishized Tagore's songs and did not pay enough attention to the complex relationship between the poet's primitivism and (inter) nationalism in music.

From an early age, Tagore revolted against rigidity in every sphere of life. In fact, most of his late poems were written "with no metre, no rhyme, no deliberate artifice."[89] Ultimately, he thought that both words and music were unable to transmit his internationalist message. Hence, in his 60s and still in search of greater honesty and vulnerability, he fanatically began to paint "primitive" (childlike) works, which like his songs were done mostly in one sitting. He believed that his paintings were a better medium for cross-cultural understanding, as they transcended the limitations of language and music. Indeed, they were mainly successful among Western modernist audiences and, in 1930, he actually remarked: "My poetry is for my countrymen, my paintings are my gift to the West."[90] In his painting, then, even more than in his music, Tagore "was freest, unimpeded and unrestricted by his equally strong moral impulse."[91] Be that as it may, both Tagore's songs and paintings show how he wrestled with the traditional and modern, the cultural and the universal. Moreover, that primitivism was not antimodern but a critical form of modernism that interactively affected metropolis and colony at the same time. Needless to say, Tagore's primitivism was very different from that of Grainger. He certainly was not completely against Western civilization. He was an internationalist, a believer in "unity in diversity," of "primitive" and modern people living together with their differences. Though he was paternalistic toward the Bengali tribal folk, he had no hierarchical racial ideas.

In 1873, Rabindranath traveled with his father through northern India. They also went to Punjab and stayed for about a month in Amritsar, where they visited the most sacred place for Sikhs, the Golden Temple, and heard Sikhs singing the hymns from their sacred scripture, the Guru Granth Sahib. Also his father invited Sikh *ragis* (musicians) to the place they were staying to play and sing for them. Overall, Sikh sacred music (*kirtan*), the topic of the next chapter, made a deep impression on Tagore, and eventually he would compose several songs under its inspiration. The parallels between *Rabindra Sangit* and Sikh *kirtan* as musical forms are intriguing at least for three reasons: first, because of the relationship with folk music; second, because of the strong relationship between music and words; and, third, because of the involvement in discussions about "authenticity" and "spirituality" in music. In comparison to *Rabindra Sangit*, however, the case of Sikh *kirtan,* because of its centrality to Sikhism, even more highlights the moral tensions between tradition and change.

5
Sikh Sacred Music: Identity, Aesthetics, and Historical Change

Sikh sacred music, empire and historiography

In 1781, the well-known British Orientalist Charles Wilkins, who together with William Jones cofounded the Asiatic Society of Bengal in 1784, visited Harmandir Sahib gurdwara in Patna, the birthplace of the last of the ten Sikh Gurus, Guru Gobind Singh. Among his observations published in the society's *Asiatick Researches* (1788), there is the following description of a public reading of the Sikh sacred scripture, the Guru Granth Sahib:

> An old man, with a reverend silver beard, kneeled down before the desk with his face towards the altar; and on one side of him sat a man with a small drum, and two or three with cymbals. The book was now opened, and the old man began to chant to the tune of the drum and cymbals; and, at the conclusion of every verse, most of the congregation joined chorus in a response, with countenances exhibiting great marks of joy. Their tones were by no means harsh; the time was quick; and I learnt that the subject was a Hymn in praise of the unity, the omnipresence, and the omnipotence, of the Deity.[1]

A 100 years later, Max Arthur Macauliffe (1841–1913), the Irish Orientalist and authority on Sikhism, wrote in the *Calcutta Review* (1881) how Muslim musicians at the Golden Temple in Amritsar chanted all day long "to accompaniment of *sitar* and *sarangi* the secular or profane songs of their religion and calling, to unlock the hearts and sympathies of the Sikh visitors of the holy temple."[2] Presumably these two vignettes are surprising to most contemporary readers because one is generally used to see three Sikh (never

Muslim!) musicians, two playing the harmonium and one *tabla*, in gurdwaras around the world. Among other things, I will discuss in this chapter the institutionalization and canonization of Sikh sacred music since the Singh Sabha reformation, when modern Sikhism was defined during the imperial encounter as part of "something akin to a Punjabi Enlightenment."[3] The topic is critical because devout Sikhs regard the performing of or listening to the hymns of the Guru Granth Sahib, known as *kirtan*, as the primary form of worship and a "spiritual" source of which the meaning goes beyond words. The ten Sikh Gurus maintained that *kirtan* was the ideal way to achieve union with God and to break the cycle of reincarnation by conquering the vices of lust, anger, greed, worldly attachment, and pride. For Sikhs, the Guru Granth Sahib, in the absence of a living human Guru, is the eternal embodiment of the Guru, a divine living guide and the prime focus of worship. The scripture is unique as the world's largest original collection of sacred hymns, arranged according to 31 *ragas* in which they are to be sung. The orally transmitted repertoire of compositions by six Sikh Gurus, as well as fifteen medieval poet-saints of Bhakti, Sant, and Sufi origins developed between the fifteenth to the eighteenth centuries. Because there was no common system of musical notation, the Gurus named particular *ragas*, which according to tradition were aesthetically tied up with specific moods, sentiments, and so on, to help in memorization. Significantly, however, they did not impose any stringent rules for the performance of these *ragas*.

With music being such an important component of the Sikh tradition, it is surprising that the study of the relationship between music and empire has been almost completely ignored in historiography. For example, in the best book on the Singh Sabha reformation, Harjot Oberoi did not pay any attention to it.[4] The same, in fact, accounts for my own work on this period, though I subsequently published a few articles on the subject.[5] Both Gurinder Singh Mann and Pashaura Singh discussed the modern organization of the Sikh hymns and their underlying *ragas* in their studies but did so explicitly from the perspective of the canonization of the Granth Sahib as a scripture rather than of the performance of *kirtan* since the imperial encounter.[6] Presently, however, Pashaura Singh is working on a research project called "Sacred Melodies: History, Theory and the Performance of Sikh Kirtan," which up till now has resulted into two articles.[7] Following the first ever conference about Sikh sacred music held at New York's Hofstra University in 2010, two special issues of the main academic journal in the field, *Sikh Formations*, were devoted to the subject, though rather than historical studies, the majority of the articles concerned contemporary performance practices and were written from a philosophical and/or anthropological point of view.[8] Other books on Sikh *kirtan* in English simply fail from the viewpoint of (imperial) history.[9] The same accounts for the Punjabi texts, which principally are collections of musical repertoire notations.[10]

By and large, the making of modern Sikh sacred music remains a vital subject to this book, while it brings to the fore certain aspects of the modernization of Indian music even better than in the cases of the Hindustani and Carnatic music traditions because of the intimate connection between the sacred word and sound of the Guru Granth Sahib as well as Sikh identity politics. Also it is particularly important because, as a musical style, *kirtan* essentially lies in between Hindustani "classical" and folk music, which of course also is one of the reasons why its study began only very recently. To give but two examples: some of the poetic forms of the hymns of the Guru Granth Sahib have their origin in folk traditions and the melodies of some hymns are based on Punjabi folk melodies and rhythmic cycles. On the whole, then, as already said, the subject of Sikh sacred music takes some of the issues discussed in relation to the "invented" tradition of *Rabindra Sangit* one step further because Sikhism concerns a "real" tradition. The aim of this chapter is twofold. On the one hand, it explores what remains of the cultural, if not transcendental, meaning of *kirtan* in the light of identity politics since the Singh Sabha reformation. On the other, it investigates the possibilities for the study of Sikh sacred music as "world music," if only because this has become an essential topic, now that *kirtan* is officially taught also at a Western University, namely, by Francesca Cassio at the Music Department of Hofstra University, New York. To put it differently, it tries to find answers to questions such as: What is cultural and what is universal in the study of *kirtan*, and what is part of Sikh identity politics of difference?; To what extent do identity politics and ancient Sanskrit music theories hinder the study of *kirtan* as "world music," and how is this related to the Sikh resistance against the translation of the Guru Granth Sahib into English or any other language?

Singh Sabha identity politics, Western Orientalism, and musicological research

In 1873, the first Singh Sabha was established by elitist Sikhs in Amritsar and it was soon followed by similar associations (*sabhas*) throughout Punjab. These together set up the Chief Khalsa Diwan in 1902. This council became the main voice for the Singh Sabhaites, who were heavily influenced by print culture and defined Sikhism in response to a fast-changing colonial culture and self-assertive Christian, Hindu, and Muslim communities in an emerging public sphere. To the Singh Sabhaites, the Sikh tradition had to be rationally defined for the community to be morally strong and heading toward the future. It was in this context also that the celebrated Singh Sabha scholar and Sikh encyclopaedia writer Kahn Singh Nabha (1861–1938) wrote his famous tract *Ham Hindu Nahin* or We Are Not Hindus (1897). One critical result of the Singh Sabha reformation was the standardization of the Guru Granth Sahib as they authorized the so-called Damdama version in terms of page length, numbering, and the use of Gurmukhi (the Punjabi script), whatever the language the original hymn was composed in. In doing so, importantly, they set aside all other versions of the scripture that were in use earlier.[11] In 1899, the reformers established Khalsa College in Amritsar for the teaching of modern subjects besides Sikh history and Punjabi in response to the creation of similar institutions by the Hindu and Muslim communities in Punjab. Further, Sikh manuals of ritual, historical works, and novels were written, printed, and widely circulated to strengthen the supposedly pure Sikh identity. All this led to the creation of what I have labeled a Singh Sabha "moral language" that often coincided with the goals of the British civilizing mission.[12] In these fast-changing social and cultural settings, then, *kirtan* was increasingly taught in modern institutional settings. The Chief Khalsa Diwan trained kirtanists, besides *granthis* (scripture readers) and preachers, for example at the Central Khalsa Yateemkhana (orphanage) in Amritsar since 1904 and the Khalsa Pracharak Vidyalaya in Taran Taran since 1906.[13] This development continued under the authority of the Shiromani Gurdwara Parbandhak Committee (SGPC), which in 1925 took over the leadership from the Chief Khalsa Diwan as the main modern orthodox Sikh organization. From 1927 onward, kirtanists were trained under the supervision of the SGPC at Shahid Sikh Missionary College, Amritsar, which also made *ragi jathas* (groups of professional singers of *kirtan*) rotate from one historic gurdwara to the other. In addition, kirtanists developed into public figures, independent of princely patrons, and Sikh sacred music became a commodity, whereby the chief *ragi* at the Golden Temple between 1910 and 1930, Bhai Moti, charged the highest fee for a public *kirtan*.[14]

Significantly, the modern processes of rationalization and canonization of *kirtan* also were influenced by contemporary Western Orientalist and musicological works. In 1869, the staunchly Protestant Ernest Trumpp was employed by the India Office in London to translate the Granth Sahib from Gurmukhi into English. In 1877, he completed a translation of one-third of the scripture. In *The Adi Granth or the Holy Scripture of the Sikhs*, he was overall derogative about the Sikh tradition and, much to the disappointment of reformist Sikhs, stressed its Hindu character. Explicitly, he was negative about the scripture's division into specific *ragas* and after providing a list of them stated:

> The verses of the different Gurus have been distributed into these fore-mentioned Rags, apparently without any leading principle, as hardly any verse is internally connected with another. The name of the Rag is, therefore, a mere superscription, without any reference to its contents [...] No system or order is, therefore, to be looked for in any of the Rags. In the first four Rags the most important matter was collected, and they are, therefore, also comparatively of the largest compass; the following minor Rags seem to be a second gathering or gleaning, as materials offered themselves, no attention being paid to the contents, but only to the bulky size of the Granth. By thus jumbling together whatever came to hand, without any judicious selection, the Granth has become an exceedingly incoherent and wearisome book.[15]

Ever since, for both reformist Sikhs and Western Orientalists with a more positive attitude toward the Sikh *Panth* (community), Trumpp's book was something that had to be confronted and proven wrong. The first Westerner who took up the challenge was the Orientalist and member of the Royal Asiatic Society Frederic Pincott. In 1886, he responded to Trumpp in an article in the *Journal of the Royal Asiatic Society*, wherein he argued that the organization of the hymns of the Granth Sahib followed a clear rational structure: "firstly, on the tunes to which the poems were sung; secondly, on the nature and metre of the poems themselves; thirdly, on their authorship; and, fourthly, on the clef or key deemed appropriate to them."[16] Leading Singh Sabhaites must have known about Pincott's article because he lobbied for them in London and was directly involved in the founding of the Khalsa College in Amritsar. My point however is that the writings of Trumpp and Pincott brought the discussion about the underlying musical structure of the Guru Granth Sahib to the front as part of the dominant nineteenth-century search for scientific authority.

While Trumpp developed a tense relationship with the Sikh community, Max Arthur Macauliffe worked on a translation of the Granth Sahib from 1893 to 1909 with the help of Singh Sabhaites such as Kahn Singh Nabha, Bhai Ditt Singh, Bhai Hazara Singh (author of a dictionary of the Guru Granth Sahib), and Bhai Prem Singh (chief *ragi* at the Golden Temple). Macauliffe sent the proofs of his Orientalist tome of six volumes, *The Sikh Religion: Its Gurus, Sacred Writings and Authors* (1909) "to select Sikhs residing in different parts of the province with a request for opinion and critical suggestions," wrote the well-known Sikh reformer Bhai Lakshman Singh, who himself also cooperated in the scheme.[17] After he collected all commentaries, he rented a bungalow in Amritsar and, during a month or so, submitted each and every line to an invited group of influential Sikhs before deciding on a final translation.[18] According to Macauliffe the task was particularly difficult because all Sikhs involved gave him different translations and he had to decide "between rival and contradictory versions."[19] In the end, he turned to Kahn Singh Nabha for advice and accordingly the book is as much a product of this Singh Sabha scholar as it is of Macauliffe. Nabha even accompanied Macauliffe to London "to assist in the publication of this work and in reading the proofs thereof."[20] Later, the Irishman also assigned to him the copyright of the book. Ultimately, *The Sikh Religion* came to reflect the viewpoint of the Singh Sabhaites, though there were some tensions with more traditional Sikhs in Amritsar, who themselves hoped to bring out a translation.[21] Significantly, the making of the book was financially supported by several Punjabi Sikh princes, the traditional patrons of the arts, including Hira Singh, the raja of Nabha, and Rajinder Singh, the maharaja of Patiala, at whose court there emerged an important *khayal gharana* after the 1857 Revolt, when one of the greatest *khayal* singers, Tanras Khan, fled the Delhi court of the last Mughal emperor Bahadur Shah and sought refuge in Patiala.

On the whole, Macauliffe paid more attention than Trumpp and Pincott to the *ragas* of the Guru Granth Sahib. In line with the idea existing among comparative musicologists that Hindustani music was doomed, he believed that the 31 *ragas* of the Granth Sahib "were merging into oblivion."[22] For that reason, he had them not only collected "with much difficulty" by the master-kirtanist Mahant Gajja

Singh (1850–1914), the music teacher of both Kahn Singh Nabha and the maharaja of Patiala, Bhupinder Singh, but also notated in Western staff notation by a professional musician and included it in the fifth volume of *The Sikh Religion*. Typical of the times, when Macauliffe writes about these notations, he implicitly refers to the theory of the contemporary ancestor and the Greek modes:

> Though they may sound bizarre to European ears, they will be appreciated by the Sikhs and by many European lovers of art who regret the loss of the music to which the Odes of Pindar and Sappho and the choral exercises of the Greek tragedians were sung.[23]

Interestingly, Macauliffe emphasized that the 31 *ragas* were sung differently throughout India and, hence, he included for comparison 8 *ragas* from Sourindro Mohun Tagore's "collection of Indian airs" made for the coronation of the king-emperor (figure 5.1).[24] I do not know exactly which one of Tagore's numerous works he used but the point is that Macauliffe, Kahn Singh Nabha, Gajja Singh, and other Sikhs collaborating in the project were conscious of the musicological context of their notations. For further information about the 31 *ragas* of the Guru Granth Sahib for instance, Macauliffe also referred to Tagore's "learned works on Indian music."[25]

In the footsteps of the writings of Trumpp, Pincott, and Macauliffe, reformist Sikhs began to write about the musical organization of the Guru Granth Sahib and, increasingly, the "authentic" performance of *kirtan*. Among them were the leading Singh Sabhaite and Sikh literary figures, Bhai Vir Singh (1872–1957), and his father Charan Singh, as well as the famous early twentieth-century kirtanists Bhai Prem Singh and Professor Sunder Singh.[26] In 1922, Prem Singh, who first worked at the Patiala court and later was appointed chief *ragi* at the Golden Temple, published his *Gurmat Ratan Sangeet Bhandar*, which includes, among other compositions, one typical *sabad* in each of the 31 *ragas* of the Granth Sahib in Western staff notation. In addition, as Pashaura Singh recently argued, Kahn Singh Nabha and Bhai Vir Singh were busy defining the number of musical "sittings" (*chaunkis*) to sing *kirtan* as part of liturgical routine at the Golden Temple.[27] Instead of the original eight musical sessions that were established by Guru Arjan after he installed the Guru Granth Sahib in the *sanctum sanctorum* in 1604, Kahn Singh Nabha and Bhai Vir Singh brought the number to four and five respectively.

TODI

The following is another version of this Rāg :–

Figure 5.1   Rag Todi with Sourindro Mohun Tagore's alternative version from M.A. Macauliffe, *The Sikh Religion: Its Gurus, Sacred Writings and Authors*, Vol. 5, Oxford: Oxford University Press, 1909.

Then again, the making of modern *kirtan* was influenced by the patronage of the maharajas of Patiala, especially maharaja Bhupinder Singh. The earlier mentioned Mahant Gajja Singh enjoyed his patronage and actually represented the Patiala (*khayal*) *gharana* at the Delhi *darbar* of 1911. Encouraged by the maharaja, he also took up the project of recording the *ragas* of the Granth Sahib, but unfortunately he died before it was finished. In 1917, maharaja Bhupinder Singh's authoritative position within the *Panth* and role as a music patron became particularly clear when a controversy arose about whether the last composition of the Guru Granth Sahib, the *Raga Mala* (Garland of *Ragas*), a catalogue of 84 *ragas*, was to be separated from the scripture or not. Among others, Bhai Vir Singh favored its inclusion but Macauliffe, Kahn Singh Nabha, and influential Singh Sabhaites like Bhai Ditt Singh and Gurmukh Singh were against it. Bhupinder Singh self-confidently stepped forward in the debate by backing up the Chief Khalsa Diwan in its claim against its removal.[28] Till date, the status of the *Raga Mala* in the Granth Sahib is undecided. The standard manual of the Sikh code of conduct, the *Rahit Maryada* (first issued in 1950), leaves the question open, but normally the composition is not recited in the "unbroken readings" (*akhand paths*) of the Guru Granth Sahib at the Golden Temple.

Over the centuries, the *ragas* of the Guru Granth Sahib were passed on orally to different generations of *ragis* belonging to various lineages and Sikh institutions of learning (*taksals*). In fact, Ajit Singh Paintal argued that the Sikh *ragis* and Muslim *rababis*, whose musical lineage goes back to the days of first Guru Nanak's Muslim accompanist Mardana, "did not confine themselves to the *ragas* used by the Sikh Gurus."[29] In any case, they were definitely sung in variable tone pitch, performed in the light of changing musical styles, and accompanied by different stringed instruments (like the *rabab, sarangi, sarinda, taus, dilruba, tanpura,* and *sitar*) and drums (like the *dhadd, mridang, dholak,* and *pakhavaj*). Without doubt, therefore, the simply notated scales of *ragas* in Western staff notation by Macauliffe and Singh Sabhaites solely reflected the contemporary intellectual climate of assertively defining the Sikh self rather than the reality of the largely improvised *raga* melodies. Also they notated these *ragas* to give their work some scientific authority. What remains ironic in view of Singh Sabha identity politics is that the Western harmonium became the standard accompanying instruments used in the performance of Sikh sacred music.

As leading Singh Sabhaites propagated an exclusive and homogenous Sikhism, *kirtan* was incorporated within distinctive high cultural community boundaries, whereby the orthodox Sikh moral self was represented in opposition to a shared, cross-religious, and cross-caste popular Punjabi culture. Singh Sabhaites found many aspects of Punjabi popular culture morally repulsive: the erotic references that were part of the *qisse* (folk tales), Hindu *bhajans* (devotional songs), Muslim *ghazals* (poetry set to music, expressing both spiritual and worldly love), female folk singing and dancing (*giddha*), and so on. This negative Singh Sabha moral agenda certainly contrasted with the fact that all Sikh Gurus sang both in contemporary north-Indian "classical" and folk music styles. Hence, it forms a point of recognition between the Singh Sabha moral language and the British civilizing mission. Also telling here remains the multifaceted and ambiguous relationship between the popular Sikh *dhadi* bards and the *Panth* since the early twentieth century.[30] More immediately, the emergence of a growing consensus among orthodox Sikhs about the "authentic" performance of *kirtan* led to a disapproval of a long tradition of Sikh sacred music performances by professional Muslim *mirasi* musicians, the earlier mentioned *rababis*. Before the reformist activities of Kahn Singh Nabha, Bhai Vir Singh, and others, the traditional liturgical cycle at the Golden Temple still existed of eight "sittings" of *ragis* and seven "sittings" of *rababis*.[31] This narrowing down of the rich Punjabi cultural setting out of which *kirtan* emerged became decisive when the improvisational, if not folk, *rababi* musical tradition was officially designed as being non-Sikh in the *Rahit Maryada,* and this was accentuated further, of course, as a result of the partition of British India, when the majority of the *rababis* fled to Pakistan and were separated from the mainstream of Sikhism.[32] One can understand the disappointment of Bhai Ghulam Muhammad Chand (b. 1927), from the family of Bhai Mardana, when during a recent concert tour in India, he was not allowed to perform at the Golden Temple, like his forefathers did.[33]

Presently, the SGCP continues to employ *ragis* to perform "authentic" *kirtan* at the Golden Temple as well as (historic) gurdwaras in India and overseas. Also it regularly arranges contests in Punjab, supposedly to maintain and raise the quality of *kirtan* performances, whereby the winners are recorded and/or broadcasted. At the same time, there now is more variety in *kirtan* performance than ever before with the Sikh hymns being sung in a semi-classical style, played by brass bands, accompanied by Anglo-American Sikh string arrangements, and so on. In recent decades, orthodox Sikhs above all reacted negatively when *kirtan* was performed in *ragas* that were different from those specified in the Guru Granth Sahib or in lighter popular styles, resembling film music or Punjabi folk songs. Other Sikhs objected to the broadcast of *kirtan* through mass media (television, radio, Internet, and so on) because in their view the hymns should be sung congregationally rather than listened to at home. Intriguing in connection to these complaints about the lack of "authenticity" in contemporary *kirtan* performances is the recently released set of six CDs, *Har Sachche Takht Rachaya*,[34] because it directly links *kirtan* performance traditions to the five Sikh *Takhts* (seats of worldly authority), of which the Akal Takht in Amritsar is paramount, and those in Patna, Nanded, and Nankana are not controlled by the SGCP. Bhai Balwinder Singh Rangila, an influential *ragi*, who runs the Gurmat Sangit Academy in Chandigarh, was the consultant for the repertoire and recording. As all CDs are accompanied with commentary by the respective *Takht's* chief priest (*jathedar*), the set is sort of authoritative from an orthodox Sikh perspective. Having said this, however, the recordings use no traditional stringed instruments, except the *sitar*. On the contrary, the Western guitar is used at several CDs. Also interesting to note is that Amritsar's Akal Takht is represented by *dhadi* (troubadour) singer Bhai Tarlochan Singh Bhammaddi and his group of musicians, as the *dhadi* tradition of "folk" songs about Sikh martyrdom and suffering became linked to this institution. Indeed, following the modern processes of institutionalization and canonization of Sikh sacred music, the main tension in the performance of *kirtan* has been between a desire for classicization and an urge toward popularization; in other words, between the invention of an "authentic" tradition and a being with the times. In what follows, then, I will discuss how one oral lineage in *kirtan* that is still important today, namely, the one from Bhai Jawala Singh (1892–1952), through his sons Bhai Avtar Singh (1925–2006) and Bhai Gurcharan Singh (b. 1915), down to Bhai Baldeep Singh, knowingly or unknowingly, became involved in the long-term historical processes of institutionalization and canonization of *kirtan*, as well as Sikh identity politics, following the Singh Sabha reformation.

The Bhai Jawala Singh lineage in *Kirtan* in historical context

Undeniably, the Bhai Jwala Singh-lineage in *kirtan* is much respected within the *Panth*. So, for example, it is commonly accepted that it has a direct historical connection back to the time of fifth Guru Arjan (1563–1606): Avtar Singh and Gurcharan Singh always call(ed) themselves eleventh-generation exponents of *kirtan* (figure 5.2). Also, the

Figure 5.2   Bhai Jawala Singh on the harmonium, Bhai Avtar Singh on the *taus*, and Bhai Gurcharan Singh on the *tabla* at Dera Sahib gurdwara in Lahore, 1935 (Courtesy of Bhai Baldeep Singh).

Central Sikh Museum in Amritsar's Golden Temple exhibits paintings of Jawala Singh and Avtar Singh as well as the harmonium used by Jawala Singh at Lahore's Dera Sahib gurdwara. Actually, Jawala and his sons became known as the torchbearers of the *dhrupad* tradition in *kirtan*, which had been prevalent during the times of the Gurus and indeed, ironically, at that time mostly was performed by *rababis*. This is fascinating, because over the centuries Sikh sacred music was increasingly influenced by Hindustani *khayal*, to the extent that by the turn of the twentieth century, the *ragis* at two centers of important *kirtan* traditions, the Golden Temple and the Nankana Sahib gurdwara in Guru Nanak's birthplace near Lahore, had more or less switched to this style of singing. As the finest *dhrupad* kirtanist alive, Jawala Singh was invited several times for performances by maharaja Jagatjit Singh of Kapurthala. Also maharaja Bhupinder Singh of Patiala sent Gajja Singh for *dhrupad* lessons to Jawala Singh.

Besides studying with his father, Jawala Singh also studied with famous nineteenth-century *ragis* such as Bhai Sarda Singh and Bhai Rangi Ram. In addition, he was a key member of the Singh Sabha movement, who, for example, took part in the Gurdwara Reform Movement (1920–1925) and underwent imprisonment for his involvement in several campaigns organized by the Akali Dal, a religious-political party founded in 1920, which considers itself the principal representative of Sikhs. He received the lucrative offer from the SGPC to become the chief *ragi* at the Golden Temple, which he declined. Though he often performed at the Sikh holiest shrine and other historic gurdwaras, as a freelancer based in the small rural town of Sultanpur Lodi, he more or less always kept the SGPC at bay. During the 1930s, nonetheless, he was chosen as the president of an association of kirtanists and, in 1942, he presided over the first All India *Ragis* Conference held in Amritsar. In these roles and generally as head of his lineage, he undoubtedly had an influence on the modern performance practice and canonization of *kirtan*. Like most of his contemporaries, Jawala Singh switched to the harmonium as his main accompanying instrument around the time of the First World War. As they were taught by their father, Avtar Singh and Gurcharan Singh entered the tradition at a young age. Though they were equally trained in the string instruments of the time, during the late 1930s they adopted the harmonium and *tabla* as accompanying instruments to their singing. Nevertheless, when a decade later they became "B"-grade artists for All India Radio Jalandhar-Amritsar, next in hierarchy only to the illustrious *ragis*, Bhai Santa Singh and Bhai Samund Singh, Gurcharan Singh most of the time played the *tanpura* (an Indian string instrument that generally plays an accompaniment drone) rather than the harmonium during radio performances. Also, Avtar Singh switched back to playing the *taus* (string instrument, with a peacock-body sound box) during the final years of his life.

Conversely, it remains critical to mention the association between Avtar Singh and Gurcharan Singh and Patiala's Punjabi University, an institution, which in the footsteps of Khalsa College, Amritsar, to a great extent reflects the Sikh identity politics as first propagated by the Singh Sabhaites. Following the death of Bhai Santa Singh, Punjabi University's Professor Taran Singh decided to record the greatest still-living performers of Sikh sacred music for posterity. One of them was Bhai Samund Singh, and it was on his suggestion that Taran Singh also requested Avtar Singh and Gurcharan Singh, who at the time were serving as chief *ragis* at New Delhi's historic gurdwaras (a role that they performed for 37 years until their retirement in 1997), to record over 500 compositions of *kirtan* accompanied by the *tanpura*.

Unfortunately, neither these recordings nor those of Samund Singh are available anymore at Punjabi University today. When Avtar Singh and Gurcharan Singh visited Samund Singh during his final days, the master complained that the golden days of good musicians were over. This, in his opinion, was particularly caused by the SGPC's recruiting of mediocre *ragis*, whom the *sangats* (congregations) regarded more highly than the good ones. Then, as another counteract, as it were, Punjabi University in 1976 published two volumes of *kirtan* compositions in traditional notation by Avtar Singh and Gurcharan Singh: *Gurbani Sangit Prachin Rit Ratanavali*. Eventually, the brothers began to disseminate their art in Britain, the United States, and Canada.

Apart from Avtar Singh's son Kultar Singh, the Bhai Jawala Singh lineage is kept alive today by the grandnephew of Avtar and Gurcharan Singh, Bhai Baldeep Singh, a very active musician, teacher, speaker, and instrument maker. Currently, in fact, Bhai Baldeep is particularly busy with the setting up of a conservatory for the Sikh musical heritage in Sultanpur Lodhi, the important Sikh pilgrimage site where Nanak, the first Sikh Guru, lived for 14 years, and for which he received significant financial support from the Punjab government.[35] Though Baldeep Singh's personality and activities are highly individualistic, his devotion to the performance of authentic *kirtan* on traditional string instruments should be seen in the context of the contemporary revivalist Gurmat Sangit movement, as propagated, for example, by Professor Gurnam Singh, who since 2003 occupies the chair in Sikh sacred music and heads the Gurmat Sangit department at Patiala University,[36] and Professor Kartar Singh at the SGPC-run Gurmat Sangit Academy at Anandpur Sahib. While the Gurmat Sangit movement overall aims for the musicological study of Sikh sacred music, it particularly represents an artistic "return to the roots" and strives to reproduce the instrumentation, *ragas*, and musical styles of the times in which a work was composed. As a consequence of its efforts, there are fewer liberties taken with the performance of *kirtan* among the orthodoxy, and there is generally a revival of the use of traditional string instruments such as the *sarangi* and the *taus* in place of the harmonium. As to be expected, Gurnam Singh and Kartar Singh have also succeeded in reintroducing traditional stringed instruments during *kirtan* performances at the Golden Temple.

By and large, the Gurmat Sangit movement is driven by a similar genuine interest in past musical practices as that of the contemporary movement behind the "historically informed performances" of early Western classical music, though the case of Sikh sacred music certainly remains more difficult, as I will discuss later in relation to Bhai Baldeep Singh's standpoint in this field. As both the SGPC and the Delhi Sikh Gurdwara Management Committee (DSGMC), which is independent from the SGPC, do not produce official degree courses in Sikh *kirtan*, the Gurmat Sangit department at Punjabi University equally is a response to the huge demand for kirtanists worldwide and, indeed, a SOS from the SGPC.[37] The department claims to be very successful in providing jobs in gurdwaras, colleges, schools, and music academies for its students. The instance of Sikh sacred music as an oral tradition becomes all the more interesting by the fact that, in line with what happened in Hindustani music practice in general after independence, Vishnu Narayan Bhatkhande's system of notation and *that* system of *raga* classification is currently used in all renowned teaching institutions of *kirtan*, including Punjabi University's Music Department, Kartar Singh's Academy, the Shahid Sikh Missionary College, and Gyani Dyal Singh's music school at Rakab-ganj gurdwara in New Delhi. Likewise, among other authors, Gurnam Singh and Avtar Singh, Gurcharan Singh, as well as Gyani Dyal Singh used this system of notation in their collections of Sikh sacred hymns.[38] In 2012, then, Punjabi University's Gurmat Sangit department published the first dictionary of Gurmat Sangit in Punjabi, Hindi, and English.

Also, it is important to know that Gurnam Singh's chair and department are financially assisted by the Sri Guru Gian Parkash Foundation, a New Delhi–based socio-religious organization. By providing this support, the foundation aims to revive ancient Sikh musical traditions, in particular, the *kirtan* "sittings," of which all major gurdwaras have at least four each day, at the Golden temple. Until recently, the foundation was headed by Bibi Jasbir Kaur Khalsa (1947–2011), the "Doyenne of Gurmat Sangit," as Pashaura Singh called her in his eulogy.[39] Since 1977, when she accompanied Bhai Jiwan Singh's *ragi jatha* to preach the message of the Gurus in the United Kingdom, the United States, and Canada, she became somewhat of a celebrity among diasporan Sikh *sangats*. Over time, she was also financially supported by Yogi Bhajan, the charismatic but controversial leader of the Healthy, Happy, Holy Organization (3HO), to teach Punjabi language and *kirtan* to the North American Sikh converts. Back in India, Bibi Jasbir Kaur Khalsa came into contact with the Sikh ascetic Sant Sucha Singh, who himself was not a musician, but yet the archives of music at the Patiala University's Gurmat Sangit department are named after him, and the two of them established a center for the revival of authentic *kirtan* in Ludhiana. In 1991, they organized the first Aduti Gurmat Sangit Sammelan (Unique Gathering of the Performers of the Guru's view of music), where all the *ragas* of the Guru Granth Sahib were performed by various professional musicians, and a panel of judges under the supervision of the well-known Hindustani scholar-musician Dilip Chandra Vedi "tried to identify the original tradition of singing."[40] In 2004, Bibi Kaur organized a great special meeting (*darbar*) of kirtanists at Taran Taran to celebrate the four-hundredth anniversary of Guru Arjan's martyrdom. Eventually, she was honored for her service to the community, jointly by the three most authoritative Sikh institutions: the Akal Takht, the SGPC, and the Akali Dal. In 2008, she became a member of the Punjabi University Senate. More immediately, in congruence with the results of the Aduti Gurmat Sangit Sammelan and to the great delight of the SGPC, Gurnam Singh prepared 31 compositions in the "authentic" *ragas* of the Guru Granth Sahib in Bhatkhande's system of notation in his *Sikh Musicology: Sri Guru Granth Sahib and Hymns of the Human Spirit* (2001) and also recorded them with a stringed accompaniment "to establish the identity of Sikh musicology in a distinct manner."[41]

To be clear, my emphasis on these processes of institutionalization, canonization, and identity formation does not mean that I do not believe that there has been no continuity in tradition of singing from Jawala Singh to Bhai Baldeep Singh, or the *rababi* and other lineages in Sikh *kirtan* for that matter. As a historian, however, I must describe how these traditions became engulfed in processes of modernization and identity politics since the Singh Sabha reformation. Thus, I have tried to make clear how in modern times kirtanists became more or less involved with the SGPC or DSGMC, educational institutions, music conferences (where demonstrations of *kirtan* were given by eminent *ragis*), modern recording and new media technologies, changing public tastes, the Sikh diaspora, and so on. Indisputably, all these involvements had an influence on their social consciousness and music making. Typically, and in line with the myth of Hindustani music in decline, these kirtanists often declared that past performances of *kirtan* were of greater quality and, indeed, therefore more "authentic" and "spiritual." As in the case of Hindustani music, however, claims like these, together with the numerous references to ancient Sanskrit music theories, of which the authority was often reinforced by the influence of Orientalist and musicological studies, do no justice to the historical and aesthetic changes in the performance of Sikh sacred music since the imperial encounter.

Ancient Sanskrit music theories, Aesthetics and historical change

In relation to the quest for the "authentic" performance of *kirtan*, the main question that remains is, of course, to what level the music of an oral tradition, of which there are almost no written sources available, can be recreated over time. Music primarily exists in performance, and before the advent of sound recording all performances were lost the moment they finished. As the famous Hindustani musician Shiv Kumar Sharma wrote: "Change is the only permanent reality in music. Even the music of the same *gharana* changes from generation to generation. No musician can ever be a perfect xerox of his *guru*."[42] In the larger Hindustani music, almost all *ragas* "have undergone transformations over the centuries, and many of them have fallen into disuse."[43] As already said, from the time of Guru Nanak onward, *kirtan* was sung and played in variable intonation, in different musical styles, and with various instruments. Hence, Sikh scholars and musicians in search of "authentic" *kirtan* can only imagine what the music of earlier generations was like; one never knows that one is hearing the original of any kind of music because it will always be related to something that precedes it. In fact, even if it were possible to recreate the past exactly, there are aesthetic and philosophical reasons why such a recreation would be undesirable. Present-day performances must appeal to present-day tastes, and "historically informed performances" therefore are not really historical, but remakes of the past in the image of the present.

Over time, the Sikh Gurus specified the *ragas* in which they sang each hymn. Ultimately, the Guru Granth Sahib was organized into 31 subsections, each of which attributed to a particular *raga*. With a few exceptions, all of these *ragas* were common to Hindustani music. Broadly speaking, a *raga* can be defined as "a tonal framework for composition and improvisation",[44] which operates between the levels of what in Western music are called scale and melody. As a noun it derived from a Sanskrit verb with the meaning "to colour" and, accordingly, every *raga* is supposed to colour the mind, bring enjoyment, and arouse an emotional response among listeners.[45]

Even so, it remains exceptionally difficult to define *raga* in words: "One has to understand it by constant and conscious listening during actual performance. Its meaning and identity grow slowly within oneself."[46] What makes the situation even more complicated is that the open-ended melodic structure of *raga* usually is seen as being closely related, as I have already remarked in relation to the songs of Rabindranath Tagore, to the creation of an emotional mood (*rasa*), which is attained by proper performance of various attributes, some musical and some extra-musical, such as the atmosphere associated with a specific "time" of the day (*samay*). Having said this, however, many Hindustani musicians today no longer see a direct connection between a certain *raga* and a specified mood and/or time. Moreover, in the Carnatic music tradition the time theory is not strictly followed.[47] Simultaneously, as artists perform a *raga*, listeners around the world experience distinct moods with different intensities. This not only because of individual backgrounds and locations but also particularly because each *raga* is loaded with several moods, including a dominant one to which the others are subordinate, and it expresses various moods at changed tempi and different levels of melodic intensity.

In modern times, man's relationship with nature and time no doubt has changed dramatically, and much more is known about the universality of music. So do the above-mentioned ontologies of difference still make sense for an understanding of Indian music? Are they to a great extent not examples of a continuing "internal Orientalism"? Do aesthetics not change over time? Has our knowledge of Indian music not increased? In recent decades, Hindustani music scholars such as Prabha Atre, Joep Bor, and Deepak Raja have questioned the value of the *raga*-mood and *raga*-time theories for the study of Hindustani music. By using these theories, they argue, musicologists and musicians attempt to reconcile old and outdated concepts with contemporary music practice.[48] In addition, they make clear that there are theories about *raga* tone material that are based on assumptions that have no scientific foundation. One of the best examples is the earlier mentioned sonant-consonant concept (*vadi-samvadi*). This concept of a dominant and another strong note around which the *raga* exposition revolves is memorized unquestionably by students of music theory, but scholars and musicians differ greatly on the subject and find no way of putting its functionality in practice.[49] I mention the *raga*-mood, *raga*-time, and sonant-consonant theories of Hindustani music because they are often repeated in Sikh studies.[50] Likewise, scholars of Sikh music underlined that since ancient times, the twenty-two *shrutis*, together with the traditional seven notes, have had a direct influence "on the listener's mind."[51] Yet, "how can one justify applying the same age-old norms of twenty-two fixed pitches to interpret intonation in present-day *raga* performance?"[52] Evidently, these scholars reiterating ancient Sanskrit music theories struggle with the ontological difference of Sikh sacred music in its oneness with the word of the Guru Granth Sahib as a reference to the transcendent.

But how then do the tones, rhythms, moods, and time of *kirtan* relate to the word of the Guru Granth Sahib, and how should this combination of sacred music and word be studied and translated in these times of "world music"? In the performance of *kirtan*, as Verne Dusenbury wrote almost 20 years ago, "both performer and audience actively take into their persons the natural sacred sounds of the Guru" and to most Sikhs this deed is central to the "*darsan* (audience) of the Guru Granth Sahib."[53] Overall, he continues, Sikhs follow a "nondualistic" ideology of language that, in the words of Pashaura Singh, challenges "analytic dichotomies that rigidly oppose oral and written texts, or sound and meaning, or that which foresees an inevitable evolutionary movement between them."[54] More or less in congruence with Tagore's idea of *rasa* as mentioned in the previous chapter, Arvind Mandair argued that the hymns of the Sikh scripture actually might have been dictated by "aesthetic sensibilities centered on mood/emotion as opposed to conceptual thought alone."[55] Conversely, Pashaura Singh emphasized that, in line with the ancient Sanskrit theory of sacred sound (*nada*), in *kirtan*, "the physical vibrations of musical sound are inextricably connected with the spiritual world of 'unstruck melody'" and that "all the *ragas* exist eternally and some of them are merely discovered from time to time by inspired musicians."[56] Likewise, Francesca Cassio recently made a direct link between modern-day performance practice of Sikh sacred music and the ancient theory of "the yoga of sound" (*nada yoga*).[57] Interestingly, these (Orientalist) theories contrast with the reformative "anti-mantra" attitude of the nineteenth-century Singh Sabhaites, which has also been included in the *Rahit Maryada*.

Overall I believe that the concept of "sacred sound" does not further the historical, aesthetic, and musicological understanding of *kirtan*. In particular, I wonder whether the contemporary Sikh performer and listener really are able to recall the supposedly "authentic" sacred sounds of the Guru. Moreover, I often find the manner in which Sikhs authorize their ideas about "authentic" performance troublesome because it essentially turns the debate once again toward the stalemate position of "history versus tradition," which following the seminal historical research of Hew McLeod, unfortunately, for too long a time dominated the field of Sikh studies.[58] So, for example, Bhai Baldeep Singh believes that the hymns of the Guru Granth Sahib are "revealed songs" and that "a careful study of these compositions will bring to us the original *nada* (sacred sound) of the gurus, as they expressed them, and in this way the other *bani* (styles of singing the compositions of the Guru Granth Sahib), which has become silent may perhaps become alive again."[59] Though he states that "almost everything has been lost" as a result of the Singh Sabha reformation,[60] he trusts that "authentic" performances of Sikh sacred music are still possible today by listening to the "tradition bearers," whose modes of singing are directly linked to *"one single original source–the gurus themselves!"*[61] and among whom he includes himself as an exponent of the Bhai Jawala Singh lineage. The performance of *kirtan*, he continues, "does not merely make a person a great musician (*sangitagya*) but a saga, a saint!"[62] and, as a result, Sikh sacred music is not "a musicians' music and mere musicians cannot, perhaps, comprehend it."[63]

Both in the light of musicological research and imperial history, I find Bhai Baldeep Singh's statements problematic. Musicologists of early Western music, including those who believe in the stern tradition of method passed down from teacher to pupil (which, let it be clear, also exists in the West), generally assume that "authentic" music cannot be traced much farther back than the early part of the nineteenth century (and, let it be clear again, this despite the fact that for early Western music, unlike for the oral tradition of *kirtan*, musical manuscripts in staff notations and treatises about music musical theory, performance practice, and instrument making, for instance, exist). Likewise, I find Nirinjan Kaur Khalsa's argument that the oral tradition of Sikh sacred music (which she calls the *Gurbani Kirtan parampara*) since the time of the Gurus, and as specifically embodied in her opinion in Bhai Baldeep Singh, "promotes a notion of the Sikh self that transgresses normative definitions," such as those propagated by the Sikh orthodoxy (SGPC, Gurnam Singh, and so on), too idealistic.[64] Khalsa's article, as she writes herself, is a response "to the topics of authenticity and authority with *Gurbani Kirtan*" as addressed in articles in *Sikh Formations* by Bhai

Baldeep Singh and myself.[65] Though she overall supports my argu-
ments, she ultimately opposes my assumption that the modern Sikh
sacred music "cannot be understood outside the imperial encounter."[66]
Like Bhai Baldeep Singh, then, she claims that, in contrast to orthodox Sikh sacred music making since the Singh Sabha reformation,
the members of the *Gurbani Kirtan parampara* remained intellectually
unscathed by the fast-changing society around them, and their music
therefore always remained "authentic."

Bhai Baldeep Singh clearly concedes to some final and transcendental authoritative source when he states that the hymns of the
Guru Granth Sahib are "revealed songs," which supposedly follow
eternal sacred sounds that presently still can be picked up by musical
saints (for Sikhs only?) directly from "the gurus themselves." In doing
so, in my view, he adheres to a traditional "spiritual" position and so,
for me at least, provides no possibility for further discussion, because
such an interpretation, without any ground in historical evidence,
goes beyond the goals of both the disciplines of history and musicology. Indeed, his exclusive position very much reminds me of the
"holier-than-thou" or "more-authentic-than-thou" approach to early
Western music, as propagated for instance by the Western harpsi-
chordist Wanda Landowska (1879–1959), who is often quoted as saying: "You play Bach your way, I will play him Bach's way." But is there
not always a transcendent dimension to the composing or making of
music, that quintessentially nonrepresentational medium, and were/
are not all great musicians around the world therefore saints in their
own individual ways and cultural contexts? Furthermore, I find Bhai
Baldeep Singh's traditional "spiritual" position troublesome from the
perspective of imperial history because it also includes his quoting of
esoteric authors such as Hazrat Inayat Khan, "another Eastern guru
going to the West to point out its spiritual bankruptcy,"[67] and David
Tame, who indeed in *The Secret Power of Music* (1984) gave a great deal
of attention to Cyril Scott,[68] as well as his orientations toward, for
instance, clairaudience.[69] For is he not simply holding on here to the
imperial trope of "spiritual" India, which, as I have already discussed
in earlier chapters, has been fashionable since the late nineteenth
century simultaneously in India and the West, and, over time, often
went hand in hand with the Pythagorean concept of "the music of
the spheres" and "the occult power of sound?"[70]

Of course, I am fully aware of the fact that all history is written from
the perspective of the present. Even so, I still deem the discipline of

history worthwhile, simply because it makes every discussion more interesting, especially through its narratives of historical change and continuity, use of sources, or attempts to establish global connections and comparisons. From the viewpoint of intellectual history, for instance, I believe that the oral tradition of *kirtan,* as part of Sikh identity politics since the imperial encounter, underwent a process of aestheticization that to some extent was similar to what happened to "folk music" in the West.[71] Then again, unsurprisingly, I think that Sikh sacred music can be studied at best in the same way as has been done in the case of early Western music in order to provide the finest possible "historically informed performances" to both Sikh and non-Sikh audiences worldwide. Here, in comparison to Bhai Baldeep Singh, Gurnam Singh, and others, however, I definitely think that much less is possible and still many questions need to be answered. As among Hindustani singers performing *ragas*, the intonation of the immutable center of the *raga* melody, the *Sa*, is different with each performance, for example, what about Sikh *kirtan* singers of the past and present,[72] and did the harmonium not have an impact on the singing of *kirtan*, for instance, through a growing identification of the *Sa* with the pitch of the middle "C" on the keyboard? Similarly, I would like to know whether or not the playing style of *dhrupad* in Sikh sacred music was influenced by that of *khayal*, for example, at the time of Guru Gobind Singh or under the patronage of maharaja Bhupinder Singh of Patiala. This especially because, as a devotional musical style with a strong precomposed tendency, *dhrupad* not only is a particularly suitable medium for Sikh *kirtan* but also, unlike the less strict *khayal* style, places more emphasis on the text of the composition. Did the popularity of *dhrupad* in Sikh sacred music decline, as in Hindustani music in general, "because of its resistance to change, restrictions on individual creativity, and its failure to accommodate changing audience tastes?"[73] Indeed, if this is true, what is the position of the Bhai Jawala Singh lineage in *kirtan* in this context?

Contemporary changes and dilemmas: Modern media, world music, and the translation of the Sikh scripture

Recently, one of the foremost representatives of the Hindustani Kirana *gharana* (in *khayal* singing) and music scholar, Prabha Atra (b. 1932), wrote:

Before the microphone arrived on the scene, a voice which could be heard in the most distant corner of the hall was considered good. Naturally, the artistic work on the notes had to be such that it could be heard by all. The loudness of the voice being an essential feature, the notes tended to be straight, bold and the speed of the phrases slow. The microphone brought about a revolution in music. Audibility no longer remained a problem; even a breath could be heard. The tonal quality of sound assumed great importance. The artist began to think in terms of making conscious use of volume, timbre, range and speed to increase the communicative ability of his voice.[74]

Undeniably, recordings and the Internet have radically changed the environment for the creation and consumption of Sikh sacred music, and it remains surprising therefore that ethnographic research in this field still needs to be done. Microphones and recordings have made it possible to convey the finest nuances of singing and instrument playing. Accordingly, the contemporary kirtanist is more than before aesthetically concerned with the notes of the *raga*: at best, with characteristic ascending-descending movements, core phrases, and other musical technicalities. Likewise, performances of *kirtan* in modern theaters and concert halls throughout the world altered its aesthetics, and audiences generally have become more aware of differences in singing and musical styles, as they are constantly exposed to *kirtan* through recordings, television, and, indeed, the Internet, which has turned the relationship between Sikh identity and *kirtan* into a transnational one.

Predictably, the SGPC has its own Internet site,[75] where one can not only read about Sikhism and its history but also watch and listen to *kirtan* performances live from Amritsar or download hymns to one's iPhone. SikhNet Radio service,[76] in fact, allows gurdwaras around the world to broadcast their daily *kirtan* program live on the Internet. But one wonders what the Sikh orthodox think about its channel, "Western/Non-Traditional," with *kirtan* sung and played in Western style and on Western instruments, or about the fact that Sikhs can download their favourite hymn as ringtone. At the same time, one can watch and listen to numerous Sikh *kirtan* performances on YouTube. Intriguingly, these performances are accompanied by multiple viewers' comments that always are positive or by the statement that "adding comments has been disabled." This lack of critical discussion certainly is different from what generally happens in the case of both Western classical and popular music uploads. Has this perhaps something to do with the idea that Sikh sacred music transcends critical debate? If so, it would contrast with the overall eagerness of Sikhs to discuss their tradition since the late nineteenth century, especially in relation to Western scholarship on Sikhism. However, Westerners have not in fact so far written critically about the subject.

All these developments signify complex processes of aesthetic change and commodification. For the future, the question remains whether the use of recording and new media technologies will lead to a greater standardization or, following a growing individualization and privatization of *kirtan*, a pluralization of Sikh sacred music. In any case, the above-mentioned case of SikhNet Radio's "Western/ Non-Traditional" channel has already made clear the emergence of Sikh sacred music as "world music." Numerous experiments are taking place that merge *kirtan* with Western music and instruments, and this not only among the Euro-American 3HO Sikhs. Specifically, the Australian Sikh, Dya Singh, has much success with his World Music Group on stages around the world, singing *kirtan* in Punjabi with occasional English explanations. On the whole, he believes that *kirtan* is in need of "radical 'evolution' towards universality and greater acceptability." This above all because he finds its traditional performances in gurdwaras

> narrow and static music [...] played by (in the majority) less than proficient musicians who are being churned out without proper coaching from Punjab and heard by diminishing numbers of Sikh adults who listen to it not because they enjoy it but because it is one path to salvation; and even less numbers of Sikh youth and children because it is not attractive and also because the profound message it carries, is not relayed sincerely and with music palatable to the younger generation.[77]

Whatever the truth about his judgment about Sikh musicians, Dya Singh's argument about the changing tastes of young Sikhs in Punjab and the diaspora, who, willingly or not, are exposed to all kinds of music, undeniably makes sense.

Closely related to the emergence of *kirtan* as world music remains the fact that the Gurmukhi script, as well as the language in which the Guru Granth Sahib is written, is increasingly incomprehensible to young (diasporan) Sikhs. Even so, there is a strong resistance within the community to the translation of the scripture into English or any other language. Unsurprisingly, the argument goes that, because of its sacred sound, the meaning of the Guru Granth Sahib transcends that of a written text, and that translation would do injustice to "the *darsan* of the Word and the transformative attributes of sacred sounds" as experienced by Sikhs.[78] In contrast, critics argue that when Sikhs do not translate the Guru Granth Sahib, it will lead to "'bibliolatry' and 'idol worship' of a linguistically 'dead' original."[79] According to Verne Dusenbery:

> It is obviously a trade-off: either you keep the material properties of the sounds and lose the intelligibility or you attempt to retain the intelligibility by translating and, in doing so, sacrifice the sacred sounds of the Guru.[80]

But what is the alternative? Knowledge of the sacred language of the Sikh scripture always has been restricted in Punjab, and this part of the tradition will definitely not be able to continue in the long term solely on the basis of the Punjabi language and *kirtan* classes currently taught at gurdwaras in India and abroad. In any case, during the last few decades, an edition of the Guru Granth Sahib in a three-column format, including the original Gurmukhi, Roman transliteration, and an English translation, has been used as the center of worship among diasporan Sikhs and, moreover, within the Euro-American Sikh community, for an "unbroken reading" (*akhand path*) in Punjabi and in English, depending on who is reading.[81]

Christopher Shackle and Arvind Mandair have argued that, with the setting of each hymn of the Guru Granth Sahib to a defined *raga*, Sikh sacred music has some limitation placed on it "so that the spiritual aspect of the performance can be maintained."[82] But what remains of the often assumed aesthetic unity between Sikh sacred music and word in the light of the ever-changing practice of *kirtan* by individuals over time? Is this assumption not utopian because the Sikh Gurus were the only ones who sang "authentically" and everything sung afterward by others would be simply interpretations of their music and words? Did musical changes not influence the Sikh experience of *gurbani* (the word of the Guru), and how does this relate to the Sikh resistance to the translation of the Guru Granth Sahib?

Indeed, when musical changes did not interrupt the message of the Guru Granth Sahib but, on the contrary, were experienced as durable and "authentic," why would the same not apply to translations of the Sikh scripture, which have already proved to be meaningful to the contemporary Sikh community, especially in the diaspora? Once more, it seems that the controversy about the translation of the Guru Granth Sahib concerns, above all, Sikh identity politics and is directly related to the Singh Sabha reformers' utopian goal of recapturing and defining the original meaning of the Gurus' teachings, as contained in the Sikh scripture, in order to make possible a return to the "authentic" tradition. As I have argued elsewhere, this rather fundamentalist exercise was influenced to a great extent by Christian Protestantism.[83] It certainly has little to do with the ever-changing set of meanings that Sikh sacred music and word provided the community throughout the world since the imperial encounter.

Conclusion

With its dedication to creating both a higher musical and moral standard, the modernization of Sikh *kirtan* (the focus on Orientalist and musicological texts, canonization of music, professionalization of musicians, and so on) more or less can be contextualized with the transformation of Hindustani music into "classical" and national music. Alternately, there were points of recognition between the Singh Sabha moral language and the British civilizing mission in the case of Sikh sacred music as well. On the whole, the making of *kirtan* since the Singh Sabha reformation was closely connected with processes of modern Sikh identity formation. Sikhism was and still is defined in the imperial encounter, and music certainly also shaped the modern Sikh self. Without denying that *kirtan* can be a "spiritual," if not a transforming, experience for Sikhs, it unambiguously became a moral bastion for the Sikh orthodoxy in opposition to progress and commercialization. Undeniably, the study and translation of Sikh sacred music and word remains yet another challenge for Sikhs in the face of modern progress, to which there will never be a satisfactory solution for those involved. This chapter underlines that the historical study of *kirtan* has been much concealed by the orthodox Sikh search for "authenticity" and argued that one step forward is a critical approach to the authority of ancient Sanskrit music theories and aesthetics, whose influence was strengthened since the nineteenth century by

Orientalist studies and Indian national musicologists like Sourindro Mohun Tagore and Bhatkhande. Furthermore, it emphasized the importance of the study of past and present practices of *kirtan* in the light of musical, aesthetic, and societal changes since the imperial encounter. For recent times, one would particularly like to know more about the relationship between the Sikh diaspora and the developments in Sikh *kirtan* through critical discussions of Sikh sacred music education, musicians touring globally, repertoire choices, transmission through recordings and the Internet, and so on.

Ultimately, it remains fascinating to see how Sikhs will make further use of the inexhaustible hermeneutic potential of the Guru Granth Sahib and create meanings in relation to Sikh sacred music and word that have not yet been determined. In any case, as a remedy against dogmatism, it seems right to remember the openness to society of both Guru Nanak, who took the universal message of *gurbani* out to the people, as well as Guru Arjan, who in compiling the Guru Granth Sahib accepted the writing in different languages, though always in Gurmukhi script, and did not get stuck on external differences of accents, intonations, grammar, structure, or vocabulary, but instead included in the Sikh scripture whatever resonated with the voice of Nanak. Moreover, he stressed the use of classical, semiclassical, and folk tunes in *kirtan* because "he was fully aware of the needs of various sections of the *Panth* coming from different backgrounds."[84] Likewise, it may be right to emphasize that, despite the importance given in Sikh practice to communal singing and the reciting of hymns, the Guru Granth Sahib "can only ever be appropriated and understood at the level of the individual" because "no two readers or listeners will ever imbibe exactly the same meaning, simply because the existential situation of one person is different from the next,"[85] or that *kirtan* is only important in a larger environment, which includes the reading of the Guru Granth Sahib, listening to its explanation, and in the performance of service to fellow human beings. As Gurinder Singh Mann has written:

> [...] the essence of the Sikh experience of *kirtan* is not the *raga*-related component but the genuine spirit of the devotee yearning to know God and develop a relationship of his constant remembrance.[86]

Coda

> If two of the themes of 1880s Europe that informed musicol-
> ogy were the discovery and conquest of the world and the
> understanding of one's national culture, it follows almost
> logically and inevitably that a third theme, combining the
> first two, would lead to a concern with understanding the
> world that has been politically or intellectually conquered,
> contemplating the interrelationship of its cultures and their
> components. Juxtaposition of nation and world led inevita-
> bly to a need to confront and relate to the cultural "other,"
> and this need was the most direct inspiration for the devel-
> opment of ethnomusicology.
>
> (Bruno Nettl, *Nettl's Elephant: On the History
> of Ethnomusicology*, 2010)[1]

Indian music, (inter) nationalism, and comparative musicology

In his classic *The Study of Ethnomusicology: Thirty-One Issues and
Concepts* (1983; revised edition 2005), Bruno Nettl defined ethnomusicology as the study of "music in culture."[2] In variation, then, this
book is concerned with the interrelated historical study of "music
in imperial culture" in Britain and India. In different ways, it made
clear that both Britons and Indians with an interest in Indian music
tapped from a wide configuration of imperial ideas, which included
for example nationalist, evolutionary, and racial concepts, as well as
Orientalist constructions of India and the notion that the West was
the home of the modern and the scientifically advanced. In particular, it underlined the importance of the cultural interactions between
a handful of British and Indian individuals against the backgrounds
of national "classical" music making, internationalism in music, folk
music research, and the emergence of comparative musicology. By
and large, it argued that the imperial encounter led to the emergence
of aesthetics in music that often were more or less similar at once in

Britain and India as part of larger processes of (national) identity formation and rationalization. The resulting dominant musical formations and related forms of social consciousness largely followed high cultural norms and to a great extent overlapped with the modernizing goals of the British civilizing mission. Simultaneously, however, and despite the discovery of a shared Aryan heritage, mutual influences and cross-cultural quests for inspiration were generally frowned upon by the British and Indian nationalist orthodoxy.

To various degrees, Indian music reformers favored the modernization of the "classical" Hindustani and Carnatic music traditions through theoretical definition, institutionalization, canonization, (staff) notation, and so on. Examples of modern rationalization are Vishnu Narayan Bhatkhande's *that* system of *raga* classification and his criticism of the orthodox Hindu view that there was a direct link between the practice and theory of Hindustani music and the ancient and medieval treatises on music. Furthermore, the rational criticisms of Ananda Coomaraswamy and Rabindranath Tagore about the Indian singing technique not only were paternalistic but also imperialist. Essentially outside of the realm of national "classical" music making, the instances of *Rabindra Sangit* and Sikh sacred music principally show how the institutionalization of Indian music was closely connected with modern identity politics that often included an anti-imperial component, for example, through the binary opposition of Indian "spiritual" versus Western "secular" music making. Intriguingly, Western internationalists and proto-ethnomusicologists like Maud MacCarthy, Arnold Bake, Margaret Cousins, and Alain Daniélou, as well as the Orientalist Max Arthur Macauliffe in the case of the Sikhs in a different way, sympathized so much with Indian music that to different degrees they adhered, consciously or unconsciously, to Indian traditionalism and, in doing so, more or less provided a stronger basis for Indian (national) identities in music.

Particularly fascinating against this background of modernization and identity politics remains the introduction of the harmonium in Indian music. All Western protagonists in this book, as well as Indian internationalists like Coomaraswamy and Tagore, loathed the instrument because they more or less were committed to defining and preserving an "authentic" Indian musical heritage and a distinctive Indian musical aesthetic based on intonation. In contrast, Indian musical reformers like Sourindro Mohun Tagore and Vishnu Digambar Paluskar accepted the harmonium and used it in their music schools. Moreover, Bhatkhande used the 12 semitones of the harmonium as a dependable basis for his *that* music theory, though he certainly was no great lover of the instrument, and it seems that earlier in his career he took the theory of 22 *shruti* microtones quite seriously.[3] Thus, paradoxically, in the instance of the harmonium, internationalists reinforced a sense of national singularity by asserting the musical boundaries between India and the West, while national music reformers in turn quietly adopted the instrument. Bhatkhande even created a most successful scientific scheme of *raga* classification on the basis of its intonation. Be that as it may, as the example of Sikh sacred music shows so well, practicing with the harmonium and the use of Bhatkhande's system of *raga* classification and notation over the last century has led to a great deal of standardization in Hindustani music teaching and practice.

In addition, *Music and Empire in Britain and India* emphasized that proto-ethnomusicologists like Arthur Henry Fox Strangways, MacCarthy, and Bake, as well as modernist composers such as John Foulds and Percy Grainger, were involved in the mapping of the world's folk music and thus in the making of comparative musicology. As Philip Bohlman put it, folk music research reflected the modern ideologies of imperialism, nationalism, and the fundamentalist search for "authenticity" and "attracted the political left no less than the political right; it became an emblem of modernity and provided a vocabulary for its malcontents."[4] Comparative musicologists were "thinking big" and imagined folk music worldwide from a Western perspective. The Indian (folk) music research of Fox Strangways, MacCarthy, Bake, and others remains particularly interesting because they were musicians themselves. Often through their own performances, they actually propagated the music they studied, while they wanted it to become known among people and accepted as equal. Simultaneously, however, these proto-ethnomusicologists regularly adhered to imperialist ideas about Indian and other non-Western music traditions and repeatedly followed racial, evolutionary, and primitivist modes of thinking. Among modernist composers especially, the binary opposition of Western harmony versus Indian melody remains a distinctive example. Ultimately, Grainger, Foulds, and Cyril Scott saw Western harmony from an evolutionary standpoint as the world's most important musical achievement and, accordingly, used Indian/non-Western musical techniques and theories to reinvigorate Western music. Because of this sense of European superiority and, closely related, their often paternalist attitude toward Indian/non-Western music, their internationalism in music, interest in Indian philosophy (through Theosophy), anti-Western radicalism, and so on, were highly ambivalent. Otherwise, Grainger's masculine and outward world of ideas certainly was as exotic and imperial as that of the inward Theosophical worlds of Foulds and Scott.

Generally, ethnomusicologists depict their discipline as having distinctly matured during the late nineteenth century and transformed from comparative musicology into ethnomusicology, with its anthropological methodologies and distrust of grand comparative ideas, during the first half of the twentieth century. Though in comparison to Fox Strangways, MacCarthy, Bake, and others, ethnomusicologists today obviously are much more aware of the imperial history of their discipline, the question remains: To what extent is the "imperial gaze" still inherent in the discipline? As Martin Clayton wrote in relation to Fox Strangways's Indian music research:

> If there is one lesson to be learnt from examining Fox Strangways's work with 85 years' hindsight, it is that we have become much more aware of the problems that bedevilled the comparative musicology of his time, and at best work around them with considerable sophistication. But the fundamental difficulties addressed in this article have not been solved—perhaps because they cannot be solved, except in so far as greater awareness can save us to some extent from falling victim to them.[5]

Of course, ethnomusicologists have agonized over the imperial connection of their discipline for decades and for a long time have discarded such notions as evolutionism and "authenticity" in music. Even so, questions related, for example, to the representation of all the world's folk music through transcription, recording, and film; the inequality between researcher and its subject (e.g., the staging of musicians); the "authenticity" of transcribed music and its transfer of ownership; and differences in aesthetics, meaning, and identity in music, remain without resolution.[6] Likewise, in relation to the idea of comparative musicology, Bruno Nettl recently emphasized that much of what ethnomusicologists have always been doing "has had a basis in comparison."[7] Or again, as Martin Clayton put it earlier:

> The conundrum remains the same as in Fox Strangways's days: ethnomusicologists can explain their subject-matter only by implicit

comparison, by suggesting that a certain musical phenomenon is comparable to musical phenomena in other cultures or other times, and that understanding one can help us to understand others.[8]

In chorus, however, ethnomusicological research, and cross-cultural communication between Western and non-Western musicians in general, undeniably has led to a greater understanding of "what music is really doing in the world," to repeat Fox Strangways's words. In particular, Grainger, the pioneer in "world music" education, as he was referred to by the well-known ethnomusicologist John Blacking,[9] would have been delighted with the Global Music Series: "Experiencing Music, Expressing Culture." Consisting of surveys on individual musical cultures, including CDs,[10] and accompanied by two framing volumes by the general editors, Bonnie C. Wade and Patricia Shehan Campbell,[11] the series is concerned with the development of a "world music" pedagogy that "strives to reach beyond queries of 'what' and 'why' to the question of 'how'":

> [...] how music is taught/transmitted and received/learned within cultures, and how best the processes that are included in significant ways within these cultures can be preserved or at least partially retained in classrooms and rehearsal halls.[12]

Indeed, ethnomusicologists are "thinking big" again, though now finally with a focus on "world music" practice.

World music and cross-cultural communication

Throughout history, meetings of musicians from different cultures have continually resulted in a practical exchange of musical ideas and instruments. Likewise, music has always changed when people moved over time and space, as the film *Latcho Drom* (1993) made clear through the example of the historical and musical journey of the Romany people from Rajasthan to Spain.[13] An underlying idea of this book, however, is that both these processes were boosted by the imperial encounter to the effect that all music today is essentially "world music" and no music any longer is exotic or "authentic." At present, there are numerous Western performers of Indian music (Amelia Cuni, Steve Gorn, Saskia Rao-de Haas, Ken Zuckerman, and so on) and Western audiences who sometimes are better informed about Indian music than those in the subcontinent. Furthermore, non-Western music traditions are increasingly taught at Western music schools and conservatories. Deepak Raja even spoke of the existence of a Rotterdam *gharana* in relation to the Indian music studies at the world music department of the Rotterdam conservatory in the Netherlands.[14] Simultaneously, there are an incredible number of non-Westerners, though indeed comparatively few South Asians, who play Western classical and popular music.

All the same, it is often argued that non-Western traditional musicians are simply exploited by the music industry, which is subject to the whims of fashion, and that the contemporary "world music" market has a homogenizing effect, to the extent that everything starts to sound the same. According to Gerry Farrell, the popular variety of "world music" was yet another feature of Western exotic consumerism, "the aural equivalent of the package holiday."[15] As Bruno Nettl recently emphasized, elites worldwide may have become musically wealthier but "the world has become poorer musically."[16] Indeed, is the spread of Western music, as epitomized by its well-tempered scale and the idea of harmony, ultimately not a continuing feature of the imperial encounter? Has the imperial relationship between the West and the rest not become more urgent over the last century because the cultural difference and "authenticity" of the exotic non-Western musical other to a great deal have become issues of power and rhetoric, rather than of essence, partially also because the formerly colonized to a great extent aestheticized and canonized their own musical traditions? In fact, among many other north-Indian musicians and music scholars, Deepak Raja has argued that the survival of Hindustani music already has become dependent on the West "for economic sustenance, discerning audiences and scholarly input."[17]

In these circumstances, the resurgence of Indian folk music as "world music" during the last decades remains intriguing. Following upon the early indifference toward folk music among Indian elites, the independent Indian government, in its propagation of unity through diversity and the cultural and moral uplift of the population through art, began to study and collect folk music in such institutions as the Indira Gandhi National Centre for the Arts and the Sangeet Natak Akademi in New Delhi. Likewise, All Indian Radio frequently broadcasted manipulated sessions of folk music, whereby arrangements of the traditional songs were recorded with studio musicians. In addition, Indian folk musicians began to travel the world in colorful traditional clothes, first as part of the Festivals of India under the administration of the Indian Council for Cultural Relations. As a result, the ritual and social meanings of folk often were downgraded to exotic entertainment for tourists or celebration of heritage in the subcontinent and abroad. In recent decades, for example, the noted Baul singer and musician Paban Das Baul, as well as the Rajasthani Muslim hereditary professional folk musicians of the Langa and the Manganiyar castes have been most successful as "world musicians" in the West. Fundamental to the nationalization and internationalization of the music of the Langas and Manganiyars was Komal Kothari (1929–2004), the folklorist and ethnomusicologist, who for over five decades studied Rajasthani music and culture. Without questioning the great knowledge and work of Kothari, the point is that in his work with Rajasthani musicians, he not only always chose the repertoire and the musicians, but also asked them typical paternalistic questions such as:

> Instead of playing the same thing over and over again, do you ever question *what* you're playing? Can you work within your own form to stretch its possibilities, and actually *do* something instead of merely repeating what you already know?[18]

Likewise, his Rupayan Sansthan, funded by the Ford Foundation, embarked on a massive project: "the construction of 100 sindhi *sarangis* and 100 *kamaychas* (bowed string instrument) for free distribution to young Langa and Manganiyar musicians."[19] As a result of Kothari's activities, Rajasthani folk musicians are now generally on demand in the "world music" circuit and recently, for instance, they performed with the renowned Dutch Jazz saxophonist Yuri Honing and his group in India and abroad.

In comparison to India, the position of folk music in Pakistan perhaps is even more remarkable. Though the Quran does not mention anything at all about the making of music, it is generally forbidden by the Muslim clergy, who solely legitimize the quasi-mystical chanting of the Quran and the call to prayer. Even so, both Hindustani "classical" music and local popular music traditions have of course always been part of Pakistani culture. As is to be expected, however, music became much bounded by the assertion

of a national Muslim identity and the negation of anything identified in India. As a result, the Hindustani "classical" tradition ended
up in an ambivalent position.[20] Initially, it seemed that the Pakistani
government was going to support the broadcast of "classical" music.
Yet the clergy's opposition to music prevented this, mainly because
the texts of many of the classical songs were connected either with
Hindu deities or with the separation of lovers. Subsequently, the
Pakistani government adopted a more easy-going attitude, with the
result that the market for "classical music" gradually diminished,
and popular (mainly film) music became utterly dominant. In fact,
partially through the efforts of Radio Pakistan, there emerged a kind
of national "folk" music: the Sufi devotional music, *qawwali*, originally sung and played at the shrines of Sufi saints and based not on
the text of the Quran but on the poetry of Muslim Sufi and Hindu
bhakti masters. During the 1990s, *qawwali* burst into international
prominence on the "world music" scene, mainly through the efforts
of Nusrat Fateh Ali Khan (1948–1997),[21] who of course was often
criticized by orthodox Muslims regularly for his commodification
of "spiritual" Sufi music.

Then again, *Music and Empire in Britain and India* discussed how
among other British composers, Scott and Foulds appropriated
Indian music in their compositions: from Scott's sheer Orientalism
in music to the creation of Foulds's insightful progressive musical
aesthetic. For these composers, Indian culture and music became
a source of inspiration in their quests for modernist sounds. I
argued that these quests for the most part were countercultural to
the existing dominant nationalist and imperial cultural forms and,
on the contrary, followed internationalist worldviews that were
often fed by Theosophical ideas about "spirituality" and music.
As I remarked earlier, both Scott and Foulds benefitted from the
activities of Arthur Eaglefield Hull and/or the British Music Society,
which he established in 1918 "to champion the cause of British
composers and performers at home and abroad." Sixty years on, in
1979, a group of British musical enthusiasts founded a society with
exactly the same name. In contrast, however, the promotion of
British composers who had largely fallen outside the British music
canon was their specific aim. Ever since, they have regularly paid
attention to Scott, Foulds, and Grainger in their publications and,
in the cases of Scott and Foulds, even made possible some pioneering recordings of their music. In doing so, the society played a

role in the present revival of interest in the music of these three composers.[22] During the last decades, plentiful CD-recordings have been released of the music of Scott, Foulds, and Grainger, whereby indeed the Ralph Vaughan Williams Society sponsored three recordings of Scott's major orchestral works. Indubitably, the three composers have profited from the contemporary view on twentieth-century music history wherein, on the one hand, trends in composition that earlier were declared dead ends (read: did not fit into the modernist master narrative of musical evolution centered on the Stravinsky-Schoenberg axis) have become relevant again, and, on the other, the boundaries of serious and popular music are more blurred and the label "accessible" has overall ceased to be a stigma. In hindsight, Foulds and Grainger also can be classed as precursors of Western "Minimalist" musicians because of such compositions as *Gandharva Music* and *Random Round*. Conversely, the interest in Theosophy of Scott and Foulds can be more or less compared with the search for "spirituality" by the contemporary British classical composers Jonathan Harvey and John Tavener, respectively, in Tibetan Buddhism and Sufism/Greek-Orthodox Christianity.[23] Indeed, the concept of "spirituality" in music remains one of the chief examples of how human beings have created a universal language around music, that quintessentially nonrepresentational medium. Thus, famous Indian musicians such as Ravi Shankar and the south-Indian violinist L. Subramaniam continue to emphasize that their music making above all is "spiritual" worship and desires humility instead of ego.[24] But to what extent does the empire strike back here by using the imperial trope of "spiritual" India, sometimes in congruence with the trope of "the music of the spheres," as a marketing strategy on the "world music" market? In this very same context the ongoing success of Scott's esoteric writings also can be explained by the popularity of the New Age movement, which to some extent remains a follow-up of the Theosophical movement.

In the footsteps of Foulds, Western and, indeed increasingly, also non-Western classical composers, like for instance the Indian composer John Mayer (1930–2004),[25] continued to appropriate Indian music in their musical styles. But do the stylistic syntheses add further corroboration to Henry Cowell's assertion that cross-cultural appropriations draw "on those materials common to the music of all the peoples of the world?" In *Music To-Day*, Foulds made clear that

Western composers and musicians especially had to immerse them-selves in Indian music because of its improvisation:

> The Indian musician sets less value than we upon "ready-made" music. [...] music must be new-created here and now for his delectation; and from this point of view all our artist performers are not "musicians" at all, properly speaking. He regards them as something like second-hand dealers in other person's ideas.
>
> It must not be supposed, however, that the Indian musician's improvisation is either the spineless sprawl so frequently offered by our Western improvisers, or a cut-and-dried affair of rigid obe-dience to inelastic rules. Within certain fixed limits both of Raga (roughly Mode) and Tala (roughly basic rhythm) there is apparently illimitable scope for free emotional play, for mental-constructive skill, and pre-eminently for those efforts to bring both creator and participator into rapport with "higher" states of consciousness which so much of our Western music makes, and so small a pro-portion achieves.
>
> Here—in Improvisation, individual and collective—is a fertile field for the creative musician of the West, in future years.[26]

Yet, would he even now optimistically see musical improvisation as a key to cross-cultural communication, as "a way not only of gaining some understanding of the cultural other, but also of shifting your own position, constructing and reconstructing your own identity in the process,"[27] or would he be rather pessimistic instead? No doubt, Foulds would have been amazed about the crowds at the concerts of Ravi Shankar, Rajasthani folk musicians, and so on. Keeping in mind his hatred for jazz, he would have been particularly surprised to hear that when Shankar first brought Indian music to the West, he worked together with jazz musicians and praised their understanding of cer-tain aspects of Indian music. Presumably, however, he would have been much attracted to today's "fusion" efforts between Western jazz improvisers and Indian musicians, like in the case of the group Shakti, which includes the Western guitarist John McLaughlin, who since the 1960s continually turns to India for "spiritual" inspiration and, according to the Indian *tabla* genius Zakir Hussain, understands and plays both Hindustani and Carnatic music.[28] Does Shakti then prove that rather than the appropriation of tonal forms and rhythms into Western classical compositions, as in Foulds's case, improvisation instead remains the key to cross-cultural communication? Does it confirm the fact that jazz is the least imperial musical form because of its ability to change continuously and interact through improvisation with "world music"? Be it as it may, what is clear is that "music in imperial culture" needs to be incorporated into the rapidly developing field of global intellectual history because it illustrates the predicament of "world music" and, more than the realm of language, the difficulty of cross-cultural communication.

Notes

Introduction

1. Wm. Roger Louis, ed., *The Oxford History of the British Empire*, 5 volumes, Oxford: Oxford University Press, 1998–1999; Douglas M. Peers and Nandini Gooptu, ed., *India and the British Empire*, Oxford: Oxford University Press, 2012; and Stephen Howe, ed., *The New Imperial Histories Reader*, London: Routledge, 2010.
2. Besides Howe, ed., *The New Imperial Histories Reader*, see for example: Tony Ballantyne, *Orientalism and Race: Aryanism and the British Empire*, Basingstoke: Palgrave, 2002, and *Between Colonialism and Diaspora: Sikh Cultural Formations in an Imperial World*, New Delhi: Permanent Black, 2007; Elleke Boehmer, *Empire, the National, and the Postcolonial 1890–1920*, Oxford: Oxford University Press, 2002; and Peter van der Veer, *Imperial Encounters: Religion and Modernity in Britain and India*, Princeton, NJ: Princeton University Press, 2001.
3. Alain Frogley, "Rewriting the Renaissance: History, Imperialism, and British Music since 1840," *Music and Letters*, 84, 2, 2003, 256.
4. See for the term "webs of empire": Ballantyne, *Orientalism and Race* and *Between Colonialism and Diaspora*.
5. Bob van der Linden, "Music, Theosophical Spirituality, and Empire: The British Modernist Composers Cyril Scott and John Foulds," *Journal of Global History*, 3, 2, 2008, 163–182.
6. Martin Clayton, "Musical Renaissance and Its Margins in England and India, 1874–1914," in *Music and Orientalism in the British Empire, 1780s–1940s: Portrayal of the East*, ed. Martin Clayton and Bennett Zon, Aldershot: Ashgate 2007, 71–93.
7. Gerry Farrell, *Indian Music and the West*, Oxford: Oxford University Press, 1997.
8. Joep Bor, "The Rise of Ethnomusicology: Sources on Indian Music c. 1780–c. 1890," *Yearbook for Traditional Music*, 20, 1988, 51–73.
9. See for example: Bruno Nettl, *Nettl's Elephant: On the History of Ethnomusicology*, Urbana-Champaign: University of Illinois Press, 2010.
10. In *The Invention of "Folk Music" and "Art Music": Emerging Categories from Ossian to Wagner*, Cambridge: Cambridge University Press, 2007, Matthew Gelbart persuasively argued how the term "national music" was used before "folk music" and, more immediately, how the idea of Scottish "national" music (as "natural," "primitive," and "a vestige of music's ancient and Eastern roots") internationally was central to the formulation of the idea of "folk music" already before Johann Gottfried Herder coined the term *Volkslied* in 1773.
11. Cecil J. Sharp, *English Folk Song: Some Conclusions*, fourth (revised) edition, ed. Maud Karpeles, with an appreciation of Cecil Sharp by Ralph Vaughan Williams, London: Mercury, 1965 (first published 1907), 3.

12. By 1918, however, Vaughan Williams had largely abandoned composition based on folk music. See further about the complex relationship between Vaughan Williams and nationalism in music: Alain Frogley, "Constructing Englishness in Music: National Character and the Reception of Ralph Vaughan Williams," in *Vaughan Williams Studies*, ed. Alain Frogley, Cambridge: Cambridge University Press, 1996, 1–22 and *"O Thou Transcendent": The Life of Ralph Vaughan Williams*, Director Tony Palmer, Gonzo Multimedia, 2007 (DVD).

13. Ralph Vaughan Williams, *National Music and Other Essays*, Oxford: Clarendon, 1996 (second edition), 41.

14. Meirion Hughes and Robert Stradling, *The English Musical Renaissance 1840–1940: Constructing a National Music*, Manchester: Manchester University Press, 2001; Jeffrey Richards, *Imperialism and Music: Britain 1876–1953*, Manchester: Manchester University Press, 2001; and see particularly also Frogley's review of these two books: "Rewriting the Renaissance."

15. See for a list of Stanford's students and their imperial connections: Stephen Banfield, "Towards a History of Music in the British Empire: Three Export Studies," in *Britishness Abroad: Transnational Movements and Imperial Cultures*, ed. Kate Darian-Smith, Patricia Grimshaw, and Stuart Macintyre, Carlton, VIC.: Melbourne University Press, 2007, 79–86.

16. Janaki Bakhle, *Two Men and Music: Nationalism in the Making of an Indian Classical Music*, New Delhi: Permanent Black, 2005; Joep Bor and Allyn Miner, "Hindustani Music: A Historical Overview of the Modern Period," in *Hindustani Music: Thirteenth to Twentieth Centuries*, ed. Joep Bor, Françoise "Nalini" Delvoye, Jane Harvey, and Emmie te Nijenhuis, New Delhi: Manohar, 2010 (hereafter referred to as: *Hindustani Music*, ed. Bor et al.), 197–220; Clayton, "Musical Renaissance"; Bob van der Linden, "Sikh Music and Empire: The Moral Representation of Self in Music," *Sikh Formations: Religion, Culture, Theory*, 4, 1, 2008, 1–15; "Music, Theosophical Spirituality, and Empire," and "Sikh Sacred Music, Empire and World Music: Aesthetics and Historical Change," *Sikh Formations: Religion, Culture, Theory*, 7, 3, 2011, 383–397, and "History versus Tradition Again?: A Response to Bhai Baldeep Singh," *Sikh Formations: Religion, Culture, Theory*, 8, 2, 2012, 247–251; Lakshmi Subramanian, *From the Tanjore Court to the Madras Music Academy*, New Delhi: Oxford University Press, 2006, and *New Mansions for Music: Performance, Pedagogy and Criticism*, New Delhi: Social Science Press, 2008; David Trasoff, "The All-India Music Conferences of 1916–1925: Cultural Transformation and Colonial Ideology," in *Hindustani Music*, ed. Bor et al., 331–356; Amanda J. Weidman, *Singing the Classical, Voicing the Modern: The Postcolonial Politics of Music in South India*, Durham, NC: Duke University Press, 2006.

17. Walter Kaufmann, *The Ragas of North India*, Bloomington: Indiana University Press, 1968, 9.

18. Philip V. Bohlman, *World Music: A Very Short Introduction*, Oxford: Oxford University Press, 2002, 70.

19. *Jerusalem*, based on a short poem by William Blake and with music written by Parry, became England's "alternative national anthem" besides *God Save the Queen* and to a lesser extent *Land of Hope and Glory*, for indeed

surprisingly the country still has no official one! In 1922, Edward Elgar re-scored the work for orchestra and it is his version that came to be used for example at the Promenade Concerts and generally replaced Parry's own.

20. As cited in: Clayton, "Musical Renaissance," 76.
21. Sharp, *English Folk Song*, 19–20; Vaughan Williams, *National Music*, 32.
22. Sharp, *English Folk Song*, 135; Vaughan Williams, *National Music*, 23. In *The Invention of "Folk Music" and "Art Music,"* Matthew Gelbart argued how Herder was especially important for the aestheticization of "folk music" into "art music", rather than for distinguishing between "folk" and "art" by coining and voicing opinions about *Volkslied* (a concept that, in any case, he applied to poetry rather than music).
23. The Greek modes are musical scales that were in use in Western music before the emergence of the tonal or major-minor system in the seventeenth century. The easiest way to find them is to use the white keys of the piano and play from middle c up to the next c' (Ionian mode), d to d' (Dorian mode), and so on.
24. Gelbart, *The Invention of "Folk Music" and "Art Music."*
25. See further on Myers: Bennett Zon, *Representing Non-Western Music in Nineteenth Century Britain*, Rochester, NY: Rochester University Press, 2007, Part 3.
26. As cited in: Clayton, "Musical Renaissance," 79.
27. Partha Mitter, *The Triumph of Modernism: India's Artists and the Avant-Garde, 1922–1947*, London: Reaktion Books, 2007, 12.
28. Ibid., 31–34.
29. For further biographical details on Fox Strangways: Martin Clayton, "A. H. Fox Strangways and *The Music of Hindostan*: Revisiting Historical Field Recordings," *Journal of the Royal Musical Association*, 124, 1999, 86–118; Mary M. Lago, ed., *Imperfect Encounter: The Letters of Rabindranath Tagore and William Rothenstein*, Cambridge, MA: Harvard University Press, 1972; and Zon, *Representing Non-Western Music*, Part 4.
30. A. H. Fox Strangways, *The Music of Hindostan*, Oxford: Clarendon Press, 1914, vii.
31. "The India Society," *The Times*, June 11, 1910, 18. As cited in: Lago, ed., *Imperfect Encounter*, 7–8.
32. Ernest Binfield Havell came to India in 1884 to take up the position of principal at the Madras School of Arts. Between 1896 and 1905, he was principal of the Government School of Art, Calcutta. Over time, his interest turned from Indian "arts and crafts" to "fine arts" and, together with Rabindranath Tagore's nephew Abanindranath he developed a cosmopolitan national style of art and art education, which led to the so-called Bengal School of Art. Later he became friends with John Foulds and Maud MacCarthy. Like them, interestingly, he propagated the idea of India as Aryan and actually wrote *The History of Aryan Rule in India* (1918).
33. Arnold Bake, "Indian Music and Rabindranath Tagore," *Indian Art and Letters*, 5, 2, 1931, 81–102, and "Different Aspects of Indian Music," *Indian Art and Letters*, 8, 1, 1934, 60–74.
34. Suvarnalata Rao and Wim van der Meer, "The Construction, Reconstruction, and Deconstruction of Shruti," in *Hindustani Music*, ed. Bor et al., 683.

35. Fox Strangways, *The Music of Hindostan*, 127–133.
36. Ibid., v.
37. Joep Bor, *And Then There Was World Music and World Dance...* (Inaugural Lecture), Leiden University: Faculty of Arts, 2008, 29.
38. Bor and Miner, "Hindustani Music."
39. A. H. Fox Strangways, "Convention: Tagore's Songs," *The Observer*, September, 20, 1936.
40. Fox Strangways, *The Music of Hindostan*, 163–164.
41. Ibid., 5–6.
42. A. H. Fox Strangways, *Music Observed*, London: Methuen, 1936, "Indian Folksong," 16.
43. Arnold Bake, "Indian Folk-Music," *Proceedings of the Musical Association*, 63rd Sess., 1936–1937, 74.
44. Bahkle, *Two Men and Music*; Joep Bor, "The Rise of Ethnomusicology"; "Introduction," in *Hindustani Music*, ed. Bor et al., 11–16; Bor and Miner, "Hindustani Music"; Farrell, *Indian Music*.
45. Bor, "Introduction," 12.
46. Katherine Butler Schofield, "Reviving the Golden Age Again: 'Classicization,' Hindustani Music, and the Mughals," *Ethnomusicology*, 54, 3, 2010, 508–509.
47. Clayton, "Musical Renaissance," 85.
48. Bor and Miner, "Hindustani Music," 206–207.
49. Bor, "Introduction," 16.
50. Ibid., 15.
51. Trasoff, "The All-India Music Conferences."
52. Farrell, *Indian Music*, 53.
53. Bakhle, *Two Men and Music*, 7–8.
54. Ibid., 253.
55. See further on Paluskar: Bakhle, *Two Men and Music*, 253, and Bor and Miner, "Hindustani Music."
56. Grace Brockington, "Introduction: Internationalism and the Arts," in *Internationalism and the Arts in Britain and Europe at the Fin de Siècle*, ed. Grace Brockington, Bern: Peter Lang, 2009, 7.
57. Ibid., 22.
58. Gauri Viswanathan, "Ireland, India, and the Poetics of Internationalism," *Journal of World History*, 15, 1, March 2004, 8.
59. See further on the relationship between Tagore and Yeats as well as the similarities between Indian and Irish nationalisms: Louise Blakeney Williams, "Overcoming the 'Contagion of Mimicry': The Cosmopolitan Nationalism and Modernist History of Rabindranath Tagore and W. B. Yeats," *American Historical Review*, 112, 1, 2007, 69–100.
60. Alex Owen, *The Place of Enchantment: British Occultism and the Culture of the Modern*, Chicago: University of Chicago Press, 2004, 24–26.
61. Subramanian, *From the Tanjore Court* and *New Mansions for Music*; Weidman, *Singing the Classical*.
62. Viswanathan, "Ireland, India," 28.
63. Ibid., 12.
64. Catherine Candy, "Mystical Internationalism in Margaret Cousins's Feminist World," *Women's Studies International Forum*, 32, 2009, 30.

65. Ibid., 31.
66. Tagore called Madanapalle, the birthplace of Jiddu Krishnamurti, who in 1925 was proclaimed by Besant to be the new World Teacher, the Santiniketan of south-India.
67. Weidman, *Singing the Classical*, 66.
68. Joscelyn Godwin, *Harmonies of Heaven and Earth: The Spiritual Dimension of Music from Antiquity to the Avant-Garde*, Londen: Thames and Hudson, 1987.
69. As cited in: James G. Mansell, "Musical Modernity and Contested Commemoration at the Festival of Remembrance, 1923–1927," *The Historical Journal*, 52, 2, 2009, 438.
70. Literally in Sanskrit, *deva*, means "shining one," but Blavatsky introduced her own esoteric conception of the *devas* as types of angels that were progressed entities from previous planetary periods and furthered the spiritual development of mankind. They are said to communicate through means of clairaudience and meditation.
71. Matthew Harp Allen, "Rewriting the Script for South Indian Dance," *The Drama Review*, 41, 3, 1997, 64.
72. Weidman, *Singing the Classical*, 120.
73. Allen, "Rewriting the Script," 64.
74. Ibid., 83.
75. Boehmer, *Empire, the National, and the Postcolonial*, 8, emphasis in original.
76. Viswanathan, "Ireland, India."
77. Ananda K. Coomaraswamy, *Essays in National Idealism*, New Delhi: Munshiram Manoharlal, 1981 (first published 1909), "Music and Education in India," 196.
78. As cited in: Ramachandra Guha, "Introduction," in Rabindranath Tagore, *Nationalism,*, New Delhi: Penguin, 2009 (first published 1917), xxix.
79. Williams, "Overcoming," 72.
80. Ibid.
81. Allen, "Rewriting the Script," 85.
82. As reprinted in: Ananda K. Coomaraswamy, *Essays on Music*, ed. Prem Lata Sharma, New Delhi: Manohar, 2010, 61.
83. Coomaraswamy, *Essays in National Idealism*, "Indian Music," 166.
84. Ibid., "Music and Education in India," 196.
85. Ibid., 194.
86. Ibid., "Indian Music," 176, emphasis mine.
87. Ibid.,"Music and Education in India," 193–196.
88. Ibid., "Gramophones–And Why Not?" 205–206.
89. Ibid., "Music and Education in India," 199–200.
90. Maud MacCarthy, "Music in East and West," *Orpheus*, 3, 1908. As cited in: Ibid., "Indian Music," 174.
91. Coomaraswamy, *Essays in National Idealism*, "Gramophones–And Why Not?," 205.
92. Fox Strangways, *The Music of Hindostan*, 347, word added.
93. Anonymous, "A Concert of Indian Music: Ratan Devi Sings Classical Ragas and Kashmiri Songs," *New York Times*, April 14, 1916.
94. Anonymous, "Ratan Devi Sings: An Exposition of Indian 'Ragas' and Kashmiri Folk Songs," *New York Times*, March 5, 1917.

95. Ananda K. Coomaraswamy, "Introduction," in Ratan Devi and Ananda K. Coomaraswamy, *Thirty Songs from the Panjab and Kashmir*, with a foreword by Rabindranath Tagore, New Delhi: Sterling, 1994 (first published 1913), 3.
96. Coomaraswamy, *Essays in Indian Idealism*, "Indian Music," 172.
97. Coomaraswamy, "Introduction," in Devi and Coomaraswamy, *Thirty Songs*, 5–6.
98. Coomaraswamy, *Essays in Indian Idealism*, "The Deeper Meaning of the Struggle," 2.
99. Coomaraswamy, *Essays in National Idealism*, i.
100. Ananda K. Coomaraswamy, "Eastern Religions and Western Thought," *The Review of Religion*, 6, 1942, 144.
101. Ibid., 138.
102. Tagore, *Nationalism*, 71.
103. Viswanathan, "Ireland, India," 7.
104. Guha, "Introduction," in Tagore, *Nationalism*, xxxiv.
105. Tagore, *Nationalism*, 72.
106. Ibid., 74.
107. Ibid., 72.
108. Ibid., 34.
109. Sometimes the term "cultural internationalism" is used here.
110. Williams, "Overcoming," 73.
111. Ibid., 98.
112. Rabindranath Tagore, Letter to Mahatma Gandhi, April 12, 1919. As cited in Williams, "Overcoming," 99.
113. Ibid.
114. C.A. Bayly, "Afterword" in "An Intellectual History for India," ed. Shruti Kapila, Special Issue of *Modern Intellectual History*, 4, 1, 2007, 168.
115. Roger Lipsey, *Coomaraswamy: His Life and Work*, Princeton, NJ: Princeton University Press, 1977, 85.
116. Coomaraswamy, "Indian Religions," 136.
117. Georgina Born and David Hesmondhalgh, "Introduction: On Difference, Representation, and Appropriation in Music," in *Western Music and Its Others: Difference, Representation, and Appropriation in Music*, ed. Born and Hesmondhalgh, Berkeley: University of California Press, 2000, 41.
118. See for example: C. A. Bayly, *Recovering Liberties: Indian Thought in the Age of Liberalism and Empire*, Cambridge: Cambridge University Press, 2012.
119. Ibid., 23.
120. Bernard Porter, *The Absent-Minded Imperialist: Empire, Society and Culture in Britain*, Oxford: Oxford University Press, 2004; John M. MacKenzie, "Empire and Metropolitan Cultures," in *The Oxford History of the British Empire, Volume 3: The Nineteenth Century*, ed. Andrew Porter, Oxford: Oxford University Press, 1999, 270–293.
121. Vaughan Williams, *National Music* and Edward Elgar, *A Future for English Music and Other Lectures*, ed. Percy M. Young, London: Dobson, 1968.

1 Cyril Scott: "The Father of Modern British Music" and the Occult

1. Cyril Scott, *An Outline of Modern Occultism*, London: Routledge, 1974 (first published 1935), 2, emphasis in original.

2. Stephen Lloyd, "Grainger and the 'Frankfurt Group,'" *Studies in Music*, 16, 1982, 111. As cited in: Laurie J. Sampsel, *Cyril Scott: A Bio-Bibliography*, Westport, CT: Greenwood Press, 2000, 4.

3. J. W. Burrow, *The Crisis of Reason: European Thought, 1848–1914*, New Haven, CT: Yale University Press, 2000, 222.

4. Lisa Hardy, *The British Piano Sonata 1870–1945*, Woodbridge: Boydell Press, 2001, 68.

5. See for example: Bernard Porter, "Edward Elgar and Empire," *Journal of Imperial and Commonwealth History*, 29, 1, January 2001, 1–34.

6. Eugene Goossens, *Overture and Beginners: A Musical Biography*, London: Methuen, 1951, 95.

7. Dedicated to H. R. H. The Prince of Wales, *Britain's War March* includes references to the following patriotic tunes: *Rule Britannia*, *God Save the King*, and *Le Marseillaise*. As Desmond Scott made clear to me: "*Britain's War March* seems to me to be an anomaly in Scott's work. I suspect it was commissioned, but I don't know who by! Or, indeed, apart from that, why he wrote it, being the least jingoistic of men" (Personal communication, January 14, 2011).

8. Cyril Scott, *Bone of Contention: Life Story and Confessions*, London: Antiquarian Press, 1969, 83.

9. For a list of Scott's Theosophical and Indian readings, see for example: Cyril Scott, *Music: Its Secret Influence throughout the Ages*, Northamptonshire: Aquarian Press, 1985 (first published 1933), 205–206.

10. Scott, *Bone of Contention*, 132–135.

11. Scott, *Music*, 111, emphasis in original.

12. Ibid.

13. Cyril Scott, *My Years of Indiscretion*, London: Mills and Boon, 1924 and *Bone of Contention*.

14. Cyril Scott, *The Adept of Galilee: A Story and An Argument, by The Author of "The Initiate,"* London: Routledge, 1920, 113.

15. Scott, *An Outline*, 214.

16. James G. Mansell, "Music and the Borders of Rationality: Discourses of Place in the Work of John Foulds," in *Internationalism and the Arts in Britain and Europe at the Fin de Siècle*, ed. Grace Brockington, Bern: Peter Lang, 2009, 57.

17. An earlier version, *The Influence of Music on History and Morals: A Vindication of Plato* (1928), was published by the Theosophical Publishing House in London.

18. Scott, *Bone of Contention*, 234.

19. See further: Joscelyn Godwin, *Harmonies of Heaven and Earth: The Spiritual Dimension of Music from Antiquity to the Avant-Garde*, London: Thames and Hudson, 1987.

20. Scott, *Music*, 203.

21. Diana Swann, "Cyril Scott (1879–1970)," *British Music Society News*, 71, September 1996, 256. As cited in: Sampsel, *Cyril Scott*, 18. Cf. Scott, *Bone of Contention*, 223–226.

22. Scott, *Bone of Contention*, 221.

23. Cyril Scott, "Introduction," in David Anrias, *Through the Eyes of the Masters*, London: Routledge, 1932.

24. I am thankful to Desmond Scott for sending me a copy of the libretto.

25. Scott, *Music*, 97.

26. Cyril Scott, *Hymn of Unity*, Libretto, 1947.

27. Scott, *Music*, 29, emphasis in original.

28. Cyril Scott, *The Philosophy of Modernism: Its Connection with Music*, London: Waverley, 1925 (first published 1917), 95.

29. Ibid., 1.

30. Ibid., 3.

31. Ibid., 5, emphasis in original.

32. Cyril Scott, "The Two Attitudes," *Musical Quarterly*, 5, 1919, 158.

33. Scott, *Music*, 136, emphasis in original.

34. Scott, *The Philosophy of Modernism*, Appendix 3 (Percy Grainger: The Music and the Man), 135.

35. Hardy, *The British Piano Sonata*, 56.

36. Scott, *The Philosophy of Modernism*, Appendix 1 (The Occult Relationship between Sound and Colour).

37. Ibid., chapter 11 (The Hidden Aspects of Music) and Scott, *Music*, Part III (Esoteric Considerations: The Music of the Deva or Nature-Spirit Evolution).

38. Scott, *Music*, 132.

39. Ibid., 142.

40. Ibid.

41. Interestingly, in *Le Piccadilly*, Satie refers to the American popular "Tin Pan Alley" song *Hello, my Baby!* (1899), being the same tune that Percy Grainger set for piano in 1900 as *The Rag-Time Girl*.

42. Scott, *Music*, 155–157, emphasis in original.

43. Ibid., 38.

44. Ibid., 114, emphasis in original.

45. Ibid., 200.

46. Ibid.

47. Hardy, *The British Piano Sonata*, 66.

48. Scott, *Bone of Contention*, 195.

49. Arthur Eaglefield Hull, *Cyril Scott: The Man and His Works*, London: Waverley, 1925 (first published 1914). He also wrote *Modern Harmony: Its Explanation and Application*, London: Augener, 1914, which includes examples of Scott's piano music.

50. Scott, *Music*, 199–200.

51. Ralph Vaughan Williams, *National Music and Other Essays*, Oxford: Clarendon, 1996 (second edition), 3, 10.

52. Jonathan Harvey, *Music and Inspiration*, London: Faber and Faber, 1999.

53. See for example: Jonathan Bellman, ed., *The Exotic in Western Music*, Boston, MA: Northeastern University Press, 1998; Georgina Born and David Hesmondhalgh, eds., *Western Music and Its Others: Difference, Representation,*

and Appropriation in Music, Berkeley: University of California Press, 2000; Gerry Farrell, *Indian Music and the West*, Oxford: Oxford University Press, 1997; John M. Mackenzie, *Orientalism: History, Theory and the Arts*, Manchester: Manchester University Press, 1995; Timothy B. Taylor, *Beyond Exoticism: Western Music and the World*, Durham, NC: Duke University Press, 2007.

54. Taylor, *Beyond Exoticism*, 102–103.
55. Ibid., 49, 209.
56. A. H. Fox Strangways, *The Music of Hindostan*, London: Clarendon Press, 1914, 224.
57. Though Frank Bridge was the most famous contemporary British composer who set Tagore's poems to music, John Foulds's incidental music for Tagore's play *Sacrifice* (1920), scored for an optional *tanpura* (Indian lute) in addition to Western instruments and later rearranged for voice and string quintet, remains one of the earliest attempts to incorporate genuine Indian musical elements into the language of Western music.
58. Peter van der Veer, *Imperial Encounters: Religion and Modernity in Britain and India*, Princeton, NJ: Princeton University Press, 2001, 46.
59. As cited in: Harald Fischer-Tiné, "Indian Nationalism and the 'World Forces': Transnational and Diasporic Dimensions of the Indian Freedom Movement on the Eve of the First World War," *Journal of Global History*, 2, 3, 2007, 333.
60. Hardy, *The British Piano Sonata*, 59.
61. Goossens, *Overture and Beginners*, 138.
62. Ibid.
63. Ibid.
64. On Gustav Holst's relationship with Theosophy and India: Raymond Head, "Holst and India (I): 'Maya' to 'Sita,'" *Tempo*, 158, September 1986, 2–7; "Holst and India (II)," *Tempo*, 160, March 1987, 27–36; and "Holst and India (III)," *Tempo*, 166, September 1988, 35–40. See also Tony Palmer's documentary: *Holst: In the Bleak Midwinter*, Gonzo Multimedia, 2011 (DVD).
65. Raymond Head, "Astrology and Modernism in the Planets," *Tempo*, 187, December 1993, 15–22.
66. Scott, *Bone of Contention*, 12; Foulds, *Music To-day*, 276.
67. Malcolm Gillies, David Pear, and Mark Carroll, eds., *Self-Portrait of Percy Grainger*, New York: Oxford University Press, 2006, 249.
68. Head, "Astrology and Modernism."
69. Ibid.
70. Hardy, *The British Piano Sonata*, 68.
71. Alex Owen, *The Place of Enchantment: British Ocultism and the Culture of the Modern*, Chicago: University of Chicago Press, 2004.

2 Percy Grainger: Kipling, Racialism, and All the World's Folk Music

1. Graham Freeman, "'That Chief Undercurrent of My Mind': Percy Grainger and the Aesthetics of English Folk Song," *Folk Music Journal*, 9, 4, 2009, 581–617.
2. Percy Grainger, "The Impress of Personality in Unwritten Music," *Musical Quarterly*, 1, 1915. As reprinted in: Teresa Balough, ed., *A Musical Genius*

from Australia: Selected Writings by and about Percy Grainger, Nedlands: University of Western Australia, 1982, 78.

3. Percy Grainger, "My Musical Outlook," extended letter to Klimsch (1902–1904). As reprinted in: Malcolm Gillies and Bruce Clunies Ross, eds., *Grainger on Music*, Oxford: Oxford University Press, 1999, 17.

4. Ibid., 19, emphasis in original.

5. Ferruccio Busoni, *Sketch of a New Esthetic of Music*, New York: G. Schirmer, 1911 (first published 1907), 5, 34.

6. Grainger, "The Impress of Personality," 72, translation mine.

7. Percy Grainger, "Collecting with the Phonograph," *Journal of the Folk Song Society*, 3, 3, 1908. As reprinted in: Balough, ed., *A Musical Genius*, Ibid., 21, emphasis in original.

8. Mark Slobin, *Folk Music: A Very Short Introduction*, Oxford: Oxford University Press, 2011, 68.

9. Michael Yates, "Percy Grainger and the Impact of the Phonograph," *Folk Music Journal*, 4, 3, 1982, 269, 274.

10. See for example: Kay Dreyfus, ed., *The Farthest North of Humanness: Letters of Percy Grainger, 1901–1914*, London: MacMillan, 1985, 305.

11. Grainger, "The Impress of Personality," 79, emphasis in original.

12. Wilfrid Mellers, *Percy Grainger*, Oxford: Oxford University Press, 1992, 67.

13. Grainger, "The Impress of Personality," 68.

14. Ibid., 69.

15. Freeman, "That Chief Undercurrent of My Mind," 594–595.

16. Ibid., 609.

17. John Blacking, *"A Common-Sense View of All Music": Reflections on Percy Grainger's Contributions to Ethnomusicology and Music Education*, Cambridge: Cambridge University Press, 1987, xi, emphasis in original.

18. Malcolm Gillies and David Pear, eds., *The All-Round Man: Selected Letters of Percy Grainger 1914–1961*, Oxford: Clarendon Press, 1994, 143; Grainger, "The Impress of Personality," 79.

19. Gillies and Pear, eds., *The All-Round Man*, 275.

20. Malcolm Gillies, David Pear, and Mark Carroll, eds., *Self-Portrait of Percy Grainger*, New York: Oxford University Press, 2006, 17.

21. Cyril Scott, "Percy Grainger: The Music and the Man," *Musical Quarterly*, 2, 1916. As reprinted in: Cyril Scott, *The Philosophy of Modernism: Its Connection with Music*, London: Waverley, 1925 (first published 1917), Appendix III, 126–127, emphasis in original.

22. David Gilmour, *The Long Recessional: The Imperial Life of Rudyard Kipling*, London: John Murray, 2002; Ashis Nandy, *The Intimate Enemy: Loss and Recovery of Self under Colonialism*, New Delhi: Oxford University Press, 1983; and the essays in Rudyard Kipling, *Kim*, ed. by Zohreh T. Sullivan, New York: Norton, 2002.

23. David Pear, "Percy Grainger and Manliness," *Journal of Australian Studies*, 56, 1998, 109.

24. Teresa R. Balough, ed., *Comrades in Art: The Correspondence of Ronald Stevenson and Percy Grainger 1957–61*, including CD, London: Toccata Press, 2010, 101.

25. Dreyfus, ed., *The Farthest North of Humanness*, 226, 237, 240, 245.

26. Mellers, *Percy Grainger*, 16.

27. Scott, "Percy Grainger," 131–132, emphasis in original.
28. John Bird, *Percy Grainger*, Oxford: Oxford University Press, 1999 and Mellers, *Percy Grainger*.
29. Teresa Balough, "Kipling and Grainger," *Studies in Music*, 11, 1977, 75.
30. Jeffrey Richards, *Imperialism and Music: Britain 1876–1953*, Manchester: Manchester University Press, 2001, 352.
31. J. R. Watson, *The English Hymn: A Critical and Historical Study*, Oxford: Oxford University Press, 1997, 519.
32. Ibid., 520.
33. Gillies and Pear, eds., *The All-Round Man*, 177.
34. Gillies, Pear, and Carroll, eds., *Self-Portrait*, 184.
35. Gillies and Pear, eds., *The All-Round Man*, 252.
36. Gillies, Pear, and Carroll, eds., *Self-Portrait*, 176–177.
37. Ibid., 177.
38. David Cannadine, *Ornamentalism: How the British Saw Their Empire*, Oxford: Oxford University Press, 2001, 5.
39. Malcolm Gillies and David Pear, "Percy Grainger and American Nordicism," in *Western Music and Race*, ed. Julie Brown, Cambridge: Cambridge University Press, 2007, 117.
40. Alain Frogley, "'The Old Sweet Anglo-Saxon Spell': Racial Discourses and the American Reception of British Music, 1895–1933," in *Western Music and Race*, ed. Julie Brown, Cambridge: Cambridge University Press, 2007, 246.
41. Ibid., 252.
42. As cited in: Laurie J. Sampsel, *Cyril Scott: A Bio-Bibliography*, Westport, CT: Greenwood Press, 11.
43. Cecil Sharp and Olive Dame Campbell, *English Folk Songs from the Southern Appalachians*, 2 vols., ed. by Maud Karpeles, London: Oxford University Press, 1932 (first published 1917), xxxvi.
44. Slobin, *Folk Music*, 55.
45. Dreyfus, ed., *The Farthest North of Humanness*, 95, emphasis in original.
46. Bird, *Percy Grainger*, 62.
47. Percy Grainger, "Nordic Characteristics in Music," Typescript dated March 5, 1921. As reprinted in Gillies and Clunies Ross, eds., *Grainger on Music*, 131–132.
48. Percy Grainger, Typescript of radio broadcast on WEVD, New York, July 4, 1953. As reprinted in: Ibid., 260.
49. Ibid., 261.
50. Percy Grainger, "A Commonsense View of All Music," Lecture broadcast in Australia, 1935. As reprinted in: Blacking, *"A Common-Sense View of All Music,"* Appendix A, 163.
51. Gillies and Clunies Ross, eds., *Grainger on Music*, 264.
52. Tony Ballantyne, *Orientalism and Race: Aryanism and the British Empire*, Basingstoke: Palgrave, 2002.
53. Gillies and Pear, eds., *The All-Round Man*, 1.
54. Gillies and Pear, "Percy Grainger and American Nordicism," 124.
55. Percy Grainger, "Characteristics of Nordic Music," Typescript of radio broadcast on WEVD, New York, July 4, 1933. As reprinted in: Gillies and Clunies Ross, eds., *Grainger on Music*, 262.
56. Gillies and Pear, eds., *The All-Round Man*, 5.

57. Percy Grainger, "A Commonsense View of All Music," Lecture broadcast in Australia, 1935. As reprinted in: Blacking, *"A Common-Sense View of All Music,"* Appendix A, 178.
58. Gillies, Pear, and Carroll, eds., *Self-Portrait*, 68, 159.
59. Dreyfus, ed., *The Farthest North of Humanness*, 1985, 334.
60. Grainger, "Collecting with the Phonograph," 20.
61. Dreyfus, ed., *The Farthest North of Humanness*, 265.
62. A. J. Knocks, Letter to Percy Grainger, June 1, 1909, Grainger Museum, University of Melbourne. As cited in: Paul Jackson, "Percy Grainger's Aleatoric Adventures: The Rarotongan Part-Songs," *Grainger Studies: An Interdisciplinary Journal*, 2, 2012, 1.
63. Jackson, "Percy Grainger's Aleatoric Adventures," 11, emphasis in original.
64. Ibid.
65. Dreyfus, ed., *The Farthest North of Humanness*, 297.
66. Grainger, "A Commonsense View of All Music," 163.
67. Mellers, *Percy Grainger*, 49.
68. Grainger, "A Commonsense View of All Music," 157.
69. Percy Grainger, "My Musical Outlook," extended letter to Klimsch (1902–1904). As reprinted in: Gillies and Clunies Ross, eds., *Grainger on Music*, 22.
70. Percy Grainger, "The World Music of To-morrow," *Etude*, 34, 6, 1916. As reprinted in: Gillies and Clunies Ross, eds., *Grainger on Music*, 87, alternative transliteration and translation mine.
71. Michelle Wick Patterson, *Natalie Curtis Burlin: A Life in Native and African American Music*, Lincoln: University of Nebraska Press, 2010, 327. Cf. Grainger, "The Impress of Personality," 69.
72. Grainger, "The Impress of Personality," 79.
73. Patterson, *Natalie Curtis Burlin*, 195.
74. Percy Grainger, "A Commonsense View of All Music," Lecture broadcast in Australia, 1934. As cited in Balough, ed., *A Musical Genius*, ix.
75. Percy Grainger, "Can Music Become a Universal Language?" Broadcast over radio WEVD, New York, June 20, 1933. As reprinted in: Balough, ed., *A Musical Genius*, 113, emphasis in original.
76. Grainger, "The Impress of Personality," 75.
77. Ibid., 71.
78. In 1986, Barrie Gavin named his Grainger documentary *The Noble Savage*. I am thankful to Barry Peter Ould of the Percy Grainger Society for sending me a copy and his enthusiastic help in general.
79. Balough, ed., *Comrades in Art*, 184.
80. Gillies and Clunies Ross, eds., *Grainger on Music*, 375.
81. Timothy B. Taylor, *Beyond Exoticism: Western Music and the World*, Durham, NC: Duke University Press, 2007, 106.
82. Suzanne Robinson, "Percy Grainger and Henry Cowell: Concurrences between Two 'Hyper-Moderns,'" *Musical Quarterly*, 94, 3, 2011, 311.
83. Blacking, *"A Common-Sense View of All Music,"* 52.
84. Percy Grainger, "Free Music," Typescript, December 6, 1938. As reprinted in: Balough, ed., *A Musical Genius*, 143.
85. Grainger, "The Impress of Personality," 77.

86. Percy Grainger, "Democracy in Music," Manuscript dated July 9–10, 1931. As reprinted in Gillies and Clunies Ross, eds., *Grainger on Music*, 218–219.

87. Grainger, "Nordic Characteristics in Music," 132, emphasis in original.

88. Percy Grainger, Letter to Ella Strom, January 31, 1928, in Gillies and Pear, eds., *The All-Round Man*, 90, emphasis in original.

89. Rokus de Groot, "Edward Said and Polyphony," in *Edward Said: A Legacy of Emancipation and Representation*, ed. A. Iskander and H. Rustom, Berkeley: University of California Press, 2010, 204–228. See also: Ben Etherington, "Said, Grainger and the Ethics of Polyphony," in *Edward Said: The Legacy of a Public Intellectual*, ed. Ned Curthoys and Debjani Ganguly, Carlton, VIC: Melbourne University Press, 2007, 221–238.

90. Most likely under the influence of Cowell, he actually was a member of the American Communist Party for two years.

91. Percy Grainger, "Modern and Universal Impulses in Music," *Etude*, 34, 5, 1916. As reprinted in: Gillies and Clunies Ross, eds., *Grainger on Music*, 82, emphasis in original.

92. I am thankful to Desmond Scott for sending me a copy of his paper, "Cyril and Percy," which he presented at the Grainger seminar, British Library, London, February 20, 2011.

93. Grainger, "*A Commonsense View of All Music*," 151.

94. Grainger, "The World Music of To-Morrow," 87.

95. See for example: Gillies, Pear, and Carroll, eds., *Self-Portrait*, 256.

96. Ibid., 152.

3 John Foulds and Maud MacCarthy: Internationalism, Theosophy, and Indian Music

1. Swami Omananda Puri, *The Boy and the Brothers*, London: Victor Gallancz, 1959, 4.

2. Ibid., 7.

3. Ibid., 7–8.

4. *The Times*, August, 2, 1907, in New York: Public Library for the Performing Arts, M-Clippings, Maud MacCarthy.

5. Kay Dreyfus, ed., *The Farthest North of Humanness: Letters of Percy Grainger, 1901–1914*, London: MacMillan, 1985, 56, and Neil Sorrell, "From 'Harm-Omnium' to Harmonia Omnium: Assessing Maud MacCarthy's Influence on John Foulds and the Globalization of Indian Music," *Journal of the Indian Musicological Society*, 40, 2009–2010, 213.

6. See among other newspaper articles for example: *The Bystander*, July, 31, 1907, and "Maud MacCarthy Renounces the Violin," *The Musical Courier*, August, 1, 1907, in New York: Public Library for the Performing Arts, M-Clippings, Maud MacCarthy.

7. *The Times*, August, 2, 1907, in New York: Public Library for the Performing Arts, M-Clippings, Maud MacCarthy.

8. Malcolm MacDonald, *John Foulds and His Music*, London: Kahn & Averill, 1989, 21.

9. Swami Omananda Puri, *Towards the Mysteries: Being Some Teachings of the Brothers of the Holy Hierarchy, Given through the Boy*, London: Neville Spearman, 1968, 38.

10. "Maud MacCarthy Renounces the Violin," *The Musical Courier*, August, 1, 1907, in New York: Public Library for the Performing Arts, M-Clippings, Maud MacCarthy.

11. Maud Mann (Maud MacCarthy), *Some Indian Conceptions of Music*, London: Theosophical Publishing Society, 1913 (earlier version published as "Some Indian Conceptions of Music," *Proceedings of the Musical Association*, 38th Sess., 1911–1912, 41–65).

12. Ibid., 4, 18.

13. Ibid., 4–5.

14. Ibid, 5, 7.

15. Ibid., 22.

16. Ibid., 11–12.

17. Ibid., 8, emphasis in original.

18. As cited in: Sorrell, "From 'Harm-Omnium' to Harmonia Omnium," 123–124.

19. MacDonald, *John Foulds*, 57.

20. Mann, *Some Indian Conceptions of Music*, preface (no page number).

21. As cited in: Sorrell, "From 'Harm-Omnium' to Harmonia Omnium," 123, emphasis in original.

22. Mann, *Some Indian Conceptions of Music*, preface (no page number).

23. A. C. Wilson, *A Short Account of the Hindu System of Music*, Lahore: Gulab Singh and Sons, 1904.

24. Gerry Farrell, *Indian Music and the West*, Oxford: Oxford University Press, 1997.

25. See further: Puri, *The Boy and the Brothers*.

26. Ibid., 20.

27. James G. Mansell, "Musical Modernity and Contested Commemoration at the Festival of Remembrance, 1923–1927," *The Historical Journal*, 52, 2, 2009, 446.

28. Ibid., 439.

29. Ibid., 434.

30. Rachel Cowgill, "Canonizing Remembrance: Music for Armistice Day at the BBC, 1922–7," *First World War Studies*, 2, 1, 2011, 92, 96.

31. Ibid., and Mansell, "Musical Modernity."

32. Cowgill, "Canonizing Remembrance," 92.

33. Mansell, "Musical Modernity," 450.

34. The performance of *A World Requiem* on November 11, 2007, in the Royal Albert Hall and its première recording on CD met similar criticism.

35. Mansell, "Musical Modernity," 444.

36. Ibid., 448.

37. Cowgill, "Canonizing Remembrance," 88.

38. Mansell, "Musical Modernity," 444.

39. Puri, *Towards the Mysteries*, 20, emphasis in original.

40. John M. MacKenzie, "The Popular Culture of Empire in Britain," in *The Oxford History of the British Empire, Volume 4: The Twentieth Century*, ed.

Judith M. Brown and W. M. Roger Louis, Oxford: Oxford University Press, 1999, 218.

41. Cowgill, "Canonizing Remembrance," 77.
42. Percy Grainger liked "Nimrod" so much that he made an arrangement of it for a piano solo in 1953.
43. MacDonald, *John Foulds*, 57. See further on Uday Shankar: Farrell, *Indian Music*, chapter 5.
44. MacDonald, *John Foulds*, 70.
45. As cited in: Ibid., vii, emphasis in original.
46. Cyril Scott, *Music: Its Secret Influence through the Ages*, Northamptonshire: Aquarian Press, 1985 (first published 1933), 133.
47. John Foulds, *Music To-day: Its Heritage from the Past, and Legacy to the Future*, London: Ivor Nicholson and Watson, 1934, 281–282.
48. Ibid., 55.
49. Ibid., 253.
50. Ibid., 345–346.
51. Ibid., 259.
52. Ibid., 22.
53. Ibid., 166–167, emphasis in original.
54. Ibid., 103.
55. Ibid., 25, emphasis in original.
56. Ibid., 58.
57. Ibid., 17–18.
58. Ibid., 224.
59. Ibid., 179–184.
60. Ibid., 20, 253.
61. I am thankful to Ian Davis (http://www.bluntinstrument.org.uk/foulds/) for sending me a copy.
62. Mann, *Some Indian Conceptions of Music*, preface and 17.
63. Ibid., 18.
64. Ibid., preface and 17.
65. Ibid., preface.
66. Ibid., 4.
67. For this and the next paragraph: Neil Sorrell, "A Composer in the Twilight of the Raj: John Foulds (1880–1939)," *Seminar on Indian Music and the West*, Mumbai: Sangeet Natak Academy, 1996, 50–55, and "Early Western Pioneers: John Foulds and Maud MacCarthy," in *Hindustani Music: Thirteenth to Twentieth Centuries*, ed. Joep Bor, Françoise "Nalini" Delvoye, Jane Harvey, and Emmie te Nijenhuis, New Delhi: Manohar, 2010, 511–519.
68. Foulds, *Music To-day*, 48.
69. Mann, *Some Indian Conceptions of Music*, 18.
70. Foulds, *Music To-day*, 51.
71. Ibid., 49.
72. Ibid., 59–60.
73. James G. Mansell, "Music and the Borders of Rationality: Discourses of Place in the Work of John Foulds," in *Internationalism and the Arts in Britain and Europe at the Fin de Siècle*, ed. Grace Brockington, Bern: Peter Lang, 2009, 70.

74. Ibid., 70–72.
75. Mann, *Some Indian Conceptions of Music*, 22.
76. Mansell, "Music and the Borders of Rationality," 66.
77. Foulds, *Music To-day*, 52.
78. As cited in: MacDonald, *John Foulds*, 104–105.
79. MacDonald, *John Foulds*, 120, emphasis in original.
80. Ibid., emphasis in original.
81. David Lelyveld, "Upon the Subdominant: Administering Music in All-India Radio," in *Consuming Modernity: Public Culture in Contemporary India*, ed. Carol A. Breckenridge, New Delhi: Oxford University Press, 1996, 53.
82. MacDonald, *John Foulds*, 124.
83. Mann, *Some Indian Conceptions of Music*, 21.
84. H. R. Luthra, *Indian Broadcasting*, New Delhi: Publications Division, Ministry of Information and Broadcasting, Government of India, 1986, 303.
85. MacDonald, *John Foulds*, 81.
86. Amanda J. Weidman, *Singing the Classical, Voicing the Modern: The Postcolonial Politics of Music in South India*, Durham, NC: Duke University Press, 2006.
87. MacDonald, *John Foulds*, 83. Cf. Foulds, *Music To-day*, 343–344.
88. John Foulds, "An East and West Concert," *The Musical Times*, 79, no. 1146, 1938, 623.
89. Sorrell, "From 'Harm-Omnium' to Harmonia Omnium," 129.
90. MacDonald, *John Foulds*, 77.
91. Ibid., 101.
92. Cyril Scott, "Introduction," in *Through the Eyes of the Masters*, ed. David Anrias, London: Routledge, 1932.
93. Mansell, "Musical Modernity," 435.

4   Rabindranath Tagore and Arnold Bake: Modernist Aesthetics and Cross-Cultural Communication in Bengali Folk Music

1. Reba Som, *Rabindranath Tagore: The Singer and His Song*, including CD, New Delhi: Viking, 2009.
2. Rabindranath Tagore, *The Religion of Man*, London: Unwin, 1961 (first published 1931), 87–88.
3. William Radice, "Introduction," in Rabindranath Tagore, *Selected Poems*, translated and with an introduction by William Radice, New Delhi: Penguin, 1995 (first published 1985), 30.
4. Mary M. Lago, ed., *Imperfect Encounter: The Letters of Rabindranath Tagore and William Rothenstein*, Cambridge, MA: Harvard University Press, 1972, and Uma Das Gupta, ed., *A Difficult Friendship: Letters of Edward Thompson and Rabindranath Tagore*, New Delhi: Oxford University Press, 2003
5. Santidev Ghosh, *Rabindrasangeet Vichitra* (Rabindra Sangeet Miscellany), New Delhi: Concept, 2006 (first published 1972), 110.

6. See for example: Arnold Bake, Letter to Tagore, Bilthoven, November 27, 1929. Santiniketan, West Bengal: Rabindra Bhavan Archives, Visva-Bharati, Correspondence File (English), No. 20, Arnold Bake, Image 25.

7. Arnold Bake, Letter to His Mother, Santiniketan March 22, 1933. Leiden: University Library, Special Collections, Arnold Bake Archive (ABA): F48/4 (5). (All cited letters from the ABA are written in Dutch and translated by the author).

8. As cited in: William Radice, "Keys to the Kingdom: The Search for How Best to Understand and Perform the Songs of Rabindranath Tagore," in *Rabindranath Tagore: Reclaiming a Cultural Icon*, ed. Kathleen M. O'Connell and Joseph T. O'Connell, Kolkata: Visva-Bharati, 2009, 123, emphasis mine.

9. Som, *Rabindranath Tagore*, 30.

10. Arnold Bake, "Tagore and Western Music," in *Rabindranath Tagore: a Centenary Volume, 1861–1961*, New Delhi: Sahitya Akademi, 1961, 94.

11. Arnold Bake, Letter to his Mother, Calcutta, February 16, 1928, ABA: F48/4 (4).

12. Jeanne Openshaw, *Seeking Bauls of Bengal*, Cambridge: Cambridge University Press, 2004, 4.

13. Ibid., 32.

14. Charles Capwell, *The Music of the Bauls of Bengal*, Kent, OH: The Kent State University Press, 1986, 23.

15. Som, *Rabindranath Tagore*, 78.

16. Openshaw, *Seeking Bauls of Bengal*, 28.

17. Som, *Rabindranath Tagore*, 194.

18. Rabindranath Tagore, "Foreword," in Ratan Devi and Ananda K. Coomaraswamy, *Thirty Songs from the Panjab and Kashmir*, New Delhi: Sterling, 1994 (first published 1913), xiv.

19. Ibid.

20. Radice, "Keys to the Kingdom," 140–141.

21. Gerry Farrell, *Indian Music and the West*, New Delhi: Oxford University Press, 1997, 158.

22. Maud Mann (Maud MacCarthy), *Some Indian Conceptions of Music*, London: Theosophical Publishing Society, 1913, 13.

23. Pradip Kumar Sengupta, *Foundations of Indian Musicology: Perspectives in the Philosophy of Art and Culture*, New Delhi: Abhinav Publications, 1991, 96.

24. At least since the nineteenth century, it is traditionally taught that within each *raga* there is a sonant dominant note (*vadi*), which has a consonant relationship of a perfect fourth or fifth with another strong note (*samvadi*).

25. Sengupta, *Foundations of Indian Musicology*, 130.

26. Arthur Henry Fox Strangways, *The Music of Hindostan*, Oxford: Clarendon Press, 1914, 170–171.

27. The well-known ethnomusicologist and student of Arnold Bake Nazir Ali Jairazbhoy (1927–2009) was a great propagator of Bhatkhande's *that* system of *raga* classification: see especially the second edition of *The Rags of North Indian Music: Their Structure and Evolution*, Mumbai: Popular Prakashan, 2011 (first published 1971), because it includes a

reprint of his article "What Happened to Indian Music Theory? Indo-Occidentalism?" (2008).

28. Prathama Banerjee, *Politics of Time: "Primitives" and History-Writing in a Colonial Society*, New Delhi: Oxford University Press, 2006.

29. Ibid., 223.

30. Ashis Nandy, *The Intimate Enemy: Loss and Recovery of Self under Colonialism*, New Delhi: Oxford University Press, 1983, 58.

31. Banerjee, *Politics of Time*, 229.

32. Maud Karpeles (1885–1976) was the driving force behind the International Folk Music Council, which to some extent was an outgrowth of the English Folk Song and Dance Society. It was founded after the Second World War and gradually developed into an organization for the study of "world music" (since 1981 as the International Council for Traditional Music). Arnold Bake was a member of the council's executive board.

33. Arnold Bake, Letter to his Wife, London, July 31, 1934, ABA: F48/5 (7).

34. Arnold Bake, "Why I Studied Tagore's Songs," Unpublished lecture note, London, April 28, 1950, ABA: F47/2 (6); Fox Strangways, *The Music of Hindostan*, 92–99.

35. John Brough, "Obituary: Arnold Adriaan Bake," *Bulletin of the School of Oriental and African Studies*, 27, 1, 1964, 246.

36. See for instance: Arnold Bake, "Different Aspects of Indian Music," *Indian Art and Letters*, 8, 1, 1934, 60–74, and *Lectures on Indian Music*, Department of Education: Baroda State Press, 1933.

37. Bake, "Different Aspects of Indian Music," 66.

38. Bake, *Lectures on Indian Music*, 2.

39. Arnold Bake, Letter to his Wife, July 31, 1934, ABA: F48/5 (7).

40. Suvarnalata Rao and Wim van der Meer, "The Construction, Reconstruction, and Deconstruction of Shruti," in *Hindustani Music: Thirteenth to Twentieth Centuries*, ed. Joep Bor, Françoise "Nalini" Delvoye, Jane Harvey, and Emmie te Nijenhuis, New Delhi: Manohar, 2010, 687, 692.

41. Arnold Bake, *Bijdrage tot de Kennis der Voor-Indische Muziek*, Paris: Paul Geuthner, 1930, 6 (for the sake of readability, I have replaced Bake's transliteration *çrutis* with *shrutis*). Cf. Arnold Bake, "Some Aspects of the Development of Indian Music," *Proceedings of the Royal Musical Association*, 76th Sess., 1949–1950, 23–34.

42. Arnold Bake, "The Impact of Western Music on the Indian Musical System," *Journal of the International Folk Music Council*, 5, 1953, 60 and Bake, *Lectures on Indian Music*, 5.

43. Arnold Bake, "A Talk on Folk-Music," *Visva-Bharati Quarterly*, 5, 1, 1927, 148, and "Indian Music and Rabindranath Tagore," *Indian Art and Letters*, 5, 2, 1931, 85.

44. Bake, "A Talk on Folk Music," 145.

45. Arnold Bake, "Synthesis of Indian and Western Music," *The Illustrated Weekly of India*, November 5, 1961, 51.

46. Arnold Bake, "Indian Folk-Music," *Proceedings of the Musical Association*, 63rd Sess., 1936–1937, 70–71.

47. Ghosh, *Rabindrasangeet Vichitra*, 158.

48. Arnold Bake, *Twenty-Six Songs of Rabindranath Tagore*, Paris: Paul Geuthner, 1935, 30, and *Lectures on Indian Music*, 17.
49. Arthur Henry Fox Strangways, "Convention: Tagore's Songs," *The Observer*, September, 20, 1936.
50. Bake, "A Talk on Folk-Music," 146, 148.
51. Arnold Bake, Letter to his Mother, Chamba, April 18, 1926, ABA: F48/4 (4).
52. Brough, "Obituary," 253.
53. Stephen N. Hay, *Asian Ideas of East and West: Tagore and his Critics in Japan, China, and India*, Cambridge, MA: Harvard University Press, 1970.
54. Arnold Bake, Letter to his Mother, S. S. Ellora, Bandung-Batavia, September 26 1927, ABA: F48/4 (4).
55. Arnold Bake, Letter to his Mother, Santiniketan, February 26, 1929, ABA: F48/4 (4).
56. Arnold Bake, Letter to his Mother, Santiniketan, January 16, 1929, ABA: F48/4 (4).
57. Krishna Dutta and Andrew Robinson, *Rabindranath Tagore: The Myriad-Minded Man*, London: Bloomsbury, 1995, 281.
58. Arnold Bake, "Tagore," Unpublished lecture note: Friends of the Brahmo Samaj, London, May 24, 1953, ABA: F47/2 (1).
59. Michael Collins, *Empire, Nationalism and the Post-Colonial World: Rabindranath Tagore's Writings on History, Politics and Society*, New York: Routledge, 2011.
60. Bake, "Tagore and Western Music," 88.
61. Ibid., 94.
62. Arnold Bake, "Tagore: The Man and the Artist," *Indian Art and Letters*, 35, 1, 1961, 20, emphasis in original.
63. Bake, *Lectures on Indian Music*, 23.
64. As cited in Rabindranath Tagore, *The Jewel That Is Best: Collected Brief Poems*, translated with an introduction by William Radice, New Delhi: Penguin, 2011, 169.
65. Som, *Rabindranath Tagore*, 189.
66. Ibid., 142.
67. Ghosh, *Rabindrasangeet Vichitra*, 107.
68. Som, *Rabindranath Tagore*, 82.
69. Alain Daniélou, *The Way to the Labyrinth: Memories of East and West*, New York: New Directions, 1987; Rakesh Mathur, "Shiv Sharan: Not Your Typical French Hindu," *Hinduism Today*, 17, 10, 1995 (Santiniketan, West Bengal: Rabindra Bhavan Archives, Visva-Bharati, Correspondence File [English], No. 78, Alain Daniélou, Images 15–20).
70. *Tagore's Songs of Destiny: The Daniélou Collection*. Francesca Cassio (voice) and Ugo Bonessi (piano). Questz, 2009 and *Tagore's Songs of Love: The Daniélou Collection*. Francesca Cassio (voice) and Ugo Bonessi (piano). Questz, 2009.
71. Ghosh, *Rabindrasangeet Vichitra*, x.
72. Ibid., 111.
73. Ibid., 111–112.
74. Ibid.

75. Tagore, *The Religion of Man*, 222–225.
76. Bake, *Twenty Six Songs*, 25.
77. As cited in: Uma Das Gupta, ed., *The Oxford India Tagore: Selected Writings on Education and Nationalism*, New Delhi: Oxford University Press, 2009, 204.
78. Ibid.
79. Tagore, "Foreword," in Devi and Coomaraswamy, *Thirty Songs*, xiv.
80. As cited in: Das Gupta, ed., *The Oxford India Tagore*, xvi, emphasis mine.
81. As cited in: Saranindranath Tagore, "Rabindranath Tagore's Conception of Cosmopolitanism: A Reconstruction," in *Rabindranath Tagore: Reclaiming a Cultural Icon*, ed. Kathleen M. O'Connell and Joseph T. O'Connell, Kolkata: Visva-Bharati, 2009, 100.
82. Bake, "A Talk on Folk Music," 148.
83. Ralph Vaughan Williams, *National Music and Other Essays*, Oxford: Clarendon, 1996 (Second edition), "Nationalism and Internationalsm," 154.
84. Ibid., "National Music," 3, 9.
85. Ibid., "Nationalism and Internationalism," 154–155.
86. Uma Das Gupta, *Rabindranath Tagore: A Biography*, New Delhi: Oxford University Press, 2004, 78.
87. Radice, "Keys to the Kingdom," 129.
88. Ibid., 140.
89. Radice, "Introduction," in Tagore, *Selected Poems*, 34.
90. As cited in: Dutta and Robinson, *Rabindranath Tagore*, 287.
91. Radice, "Introduction," in Tagore, *Selected Poems*, 38.

5   Sikh Sacred Music: Identity, Aesthetics, and Historical Change

1. Charles Wilkins, "Observations on the Seeks and Their College" (1788). As reprinted in *Western Image of the Sikh Religion: A Source Book*, ed. Darshan Singh, New Delhi: National Book Organization, 1999, 2.
2. M. A. Macauliffe, "The Rise of Amritsar and the Alterations of the Sikh Religion" (1881). As reprinted in *Western Image of the Sikh Religion*, ed. Darshan Singh, 250.
3. C. A. Bayly, *Recovering Liberties: Indian Thought in the Age of Liberalism and Empire*, Cambridge: Cambridge University Press, 2012, 225.
4. Harjot Oberoi, *The Construction of Religious Boundaries: Culture, Identity and Diversity in the Sikh Tradition*, New Delhi: Oxford University Press, 1994.
5. Bob van der Linden, *Moral Languages from Colonial Punjab: The Singh Sabha, Arya Samaj and Ahmadiyahs*, New Delhi: Manohar, 2008; "Sikh Music and Empire: The Moral Representation of Self in Music," *Sikh Formations: Religion, Culture, Theory*, 4, 1, 2008, 1–15; "Sikh Sacred Music, Empire and World Music: Aesthetics and Historical Change," *Sikh Formations: Religion, Culture, Theory*, 7, 3, 2011, 383–397; and "History versus Tradition Again? A Response to Bhai Baldeep Singh," *Sikh Formations: Religion, Culture, Theory*, 8, 2, 2012, 247–251.
6. Gurinder Singh Mann, *The Making of Sikh Scripture*, New Delhi: Oxford University Press, 2001, and Pashaura Singh, *The Guru Granth Sahib: Canon, Meaning and Authority*, New Delhi: Oxford University Press, 2000.

7. Pashaura Singh, "Sikhism and Music," in *Sacred Sound: Experiencing Music in World Religions*, ed. Guy L. Beck, including CD, Waterloo, Ontario: Wilfrid Laurier University Press, 2006, 141–167, and "Musical *Chaunkis* at the Darbar Sahib: History, Aesthetics, and Time," in *Sikhism in Global Context*, ed. Pashaura Singh, New Delhi: Oxford University Press, 2011, 102–129.

8. *Sikh Formations: Religion, Culture, Theory*, Vols. 7, 3, 2011, and 8, 2, 2012.

9. Anonymous, *Sikh Sacred Music*, New Delhi: Sikh Sacred Music Society, 1967; Gobind Singh Mansukhani, *Indian Classical Music and Sikh Kirtan*, New Delhi: Oxford and IBH, 1982; Ajit Singh Paintal, *Nature and Place of Music in Sikh Religion and Its Affinity with Hindustani Classical Music*, PhD Dissertation, University of Delhi: Department of Music, 1972; and Gurnam Singh, *Sikh Musicology: Sri Guru Granth Sahib and Hymns of the Human Spirit*, New Delhi: Kanishka, 2001.

10. Avtar Singh and Gurcharan Singh, *Gurbani Sangit Prachin Rit Ratnavali*, 2 vols., Patiala: Punjabi University Press, 1979, and Gyani Dyal Singh, *Gurmat Sangit Sagar*, 4 vols., New Delhi: Guru Nanak Vidya Bhandar Trust, 1992.

11. Pashaura Singh, *The Guru Granth Sahib*, 232.

12. Linden, *Moral Languages from Colonial Punjab*.

13. Ajit Singh Paintal, "The Contributions of Ragis and Rababis to the Sikh Devotional Music," in *The City of Amritsar: A Study of Historical, Social and Economic Aspects*, ed. Fauja Singh, New Delhi: Oriental Publishers and Distributors, 1978, 268, 274–275, 280.

14. Ibid., 268.

15. Ernest Trumpp, *The Adi Granth or the Holy Scripture of the Sikhs*, New Delhi: Mushiram Manoharlal, 1978 (first published 1877), cxx.

16. Frederic Pincott, "The Arrangement of the Hymns of the Adi Granth, Holy Bible of the Sikhs" (1886). As reprinted in *Western Image of the Sikh Religion*, ed. Darshan Singh, 210.

17. Bhagat Lakshman Singh, *Autobiography*, ed. Ganda Singh, Calcutta: The Sikh Cultural Centre, 1965, 122.

18. Ibid., 123.

19. M. A. Macauliffe, "The Holy Writings of the Sikhs" (1898). As reprinted in *Western Image of the Sikh Religion*, ed. Darshan Singh, 321.

20. M. A. Macauliffe, *The Sikh Religion: Its Gurus, Sacred Writings and Authors*, 6 volumes, Oxford: Oxford University Press, 1909, vol. 1., xxx.

21. Bhagat Lakshman Singh, *Autobiography*, 124.

22. Macauliffe, *The Sikh Religion*, vol. 1., xxvi.

23. Ibid., xxvii.

24. Ibid., vol. 5., 333–351.

25. Ibid., vol. 1., 3.

26. Anonymous, *Sikh Sacred Music* and Paintal, "The Contributions of Ragis," 272–274.

27. Pashaura Singh, "Musical *Chaunkis*," 121–122.

28. Barbara N. Ramusack, "Punjab States, Maharajas and Gurudwaras: Patiala and the Sikh Community," in *People, Princes and Paramount Power: Society and Politics in the Indian Princely States*, ed. Robin Jeffrey, New Delhi: Oxford University Press, 1978, 182.

29. Paintal, *Nature and Place of Music*, 203.
30. Michael Nijhawan, *Dhadi Darbar: Religion, Violence, and the History of Sikh History*, New Delhi: Oxford University Press, 2006.
31. Pashaura Singh, "Musical *Chaunkis*," 119–120.
32. Navtej K. Purewal, "Sikh/Muslim Bhai-Bhai? Towards a Social History of the Rababi Tradition of Shabad," *Sikh Formations: Religion, Culture, Theory*, 7, 3, 2011, 365–382.
33. I am thankful to Tej Purewal for sending me a copy of the CD: Bhai Ghulam Muhammad Chand, *Mittar Pyare Noon: Contemporary Sounds of the Rababi Tradition of Kirtan in Lahore*, 2010, which she conceptualized and produced together with Virinder Kalra as part of her research into the *rababi* tradition.
34. *Har Sachche Takht Rachaya: History & Significance of 5 Takhts through Shabad-Kirtan & Vyakhya*, Music Today, India D 09042 A-F, 6 CDs, 2009.
35. www.anadconservatory.org.
36. www.gurmatsangeetpup.com.
37. Dharmendra Rataul, "SGPC sends SOS World over for Training of Ragis," *Indian Express*, March 13, 2006.
38. Gurnam Singh, *Sikh Musicology*; Avtar Singh and Gurcharan Singh, *Gurbani Sangit*; and Gyani Dyal Singh, *Gurmat Sangit*.
39. Pashaura Singh, "Bibi Jasbir Kaur Khalsa: Tribute to the Doyenne of Gurmat Sangeet," www.SikhChic.com, February 13, 2011.
40. Pashaura Singh, "Sikhism and Music," 163, and Gurnam Singh, *Sikh Musicology*, vi.
41. Gurnam Singh, *Sri Guru Granth Sahib: 31 Raag Darshan*, 4 CDs, Punjabi University Patiala/Amritsar: Fine Touch FTACD 2185–88, n.d.; Gurnam Singh, *Sikh Musicology*, vii.
42. Deepak Raja, *Hindustani Music: A Tradition in Transition*, with a foreword by Shiv Kumar Sharma, New Delhi: D. K. Printworld, 2005, vii.
43. Joep Bor, et al., *The Raga Guide: A Survey of 74 Hindustani Ragas*, set of 4 CDs with book, Wyastone Leys, Monmouth: Nimbus, 1999, 1.
44. Ibid., 181.
45. Ibid., 1.
46. Prabha Atre, *Enlightening the Listener: Contemporary North Indian Classical Vocal Music Performance*, including CD, New Delhi: Munshiram Manoharlal, 2000, 8.
47. Ibid., 73–74.
48. Ibid.; Bor, et al.; *The Raga Guide*; and Raja, *Hindustani Music*.
49. Bor, et al., *The Raga Guide,* and Raja, *Hindustani Music*, 132.
50. See for example: Arvind-Pal S. Mandair, *Religion and the Spectre of the West: Sikhism, India, Postcoloniality, and the Politics of Translation*, New York: Columbia University Press, 2009, 193, 361–362, Mansukhani, *Indian Classical Music*; Christopher Shackle and Arvind-Pal Singh Mandair, eds., *Teachings of the Sikh Gurus: Selections from the Guru Granth Sahib*, London: Routledge, 2005, xxiii; and Pashaura Singh, *The Guru Granth Sahib*, 127–128, and "Sikhism and Music," 157–158.
51. See for example: Mansukhani, *Indian Classical Music,* and Francesca Cassio, "The Music of the Sikh Gurus' Tradition in a Western Context:

Cross-Cultural Pedagogy and Research," *Sikh Formations: Religion, Culture, Theory*, 7, 3, 2011, 326.

52. Suvarnalata Rao and Wim van der Meer, "The Construction, Reconstruction, and Deconstruction of Shruti," in *Hindustani Music: Thirteenth to Twentieth Centuries*, ed. Joep Bor, Françoise "Nalini" Delvoye, Jane Harvey, and Emmie te Nijenhuis, New Delhi: Manohar, 2010, 693.

53. Dusenbery, Verne A., "The Word as Guru: Sikh Scripture and the Translation Controversy" (1992), in Dusenbery, *Sikhs at Large: Religion, Culture, and Politics in Global perspective*, Oxford University Press, 2008, 78–79, translation mine.

54. Pashaura Singh, *The Guru Granth Sahib*, 22.

55. Mandair, *Religion and the Spectre of the West*, 193.

56. Pashaura Singh, "Sikhism and Music," 144; cf. Shackle and Mandair, *Teachings of the Sikh Gurus*, xxx–xxxi.

57. Cassio, "The Music of the Sikh Gurus' Tradition," 331.

58. Hew McLeod, *Discovering the Sikhs: Autobiography of a Historian*, New Delhi: Permanent Black, 2004.

59. Bhai Baldeep Singh, "What Is Kirtan? Observations, Interventions and Personal Reflections," *Sikh Formations: Religion, Culture, Theory*, 7, 3, 2011, 248, translation mine.

60. Ibid., 271.

61. Ibid., 268, emphasis in original.

62. Ibid., 248.

63. Ibid., 260.

64. Nirinjan Kaur Khalsa, "Gurbani Kirtan Renaissance: Reviving Musical Memory, Reforming Sikh Identity," *Sikh Formations: Religion, Culture, Theory*, 2012, 8, 2, 2012, 201.

65. Bhai Baldeep Singh, "What Is Kirtan?"; Linden, "Sikh Music and Empire," and "Sikh Sacred Music."

66. Linden, "Sikh Music and Empire," 12.

67. Gerry Farrell, *Indian Music and the West*, Oxford: Oxford University Press, 1997, 149.

68. David Tame, *The Secret Power of Music*, Rochester, VT: Destiny Books, 1984.

69. Bhai Baldeep Singh, "What Is Kirtan?" 264.

70. Recently again, Francesca Cassio referred to the Pythagorean concept of the "music of the spheres" in "The Music of the Sikh Gurus' Tradition," 333.

71. Cf. Matthew Gelbart, *The Invention of "Folk Music" and "Art Music": Emerging Categories from Ossian to Wagner*, Cambridge: Cambridge University Press, 2007.

72. Pashaura Singh, "Sikhism and Music," 160.

73. Raja, *Hindustani Music*, 204.

74. Atre, *Enlightening the Listener*, 70.

75. www.sgpc.net.

76. www.sikhnet.com/radio.

77. http://www.sikh-history.com/sikhhist/personalities/bhai_daya_singh_aust.html.

78. Dusenbery, "The Word as Guru," 79.

79. Ibid., 73.

80. Ibid., 82.
81. Mann, *The Making of Sikh Scripture*, 136.
82. Shackle and Mandair, *Teachings of the Sikh Gurus*, xxiii.
83. Linden, *Moral Languages from Colonial Punjab*.
84. Pashaura Singh, *Life and Work of Guru Arjan: History, Memory, and Biography in the Sikh Tradition*, New Delhi: Oxford University Press, 2006, 48.
85. Shackle and Mandair, *Teachings of the Sikh Gurus*, xlv.
86. Mann, *The Making of Sikh Scripture*, 87–88.

Coda

1. Bruno Nettl, *Nettl's Elephant: On the History of Ethnomusicology*, Urbana-Champaign: University of Illinois Press, 2010, 16. Of course, Alan P. Merriam first defined the concept of the study of "music in culture" in his classic *The Anthropology of Music* (1964), though he later amended it to "music as culture."
2. Bruno Nettl, *The Study of Ethnomusicology: Thirty-One Issues and Concepts*, Urbana-Champaign: University of Illinois Press, 2005, 12.
3. Matt Rahaim, "That Ban(e) of Indian Music: Hearing Politics in The Harmonium," *Journal of Asian Studies*, 70, 3, 2011, 657–682.
4. Philip V. Bohlman, *World Music: A Very Short Introduction*, Oxford: Oxford University Press, 2002, 70.
5. Martin Clayton, "A. H. Fox Strangways and *The Music of Hindostan*: Revisiting Historical Field Recordings," *Journal of the Royal Musical Association*, 124, 1999, 115.
6. See further about these issues for example: Laurent Aubert, *The Music of the Other: New Challenges for Ethnomusicology in a Global Age,* trans. Carla Ribeiro, with a foreword by Anthony Seeger, Aldershot: Ashgate, 2007; Bohlman, *World Music*; Georgina Born and David Hesmondhalgh, eds., *Western Music and Its Others: Difference, Representation, and Appropriation in Music*, Berkeley: University of California Press, 2000; Nettl, *The Study of Ethnomusicology*; Timothy D. Taylor, *Beyond Exoticism: Western Music and the World*, Durham, NC: Duke University Press, 2007.
7. Nettl, *Nettl's Elephant*, 89.
8. Clayton, "A. H. Fox Strangways," 112.
9. John Blacking, *"A Common-Sense View of All Music": Reflections on Percy Grainger's Contribution to Ethnomusicology and Music Education*, Cambridge: Cambridge University Press, 1987.
10. The series contains two volumes on South Asia: George Ruckert, *Music in North India*, New York: Oxford University Press, 2004, and T. Viswanathan and Matthew Harp Allen, *Music in South India*, New York: Oxford University Press, 2004.
11. Bonnie C. Wade, *Thinking Musically*, New York: Oxford University Press, 2004, and Patricia Shehan Campbell, *Teaching Music Globally*, New York: Oxford University Press, 2004.
12. Campbell, *Teaching Music Globally*, 26.
13. *Latcho Drom*, Director Tony Gatlif, France: K. G. Productions, 1993 (DVD).

14. Deepak Raja, *Hindustani Music: A Tradition in Transition*, with a foreword by Shiv Kumar Sharma, New Delhi: D. K. Printworld, 2005, 35.

15. Gerry Farrell, *Indian Music and the West*, Oxford: Oxford University Press, 1997, 202.

16. Nettl, *Nettl's Elephant*, 57.

17. Raja, *Hindustani Music*, 34.

18. Rustom Barucha, *Rajasthan: An Oral History* (Conversations with Komal Kothari), New Delhi: Penguin, 2003, 240, emphasis in original. See also the accompanying CD to this book: *Rajasthan: A Musical Journey*, Jodhpur: Rupayan Sansthan Archives, 2003.

19. Ibid., 290, translation added.

20. See for the developments of Hindustani music in Pakistan: *Khayal Darpan: A Mirror of Imagination* (An Indian Filmmaker Journeys through Classical Music in Pakistan), Directed by Yousuf Saeed, Ektara 2006 (DVD).

21. *A Voice from Heaven: Nusrat Fateh Ali Khan, the Most Beautiful Voice in the World*, New York, Winstar TV & Video, 2001.

22. www.britishmusicsociety.com.

23. Jonathan Harvey, *In Quest of Spirit: Thoughts on Music*, Berkeley: University of California Press, 1999, and John Tavener, *The Music of Silence: A Composer's Testament*, London: Faber and Faber, 1999.

24. *Ravi Shankar in Portrait*. BBC: Opus Art, 2002 (DVD), and *Violin from the Heart: Biography of Dr. L. Subramaniam*. Living Media India Ltd., 2006 (DVD).

25. *Mayer, Rubbra, Britten: Works for Cello and Piano*, Guild GMCD 7114, 1995, includes Mayer's pieces *Prabhanda* (1982) for cello and piano and *Calcutta Nagar* (1993) for piano.

26. John Foulds, *Music To-day: Its Heritage from the Past, and Legacy to the Future*, London: Ivor Nicholson and Watson, 345–346.

27. Nicholas Cook, *Music: A Very Short Introduction*, Oxford: Oxford University Press, 1998, 127.

28. *Remember Shakti. The Way of Beauty*. Universal Music France, 2006 (DVD).

Chronology

1792	William Jones, *On the Musical Modes of the Hindus*
1834	N. Augustus Willard, *A Treatise on the Music of Hindoostan*
1861	Birth, Rabindranath Tagore
1873	Foundation, Amritsar Singh Sabha; Tagore in Amritsar
1875	Establishment, Theosophical Society in New York
1877	Thomas Edison invents the phonograph; Theosophical Society establishes headquarters in Adyar; Trumpp, *The Adi Granth*
1879	Birth, Cyril Scott
1880	Birth, John Foulds
1882	Birth, Percy Grainger; birth, Maud MacCarthy
1885	Ellis, *On the Musical Scales of Various Nations*
1888	Blavatsky, *The Secret Doctrine*
1891	Scott to Frankfurt for the first time
1892	Birth, Bhai Jawala Singh
1893	Parry, *The Evolution of the Art of Music*
1894–1895	Kipling, *Jungle Books*
1895	Grainger to Frankfurt
1896	Sourindro Mohun Tagore, *Universal History of Music*
1897	Kahn Singh Nabha, *Ham Hindu Nahin*
1899	Birth, Arnold Bake; first gramophone recording of Indian voice in London
1901	Grainger moves to London; Kipling, *Kim*
1902	Foundation, Chief Khalsa Diwan; first gramophone disc cut in Calcutta
1904	Fox Strangways first time India
1905	*Swadeshi* movement in Bengal
1907	Sharp, *English Folk Song*; Besant becomes president of the Theosophical Society; Curtis, *The Indians' Book*; Busoni, *Sketch of a New Esthetic of Music*
1908	Grainger, "Collecting with the Phonograph"; MacCarthy tours India
1909	Coomaraswamy, *Essays in Indian Idealism*; Macauliffe, *The Sikh Religion*; Scott, *First Piano Sonata*
1910	Foundation, India Society; Scriabin, *Promotheus*
1912	MacCarthy, "Some Indian Conceptions of Music"; Tagore, *Gitanjali*
1913	Tagore wins Nobel Prize for Literature; Devi and Coomaraswamy, *Thirty Songs from Panjab and Kashmir*
1914	Fox Strangways, *The Music of Hindostan*; Grainger emigrates to the United States; Grainger, *Colonial Song*

1915	MacCarthy meets Foulds; James and Margaret Cousins travel to India; Grainger, "The Impress of Personality in Unwritten Music"
1916	First All India Music Conference, Baroda; Grainger, *The Warriors*
1917	Scott, *The Philosophy of Modernism*; Holst, *The Planets*; Tagore, *Nationalism*
1918	Foundation, Visva-Bharati University, Santiniketan
1920	Foundation, Shiromani Gurdwara Parbandhak Committee (SGPC)
1921	Foulds, *A World Requiem*
1922	Scott, *Indian Suite*
1925	Bake visits India for the first time
1926	Foulds, *Gandharva-Music*
1927	Tagore and Bake tour Java and Bali
1928	Coomaraswamy, *Dance of Shiva*; Foulds, *Essays in the Modes*
1929	Grainger, *Recessional*; Foulds, *Dynamic Tryptych*
1930	Bake, *Bijdrage tot de Kennis der Voor-Indische Muziek*; Foulds, *Three Mantras*
1931	Hornbostel, *Music of the Orient*
1933	Scott, *Music: Its Secret Influence throughout the Ages*
1934	Foulds, *Music To-day*
1935	MacCarthy and Foulds to India; Cousins, *Music of the Orient and Occident*; Bake, *Twenty-Six Songs of Rabindranath Tagore*
1936	Establishment, Kalakshetra, Adyar
1939	Death, Foulds
1947	Partition of British India into India and Pakistan; Scott, *Hymn of Unity*
1948	Bake joins School of African and Oriental Studies
1950	Sikh Rahit Maryada
1951	Karpeles and Bake, *Manual for Folk Music Collector*
1976	Bhai Avtar Singh and Bhai Gurcharan Singh, *Gurbani Sangit Prachin Rit Ratanavali*
2001	End copyright of the Visva-Bharati Music Board on *Rabindra Sangit*
2003	Establishment, Gurmat Sangit department at Punjabi University, Patiala

Glossary of Indian Terms

bhakti   Devotionalism, with a highly emotional and personal focus on a Hindu deity

dhrupad   The original form of Hindustani music sung at the Hindu and Mughal courts in medieval times. The music was formal in structure (four parts) with strict adherence to the purity of the *raga* and *tala*, as well as regulated improvisation around the texts, which were mostly devotional and Vaishnava (devoted to Krishna) in character.

gharana   Traditional musical lineage, which operates as semiprofessional guilds in which successful maestros hand down musical learning to their sons, nephews, grandsons, and grandnephews, and sometimes to a talented male apprentice from outside the family.

khayal   The predominant vocal genre in the Hindustani music tradition, which is generally in two parts and of a more improvisational character than its predecessor, *dhrupad*, which it increasingly replaced from the early nineteenth century onward.

raga   Generalized melodic practice based on a series of five or more notes, whereby combinations of notes are identified for their individual emotive "flavor" (*rasa*) and set to a fixed structure that includes a starting note, a final note, between five and seven notes ascending and descending, the use of accidentals, flats, and sharps, and unique phrasing.

rasa   Sentiment, aesthetic potential (literally, "juice") inherent in the music

sant   Group of teachers (usually of low caste) who flourished in the fifteenth, sixteenth, and seventeenth centuries in north-India and were critical about Brahmanical authority.

sufi   Islamic mystic who seeks God directly

tala   Rhythmic cycle rather than time signature, whereby each particular cycle contains a number of *talas* (claps), *khalis* (open hands), and other blank beats called *matras*, which add up to a total that is repeated indefinitely but is variable in tempo.

Vedanta   A word used in Hindu philosophy as a synonym for the last section of the *Vedas* known also as the *Upanishads*. It follows the idea that all reality is a single principle, *Brahman*, and teaches that the believer's goal is to transcend the limitations of self-identity and realize one's unity with the *Brahman*.

Vedas   The oldest sacred texts in the world and the basis for Hindu revelation, the Vedas are a large body of Sanskrit hymns and verse that lay the foundation of Hindu rites and practices, going back nearly six thousand years. These texts were memorized for millennia by Brahmins and contain the seeds of Indian musical thought.

Selected Discography

Cyril Scott

Moods & Impressions: Piano Music by Cyril Scott. Christopher Howell (piano). Tremula 104–2, 1994 [**Impressions from the Junglebook**].

Cyril Scott: Complete Piano Music, Volume One, Suites & Miniatures. Leslie De'Ath (piano). Dutton CDLX 7150, 2 CDs, 2005 [**Soirée Japonaise; Sphinx; Indian Suite; Caprice Chinois; Lotus Land**].

Cyril Scott: Complete Piano Music, Volume Two, Complete Piano Sonatas. Leslie De'Ath (piano). Dutton CDLX 7155, 2005.

Cyril Scott: Sonata Lyrica and Other Works for Violin and Piano. Clare Howick (violin) and Sophia Rahman (piano). Dutton CDLX 7200, 2007 [**Lotus Land; Tallahassee Suite**].

Songs of Quest and Inspiration: Cyril Scott—Ralph Vaughan Williams. Robbert Muuse (baritone)/Micha van Weers (piano). Challenge Classics 72527, 2011 [**An Eastern Lament; Picnic; Ballad of Fair Helen of Kirkconnell**].

Percy Grainger

Percy Grainger: The Complete Piano Music. Martin Jones (piano). Nimbus NI 1767, 5 CDs, 1997 [**Beautiful Fresh Flower; Colonial Song; Country Gardens; Sussex Mummers' Christmas Carol; The Warriors; Nimrod; Rag-Time Girl**].

Salute to Percy Grainger. Peter Pears, Benjamin Britten, English Chamber Orchestra, Ambrosian Singers, and so on, London 425 159–2, 1989 [**Let's Dance Gay in Green Meadow; Bold William Taylor**].

Grainger: Jungle Book. Libby Crabtree, John Mark Ainsley, David Wilson-Johnson (soloists)/Polyphony/The Polyphony Orchestra, Stephen Layton. Hyperion CDA66863, 1996 [**Jungle Book Cycle**].

Percy Grainger/Gustav Holst

Percy Grainger: The Warriors/Gustav Holst: The Planets. Philharmonia Orchestra, John Eliot Gardiner. Deutsche Grammophon 445 860–2, 1995.

John Foulds

John Foulds: A World Requiem. Jeanne-Michèle Charbonnet, Catherine Wyn-Rogers, Stuart Skelton, Gerald Finley (soloists)/Trinity Boys Choir/Crouch End Festival Chorus/Philharmonia Chorus/BBC Symphony Chorus/BBC Symphony Ochestra, Leon Botstein. Chandos CHSA 5058 (2), 2 CDs, 2008.

John Foulds (Dynamic Triptych, Music Pictures III and so on). Peter Donohoe (piano)/City of Birmingham Symphony Orchestra, Sakari Oramo. WB 2564 62 999–2, 2006 [**Dynamic Triptych; The Song of Ram Dass; Keltic Lament**].

John Foulds (Mirage, Three Mantras and so on) Susan Bickley and Daniel Hope (soloists)/ City of Birmingham Symphony Orchestra/City of Birmingham Youth Chorus, Sakari Oramo. WB 2564 61525, 2004 [**Three Mantras; Lyra Celtica**].

John Foulds: Music for Solo Piano. Peter Jacobs (piano). Altarus AIR-CD-9001, 1992 (first released 1984) [**Essays in the Modes; Gandharva Music**].

John Foulds, Volume 2 (Music-Pictures, Henry VIII Suite and so on). BBC Concert Orchestra, Ronald Corp. Dutton CDLX 7260, 2010 [**The Florida Spiritual; Indian Suite**].

John Foulds, *Chamber Music.* Endellion String Quartet. Pearl SHE CD 9564, 1981 [**Quartetto Intimo**].

English Cello Sonatas: Foulds/Walker/Bowen. Jo Cole (Cello) and John Talbot (piano). British Music Society 423CD, 1998 [**Cello Sonata**].

Rabindra Sangit

The Voice of Rabindranath Tagore: The Complete Hindusthan Recordings 1932–1939. Calcutta: Hindusthan Musical Products Ltd, IP-6040, 1997.

Rabindra Sangeet, 2 Volumes, Doordarshan Archives, 2006, with performances by Debabrata Biswas, Santidev Ghosh, Suchitra Mitra, Hemanta Mukhopadhyay, Sagar Sen, among others (DVD).

Tagore's Songs of Destiny: The Daniélou Collection. Francesca Cassio (voice) and Ugo Bonessi (piano). Questz, 2009.

Tagore's Songs of Love: The Daniélou Collection. Francesca Cassio (voice) and Ugo Bonessi (piano). Questz, 2009.

Sikh Sacred Music

Bhai Avtar Singh, *Gurmat Sangeet,* Music Today, India CD GM99004 A&B, 2 CDs, 1999.

Har Sachche Takht Rachaya: History & Significance of 5 Takhts through Shabad-Kirtan & Vyakhya. Music Today, India CD 09042 A-F, 6 CDs, 2009.

Bhai Ghulam Muhammad Chand, *Mittar Pyare Noon: Contemporary Sounds from the Rababi Tradition of Kirtan from Lahore,* 2010 (available from: www.saanjhpunjab.info).

Gurnam Singh, *Sri Guru Granth Sahib: 31 Raag Darshan,* 4 CDs, Punjabi University Patiala/Amritsar: Fine Touch FTACD 2185–88, n.d.

Other

Mayer, Rubbra, Britten: Works for Cello and Piano, Guild GMCD 7114, 1995 [**Prabhanda; Calcutta Nagar**].

Rajasthan: A Musical Journey, Jodhpur: Rupayan Sansthan Archives CD, 2003.

Documentaries

The Noble Savage: Percy Grainger, Director Barrie Gavin, Central TV Films, 1986.

Holst: In the Bleak Midwinter, Director Tony Palmer, Gonzo Multimedia, 2011 (DVD).

A Voice from Heaven: Nusrat Fateh Ali Khan, the Most Beautiful Voice in the World, New York, Winstar TV & Video, 2001 (DVD).

Khayal Darpan: A Mirror of Imagination (An Indian Filmmaker Journeys through Classical Music in Pakistan), Directed by Yousuf Saeed, Ektara 2006 (DVD).

Latcho Drom, Director Tony Gatlif, France: K. G. Productions, 1993 (DVD).

Remember Shakti. The Way of Beauty, Universal Music France, 2006 (DVD).

Ravi Shankar in Portrait, BBC: Opus Art, 2002 (DVD).

Violin from the Heart: Biography of Dr. L. Subramaniam, Living Media India Ltd., 2006 (DVD).

"O Thou Transcendent": The Life of Ralph Vaughan Williams, Director Tony Palmer, 2007 (DVD).

Works Cited

Manuscript Sources

Leiden University Library, Institute Kern Collection:
Arnold Bake Archive
New York Public Library for the Performing Arts:
M-Clippings, Maud MacCarthy
Rabindra Bhavan Archives, Visva-Bharati (Santiniketan), West Bengal:
Correspondence File (English), No. 20, Arnold Bake
Correspondence File (English), No. 78, Alain Daniélou

Published Materials

Allen, Matthew Harp, "Rewriting the Script for South Indian Dance," *The Drama Review*, 41, 3, 1997: 63–100.

Anonymous, "A Concert of Indian Music: Ratan Devi Sings Classical Ragas and Kashmiri Songs," *New York Times*, April 14, 1916.

—— "Ratan Devi Sings: An Exposition of Indian 'Ragas' and Kashmiri Folk Songs," *New York Times*, March 5, 1917.

—— *Sikh Sacred Music*, New Delhi: Sikh Sacred Music Society, 1967.

Atre, Prabha, *Enlightening the Listener: Contemporary North Indian Classical Vocal Music Performance*, including CD, New Delhi: Munshiram Manoharlal, 2000.

Aubert, Laurent, *The Music of the Other: New Challenges for Ethnomusicology in a Global Age* (Translated by Carla Ribeiro), With a foreword by Anthony Seeger, Aldershot: Ashgate, 2007.

Bake, Arnold, "A Talk on Folk-Music," *Visva-Bharati Quarterly*, vol. 5, July 1927, 144–148.

—— *Bijdrage tot de Kennis der Voor-Indische Muziek*, Paris: Paul Geuthner, 1930.

—— "Indian Music and Rabindranath Tagore," *Indian Art and Letters*, 5, 2, 1931, 81–102.

—— *Lectures on Indian Music*, Department of Education: Baroda State Press, 1933.

—— "Different Aspects of Indian Music," *Indian Art and Letters*, 8, 1, 1934, 60–74.

——*Twenty-Six Songs of Rabindranath Tagore*, Paris: Paul Geuthner, 1935.

——"Indian Folk Music," *Proceedings of the Musical Association*, 63rd Sess., 1936–1937, 65–77.

——, "Some Aspects of the Development of Indian Music," *Proceedings of the Royal Musical Association*, 76th Sess., 1949–1950, 23–34.

——, "The Impact of Western Music on the Indian Musical System," *Journal of the International Folk Music Council*, 5, 1953, 57–60.

Bake, Arnold, "Tagore and Western Music," in *Rabindranath Tagore: A Centenary Volume*, 1861–1961, New Delhi: Sahitya Akademi, 1961, 88–95.

———, "Tagore: The Man and the Artist," *Indian Art and Letters*, 35, 1, 1961, 10–20.

———, "Synthesis of Indian and Western Music," *The Illustrated Weekly of India*, November 5, 1961, 51.

Bakhle, Janaki, *Two Men and Music: Nationalism in the Making of an Indian Classical Tradition*, New Delhi: Permanent Black, 2005.

Ballantyne, Tony, *Orientalism and Race: Aryanism and the British Empire*, Basingstoke: Palgrave, 2002.

——— *Between Colonialism and Diaspora: Sikh Cultural Formations in an Imperial World*, New Delhi: Permanent Black, 2007.

Balough, Teresa, ed., *A Musical Genius from Australia: Selected Writings by and about Percy Grainger*, Nedlands: University of Western Australia, 1982.

———, ed., *Comrades in Art: The Correspondence of Ronald Stevenson and Percy Grainger 1957–61*, including CD, London: Toccata Press, 2010.

Banerjee, Prathama, *Politics of Time: "Primitives" and History-Writing in a Colonial Society*, New Delhi: Oxford University Press, 2006.

Banfield, Stephen, "Towards a History of Music in the British Empire: Three Export Studies," in *Britishness Abroad: Transnational Movements and Imperial Cultures*, ed. Kate Darian-Smith, Patricia Grimshaw, and Stuart Macintyre, Carlton, VIC: Melbourne University Press, 2007, 63–89.

Barucha, Rustom, *Rajasthan: An Oral History* (Conversations with Komal Kothari), New Delhi: Penguin, 2003.

Bayly, C. A., "Afterword," in "An Intellectual History for India," ed. Shruti Kapila, Special Issue of *Modern Intellectual History*, 4, 1, 2007, 163–169.

———, *Recovering Liberties: Indian Thought in the Age of Liberalism and Empire*, Cambridge: Cambridge University Press, 2012.

Bearman, C. J., "Percy Grainger, the Phonograph, and the Folk Song Society," *Music and Letters*, 84, 3, 2003, 434–455.

Bellman, Jonathan, ed., *The Exotic in Western Music*, Boston, MA: Northeastern University Press, 1998.

Bird, John, *Percy Grainger*, Oxford: Oxford University Press, 1999.

Blacking, John, *"A Common-Sense View of All Music": Reflections on Percy Grainger's Contribution to Ethnomusicology and Music Education*, Cambridge: Cambridge University Press, 1987.

Boehmer, Elleke, *Empire, the National, and the Postcolonial 1890–1920*, Oxford: Oxford University Press, 2002.

Bohlman, Philip V., *World Music. A Very Short Introduction*, Oxford: Oxford University Press, 2002.

Bor, Joep, "The Rise of Ethnomusicology: Sources on Indian Music c. 1780–c. 1890," *Yearbook for Traditional Music*, 20, 1988, 51–73.

———, et al., *The Raga Guide: A Survey of 74 Hindustani Ragas*, set of 4 CDs with book, Wyastone Leys, Monmouth: Nimbus, 1999.

———, *And Then There Was World Music and World Dance...* (Inaugural Lecture), Leiden University: Faculty of Arts, 2008.

———, "Introduction," in *Hindustani Music: Thirteenth to Twentieth Centuries*, ed. Joep Bor, Françoise "Nalini" Delvoye, Jane Harvey, and Emmie te Nijenhuis, New Delhi: Manohar, 2010, 11–16.

Bor, Joep, and Allyn Miner, "Hindustani Music: A Historical Overview of the Modern Period," in *Hindustani Music: Thirteenth to Twentieth Centuries*, ed. Joep Bor, Françoise "Nalini" Delvoye, Jane Harvey, and Emmie te Nijenhuis, New Delhi: Manohar, 2010, 197–220.

Born, Georgina, and David Hesmondhalgh, eds., *Western Music and Its Others: Difference, Representation, and Appropriation in Music*, Berkeley: University of California Press, 2000.

Brockington, Grace, "Introduction: Internationalism and the Arts," in *Internationalism and the Arts in Britain and Europe at the Fin de Siècle*, ed. Grace Brockington, Bern: Peter Lang, 2009, 1–26.

Brough, John, "Obituary: Arnold Adriaan Bake," *Bulletin of the School of Oriental and African Studies*, 27, 1, 1964, 246–264.

Burrow, J. W., *The Crisis of Reason: European Thought, 1848–1914*, New Haven, CT: Yale University Press, 2000.

Busoni, Ferruccio, *Sketch of a New Esthetic of Music*, New York: G. Schirmer, 1911 (first published 1907).

Campbell, Patricia Shehan, *Teaching Music Globally*, New York: Oxford University Press, 2004.

Candy, Catherine, "Mystical Internationalism in Margaret Cousins's Feminist World," *Women's Studies International Forum*, 32, 2009, 29–34.

Cannadine, David, *Ornamentalism: How the British Saw Their Empire*, Oxford: Oxford University Press, 2001.

Capwell, Charles, *The Music of the Bauls of Bengal*, Kent, Ohio: The Kent State University Press, 1986.

Cassio, Francesca, "The Music of the Sikh Gurus' Tradition in a Western Context: Cross-Cultural Pedagogy and Research," *Sikh Formations: Religion, Culture, Theory*, 7, 3, 2011, 313–337.

Clayton, Martin, "A. H. Fox Strangways and *The Music of Hindostan*: Revisiting Historical Field Recordings," *Journal of the Royal Musical Association*, 124, 1999, 86–118.

———, "Musical Renaissance and Its Margins in England and India, 1874–1914," in *Music and Orientalism in the British Empire, 1780s–1940s: Portrayal of the East*, ed. Martin Clayton and Bennett Zon, Aldershot: Ashgate, 2007, 71–93.

Collins, Michael, *Empire, Nationalism and the Post-Colonial World: Rabindranath Tagore's Writings on History, Politics and Society*, New York: Routledge, 2011.

Cook, Nicholas, *Music: A Very Short Introduction*, Oxford: Oxford University Press, 1998.

Coomaraswamy, Ananda K., *Essays in Indian Idealism*, New Delhi: Munshiram Manoharlal, 1981 (first published 1909).

———, "Eastern Religions and Western Thought," *The Review of Religion*, 6, 1942, 129–145.

——— *Essays on Music*, ed. Prem Lata Sharma, New Delhi: Manohar, 2010.

Cowgill, Rachel, "Canonizing Remembrance: Music for Armistice Day at the BBC, 1922–7," *First World War Studies*, 2, 1, 2011, 75–107.

Daniélou, Alain, *The Way to the Labyrinth: Memories of East and West*, New York: New Directions, 1987.

Das Gupta, Uma, ed., *A Difficult Friendship: Letters of Edward Thompson and Rabindranath Tagore*, New Delhi: Oxford University Press, 2003.

Das Gupta, Uma, ed., *Rabindranath Tagore: A Biography*, New Delhi: Oxford University Press, 2004.

———, ed., *The Oxford India Tagore: Selected Writings on Education and Nationalism*, New Delhi: Oxford University Press, 2009.

Devi, Ratan, and Ananda K. Coomaraswamy, *Thirty Songs from the Panjab and Kashmir*, with a foreword by Rabindranath Tagore, New Delhi: Sterling, 1994 (first published 1913).

Dreyfus, Kay, ed., *The Farthest North of Humanness: Letters of Percy Grainger 1901–1914*, Melbourne: MacMillan, 1985.

Dusenbery, Verne A., "The Word as Guru: Sikh Scripture and the Translation Controversy" (1992), in Dusenbery, *Sikhs at Large: Religion, Culture, and Politics in Global perspective*, Oxford University Press, 2008, 72–91.

Dutta, Krishna, and Andrew Robinson, *Rabindranath Tagore: The Myriad-Minded Man*, London: Bloomsbury, 1995.

Elgar, Edward, *A Future for English Music and Other Lectures*, ed. Percy M. Young, London: Dobson, 1968.

Etherington, Ben, "Said, Grainger and the Ethics of Polyphony," in *Edward Said: The Legacy of a Public Intellectual*, ed. Ned Curthoys and Debjani Ganguly, Carlton, VIC: Melbourne University Press, 2007, 221–238.

Farrell, Gerry, *Indian Music and the West*, Oxford: Oxford University Press, 1997.

Fischer-Tiné, Harald, "Indian Nationalism and the 'World Forces': Trans-national and Diasporic Dimensions of the Indian Freedom Movement on the Eve of the First World War," *Journal of Global History*, 2, 3, 2007, 325–344.

Foulds, John, *Music To-day: Its Heritage from the Past, and Legacy to the Future*, London: Ivor Nicholson and Watson, 1934.

———, "An East and West Concert," *The Musical Times*, 79, 1146, 1938, 623.

Fox Strangways, A. H., *The Music of Hindostan*, London: Clarendon Press, 1914.

———, *Music Observed*, London: Methuen, 1936.

———, "Convention: Tagore's Songs," *The Observer*, September, 20, 1936.

Freeman, Graham, "'That Chief Undercurrent of My Mind': Percy Grainger and the Aesthetics of English Folk Song," *Folk Music Journal*, 9, 4, 2009, 581–617.

Frogley, Alain, "Constructing Englishness in Music: National Character and the Reception of Ralph Vaughan Williams," in *Vaughan Williams Studies*, ed. Alain Frogley, Cambridge: Cambridge University Press, 1996, 1–22.

———, "Rewriting the Renaissance: History, Imperialism, and British Music since 1840," *Music and Letters*, 84, 2, 2003, 241–257.

———, "'The Old Sweet Anglo-Saxon Spell': Racial Discourses and the American Reception of British Music, 1895–1933," in *Western Music and Race*, ed. Julie Brown, Cambridge: Cambridge University Press, 2007, 244–257.

Gelbart, Matthew, *The Invention of "Folk Music" and "Art Music": Emerging Categories from Ossian to Wagner*, Cambridge: Cambridge University Press, 2007.

Ghosh, Santidev, *Rabindrasangeet Vichitra* (Rabindra Sangeet Miscellany), New Delhi: Concept, 2006 (first published 1972).

Gillies, Malcolm, and David Pear, eds., *The All-Round Man: Selected Letters of Percy Grainger 1914–1961*, Oxford: Clarendon Press, 1994.

———, and Bruce Clunies Ross, eds., *Grainger on Music*, Oxford: Oxford University Press, 1999.

———, David Pear, and Mark Carroll, eds., *Self-Portrait of Percy Grainger*, New York: Oxford University Press, 2006.

———, and David Pear, "Percy Grainger and American Nordicism," in *Western Music and Race*, ed. Julie Brown, Cambridge: Cambridge University Press, 2007, 115–124.

Gilmour, David, *The Long Recessional: The Imperial Life of Rudyard Kipling*, London: John Murray, 2002.

Godwin, Joscelyn, *Harmonies of Heaven and Earth: The Spiritual Dimension of Music from Antiquity to the Avant-Garde*, London: Thames and Hudson, 1987.

Goossens, Eugene, *Overture and Beginners: A Musical Autobiography*, London: Methuen, 1951.

Groot, Rokus de, "Edward Said and Polyphony," in *Edward Said: A Legacy of Emancipation and Representation*, ed. A. Iskander and H. Rustom, Berkeley: University of California Press, 2010, 204–228.

Hardy, Lisa, *The British Piano Sonata 1870–1945*, Woodbridge: Boydell Press, 2001.

Harvey, Jonathan, *Music and Inspiration*, London: Faber and Faber, 1999.

———, *In Quest of Spirit: Thoughts on Music*, Berkeley: University of California Press, 1999.

Hay, Stephen N., *Asian Ideas of East and West: Tagore and His Critics in Japan, China, and India*, Cambridge, MA: Harvard University Press, 1970.

Head, Raymond, "Holst and India (I): 'Maya' to 'Sita,'" *Tempo*, 158, September 1986, 2–7.

———, "Holst and India (II)," *Tempo*, 160, March 1987, 27–36.

———, "Holst and India (III)," *Tempo*, 166, September 1988, 35–40.

———, "Astrology and Modernism in The Planets," *Tempo*, 187, December 1993, 15–22.

Howe, Stephen, ed., *The New Imperial Histories Reader*, London: Routledge, 2010.

Hughes, Meirion, and Robert Stradling, *The English Musical Renaissance 1840–1940: Constructing a National Music*, Manchester: Manchester University Press, 2001.

Hull, Arthur Eaglefield, *Cyril Scott: The Man and His Works*, London: Waverley, 1925 (first published 1914).

———, *Modern Harmony: Its Explanation and Application*, London: Augener, 1914.

Jackson, Paul, "Percy Grainger's Aleatoric Adventures: The Rarotongan Part-Songs," *Grainger Studies: An Interdisciplinary Journal*, 2, 2012, 1–32.

Jairazbhoy, Nazir Ali, *The Rags of North Indian Music: Their Structure and Evolution*, Mumbai: Popular Prakashan, 2011 (first published 1971).

Karpeles, Maud, and Arnold Bake, *Manual for Folk Music Collectors*, London: International Folk Music Council, 1951.

Kaufmann, Walter, *The Ragas of North India*, Bloomington: Indiana University Press, 1968.

Khalsa, Nirinjan Kaur, "Gurbani Kirtan Renaissance: Reviving Musical Memory, Reforming Sikh Identity," *Sikh Formations: Religion, Culture, Theory*, 2012, 8, 2, 2012, 199–229.

Kipling, Rudyard, *Kim*, ed. Zohreh T. Sullivan, New York: Norton, 2002.

Lago, Mary M., ed., *Imperfect Encounter: The Letters of Rabindranath Tagore and William Rothenstein*, Cambridge, MA: Harvard University Press, 1972.

Lelyveld, David, "Upon the Subdominant: Administering Music in All-India Radio," in *Consuming Modernity: Public Culture in Contemporary India*, ed. Carol A. Breckenridge, New Delhi: Oxford University Press, 1996, 49–65.

Linden, Bob van der, "Sikh Music and Empire: The Moral Representation of Self in Music," *Sikh Formations: Religion, Culture, Theory*, 4, 1, 2008, 1–15.

———, "Music, Theosophical Spirituality and Empire: The British Modernist Composers Cyril Scott and John Foulds," *Journal of Global History*, 3, 2, 2008, 163–182.

———, *Moral Languages from Colonial Punjab: The Singh Sabha, Arya Samaj and Ahmadiyahs*, New Delhi: Manohar, 2008.

———, "Percy Grainger and Empire: Kipling, Racialism and All the World's 'Folk Music,'" *British Music: The Journal of the British Music Society*, 32, 2010, 13–24.

———, "Sikh Sacred Music, Empire and World Music: Aesthetics and Historical Change," *Sikh Formations: Religion, Culture, Theory*, 7, 3, 2011, 383–397.

———, "History versus Tradition Again?: A Response to Bhai Baldeep Singh," *Sikh Formations: Religion, Culture, Theory*, 8, 2, 2012, 247–251.

Lipsey, Roger, *Coomaraswamy: His Life and Work*, Princeton, NJ: Princeton University Press, 1977.

Louis, Wm. Roger, general ed., *The Oxford History of the British Empire*, 5 volumes, Oxford: Oxford University Press, 1998–1999.

Luthra, H. R., *Indian Broadcasting*, New Delhi: Publications Division, Ministry of Information and Broadcasting, Government of India, 1986.

Macauliffe, M. A., "The Rise of Amritsar and the Alterations of the Sikh Religion" (1881), as reprinted in *Western Image of the Sikh Religion: A Source Book*, ed. Darshan Singh, New Delhi: National Book Organization, 1999, 247–267.

———, "The Holy Writings of the Sikhs" (1898), as reprinted in *Western Image of the Sikh Religion: A Source Book*, ed. Darshan Singh, New Delhi: National Book Organization, 1999, 285–326.

———, *The Sikh Religion. Its Gurus, Sacred Writings and Authors*, 6 volumes, Oxford: Oxford University Press, 1909.

MacDonald, Malcolm, *John Foulds and His Music*, London: Kahn & Averill, 1989.

MacKenzie, John M., *Orientalism: History, Theory and the Arts*, Manchester: Manchester University Press, 1995.

———, "Imperial and Metropolitan Cultures," in *The Oxford History of the British Empire, Volume 3: The Nineteenth Century*, ed. Andrew Porter, Oxford: Oxford University Press, 1999, 270–293.

———, "The Popular Culture of Empire in Britain," in *The Oxford History of the British Empire, Volume 4: The Twentieth Century*, ed. Judith M. Brown and Wm Roger Louis, Oxford: Oxford University Press, 1999, 212–231.

Mandair, Arvind-Pal S., *Religion and the Spectre of the West: Sikhism, India, Postcoloniality, and the Politics of Translation*. New York: Columbia University Press, 2009.

Mann, Gurinder Singh, *The Making of Sikh Scripture*, New Delhi: Oxford University Press, 2001.

Mann, Maud (Maud MacCarthy), *Some Indian Conceptions of Music*, London: Theosophical Publishing Society, 1913.

Mansell, James G., "Musical Modernity and Contested Commemoration at the Festival of Remembrance, 1923–1927," *The Historical Journal*, 52, 2, 2009, 433–454.

———, "Music and the Borders of Rationality: Discourses of Place in the Work of John Foulds," in *Internationalism and the Arts in Britain and Europe at the Fin de Siècle*, ed. Grace Brockington, Bern: Peter Lang, 2009, 49–75.

Mansukhani, Gobind Singh, *Indian Classical Music and Sikh Kirtan*, New Delhi: Oxford and IBH, 1982.

McLeod, Hew, *Discovering the Sikhs: Autobiography of a Historian*, New Delhi: Permanent Black, 2004.

Mellers, Wilfred, *Percy Grainger*, Oxford: Oxford University Press, 1992.

Merriam, Alan P., *The Anthropology of Music*, Evanston, Ill.: Northwestern University Press, 1964.

Mitter, Partha, *The Triumph of Modernism: India's Artists and the Avant-Garde, 1922–1947*, London: Reaktion Books, 2007.

Nandy, Ashis, *The Intimate Enemy: Loss and Recovery of Self under Colonialism*, New Delhi: Oxford University Press, 1983.

Nettl, Bruno, *The Study of Ethnomusicology: Thirty-One Issues and Concepts*, Urbana-Champaign: University of Illinois Press, 2005.

———, *Nettl's Elephant: On the History of Ethnomusicology*, with a foreword by Anthony Seeger, Urbana-Champaign: University of Illinois Press, 2010.

Nijhawan, Michael, *Dhadhi Darbar: Religion, Violence, and the Performance of Sikh History*, New Delhi: Oxford University Press, 2006.

Oberoi, Harjot, *The Construction of Religious Boundaries: Culture, Identity and Diversity in the Sikh Tradition*, New Delhi: Oxford University Press, 1994.

Openshaw, Jeanne, *Seeking Bauls of Bengal*, Cambridge: Cambridge University Press, 2004.

Owen, Alex, *The Place of Enchantment: British Occultism and the Culture of the Modern*, Chicago: University of Chicago Press, 2004.

Paintal, Ajit Singh, "The Contribution of Ragis and Rababis to the Devotional Music," in *The City of Amritsar. A Study of Historical, Social and Economic Aspects*, ed. Fauja Singh, New Delhi: Oriental Publishers and Distributors, 1978, 256–281.

Patterson, Michelle Wick, *Natalie Curtis Burlin: A Life in Native and African American Music*, Lincoln: University of Nebraska Press, 2010.

Pear, David, "Percy Grainger and Manliness," *Journal of Australian Studies*, 56, 1998, 106–115.

Peers, Douglas M., and Nandini Gooptu, ed., *India and the British Empire*, Oxford: Oxford University Press, 2012.

Pincott, Frederic, "The Arrangement of the Hymns of the Adi Granth, Holy Bible of the Sikhs" (1886), as reprinted in *Western Image of the Sikh Religion:*

A Source Book, ed. Darshan Singh, New Delhi: National Book Organization, 1999, 185–211.

Porter, Bernard, "Edward Elgar and Empire," *Journal of Imperial and Commonwealth History*, 29, 1, January 2001, 1–34.

———, *The Absent-Minded Imperialists: Empire, Society and Culture in Britain*, Oxford: Oxford University Press, 2004.

Purewal, Navtej K., "Sikh/Muslim Bhai-Bhai?: Towards a Social History of the Rababi Tradition of Shabad," *Sikh Formations: Religion, Culture, Theory*, 7, 3, 2011, 365–382.

Puri, Swami Omananda (Maud MacCarthy), *The Boy and the Brothers*, London: Victor Gallancz, 1959.

———, *Towards the Mysteries: Being Some Teachings of the Brothers of the Holy Hierarchy, Given Through the Boy*, London: Neville Spearman, 1968.

Radice, William, "Keys to the Kingdom: The Search for How Best to Understand and Perform the Songs of Rabindranath Tagore," in *Rabindranath Tagore: Reclaiming a Cultural Icon*, ed. Kathleen M. O'Connell and Joseph T. O'Connell, Kolkata: Visva-Bharati, 2009, 123–147.

Rahaim, Matt, "That Ban(e) of Indian Music: Hearing Politics in The Harmonium," *Journal of Asian Studies*, 70, 3, 2011, 657–682.

Raja, Deepak, *Hindustani Music: A Tradition in Transition*, with a foreword by Shiv Kumar Sharma, New Delhi: D. K. Printworld, 2005.

Ramusack, Barbara N., "Punjab States, Maharajas and Gurudwaras: Patiala and the Sikh Community," in *People, Princes and Paramount Power: Society and Politics in the Indian Princely States*, ed. Robin Jeffrey, New Delhi: Oxford University Press, 1978, 170–204.

Rao, Suvarnalata, and Wim van der Meer, "The Construction, Reconstruction, and Deconstruction of Shruti," in *Hindustani Music: Thirteenth to Twentieth Centuries*, ed. Joep Bor, Françoise "Nalini" Delvoye, Jane Harvey and Emmie te Nijenhuis, New Delhi: Manohar, 2010, 673–696.

Rataul, Dharmendra, "SGPC sends SOS World over for Training of Ragis," *Indian Express*, March 13, 2006.

Richards, Jeffrey, *Imperialism and Music: Britain 1876–1953*, Manchester: Manchester University Press, 2001.

Robinson, Suzanne, "Percy Grainger and Henry Cowell: Concurrences between Two 'Hyper-Moderns,'" *Musical Quarterly*, 94, 3, 2011, 278–324.

Ruckert, George, *Music in North India*, including CD, New York: Oxford University Press, 2004.

Sampsel, Laurie J., *Cyril Scott: A Bio-Bibliography*, Westport, CT: Greenwood Press, 2000.

Schofield, Katherine Butler, "Reviving the Golden Age Again: 'Classicization,' Hindustani Music, and the Mughals," *Ethnomusicology*, 54, 3, 2010, 484–517.

Scott, Cyril, *The Philosophy of Modernism: Its Connection with Music*, London: Waverley, 1925 (first published 1917).

———, "The Two Attitudes," *Musical Quarterly*, 5, 1919, 149–159.

———, *The Adept of Galilee: A Story and An Argument by The Author of "The Initiate,"* London: Routledge, 1920.

———, *My Years of Indiscretion*, London: Mills and Boon, 1924.

———, "Introduction," in David Anrias, *Through the Eyes of the Masters*, London: Routledge, 1932.

———, *Music: Its Secret Influence Throughout the Ages*, Northamptonshire: Aquarian Press, 1985 (first published 1933).

———, *An Outline of Modern Occultism*, London: Routledge, 1974 (first published 1935).

———, *Bone of Contention: Life Story and Confessions*, London: Antiquarian Press, 1969.

Sengupta, Pradip Kumar, *Foundations of Indian Musicology: Perspectives in the Philosophy of Art and Culture*, New Delhi: Abhinav Publications, 1991.

Shackle, Christopher, and Arvind-Pal Singh Mandair, eds., *Teachings of the Sikh Gurus: Selections from the Guru Granth Sahib*, London: Routledge, 2005.

Sharp, Cecil, J., *English Folk Song: Some Conclusions*, fourth (revised) edition ed. Maud Karpeles, with an appreciation of Cecil Sharp by Ralph Vaughan Williams, London: Mercury Books, 1965 (first published 1907).

Sharp, Cecil, J, and Olive Dame Campbell, *English Folk Songs from the Southern Appalachians*, 2 vols., ed. Maud Karpeles, London: Oxford University Press, 1932 (first published 1917).

Singh, Avtar, and Gurcharan Singh, *Gurbani Sangit Prachin Rit Ratnavali*, 2 volumes, Patiala: Punjabi University Press, 1979.

Singh, Bhai Baldeep, "What Is Kirtan? Observations, Interventions and Personal Reflections," *Sikh Formations: Religion, Culture, Theory*, 7, 3, 2011, 245–295.

Singh, Gyani Dyal, *Gurmat Sangit Sagar*, 4 volumes, New Delhi: Guru Nanak Vidya Bhandar Trust, 1992.

Singh, Gurnam, *Sikh Musicology: Sri Guru Granth Sahib and Hymns of the Human Spirit*, New Delhi: Kanishka, 2001.

Singh, Bhagat Lakshman, *Autobiography*, ed. Ganda Singh, Calcutta: The Sikh Cultural Centre, 1965.

Singh, Pashaura, *The Guru Granth Sahib: Canon, Meaning and Authority*, New Delhi: Oxford University Press, 2000.

———, *Life and Work of Guru Arjan: History, Memory, and Biography in the Sikh Tradition*, New Delhi: Oxford University Press, 2006.

———, "Sikhism and Music," in *Sacred Sound: Experiencing Music in World Religions*, ed. Guy L. Beck, including CD, Waterloo, Ontario: Wilfrid Laurier University Press, 2006, 141–167.

———, "Musical *Chaunkis* at the Darbar Sahib: History, Aesthetics, and Time," in *Sikhism in Global Context*, ed. Pashaura Singh, New Delhi: Oxford University Press, 2011, 102–129.

Slobin, Mark, *Folk Music: A Very Short Introduction*, Oxford: Oxford University Press, 2011.

Som, Reba, *Rabindranath Tagore: The Singer and His Song*, including CD, New Delhi: Viking, 2009.

Sorrell, Neil, "A Composer in the Twilight of the Raj: John Foulds (1880–1939)," *Seminar on Indian Music and the West*, Mumbai: Sangeet Natak Academy, 1996, 50–55.

———, "Early Western Pioneers: John Foulds and Maud MacCarthy," in *Hindustani Music: Thirteenth to Twentieth Centuries*, ed. Joep Bor, Françoise

"Nalini" Delvoye, Jane Harvey and Emmie te Nijenhuis, New Delhi: Manohar, 2010, 511–519.

Sorrell, Neil, "From 'Harm-omnium' to Harmonia Omnium: Assessing Maud MacCarthy's Influence on John Foulds and the Globalization of Indian Music," *Journal of the Indian Musicological Society*, 40, 2009–2010, 110–130.

Subramanian, Lakshmi, *From the Tanjore Court to the Madras Music Academy*, New Delhi: Oxford University Press, 2006.

———, *New Mansions for Music: Performance, Pedagogy and Criticism*, New Delhi: Social Science Press, 2008.

Tagore, Rabindranath, *Nationalism*, with an introduction by Ramachandra Guha, New Delhi: Penguin, 2009 (first published 1917).

———, *The Religion of Man*, London: Unwin, 1961 (first published 1931).

———, *Selected Poems*, translated and with an introduction by William Radice, New Delhi: Penguin, 1995 (first published 1985).

———, *The Jewel That Is Best: Collected Brief Poems*, translated and with an introduction by William Radice, New Delhi: Penguin, 2011.

Tagore, Saranindranath, "Rabindranath Tagore's Conception of Cosmopolitanism: A Reconstruction," in *Rabindranath Tagore: Reclaiming a Cultural Icon*, ed. Kathleen M. O'Connell and Joseph T. O'Connell, Kolkata: Visva-Bharati, 2009, 93–110.

Tame, David, *The Secret Power of Music*, Rochester, VT: Destiny Books, 1984.

Tavener, John, *The Music of Silence: A Composer's Testament*, London: Faber and Faber, 1999.

Taylor, Timothy D., *Beyond Exoticism: Western Music and the World*, Durham, NC: Duke University Press, 2007.

Trasoff, David, "The All-India Music Conferences of 1916–1925: Cultural Transformation and Colonial Ideology," in *Hindustani Music: Thirteenth to Twentieth Centuries*, ed. Joep Bor, Françoise "Nalini" Delvoye, Jane Harvey, and Emmie te Nijenhuis, New Delhi: Manohar, 2010, 331–356.

Trumpp, Ernest, *The Adi Granth or the Holy Scripture of the Sikhs translated from the Original Scripture with Introductory Essays*, New Delhi: Munshiram Manoharlal, 1978 (first published 1877).

Vaughan Williams, Ralph, *Nationalist Music and Other Essays*, Oxford: Clarendon, 1996 (Second Edition).

Veer, Peter van der, *Imperial Encounters: Religion and Modernity in India and Britain*, Princeton, NJ: Princeton University Press, 2001.

Viswanathan, Gauri, "Ireland, India, and the Poetics of Internationalism," *Journal of World History*, 15, 1, March 2004, 7–30.

Viswanathan, T., and Matthew Harp Allen, *Music in South India*, including CD, New York: Oxford University Press, 2004.

Wade, Bonnie C., *Thinking Musically*, including CD, New York: Oxford University Press, 2004.

Watson, J. R., *The English Hymn: A Critical and Historical Study*, Oxford: Oxford University Press, 1997.

Weidman, Amanda J., *Singing the Classical, Voicing the Modern: The Postcolonial Politics of Music in South India*, Durham, NC: Duke University Press, 2006.

Wilkins, Charles, "Observations on the Seeks and Their College" (1788), as reprinted in *Western Image of the Sikh Religion: A Source Book*, ed. Darshan Singh, New Delhi: National Book Organization, 1999, 1–5.

Williams, Louise Blakeney, "Overcoming the 'Contagion of Mimicry': The Cosmopolitan Nationalism and Modernist History of Rabindranath Tagore and W. B. Yeats," *American Historical Review*, 112, 1, 2007, 69–100.

Wilson, A. C., *A Short Account of the Hindu System of Music*, Lahore: Gulab Singh and Sons, 1904.

Yates, Michael, "Percy Grainger and the Impact of the Phonograph," *Folk Music Journal*, 4, 3, 1982, 265–275.

Zon, Bennett, *Representing Non-Western Music in Nineteenth-Century Britain*, Rochester, NY: University of Rochester Press, 2007.

Unpublished Materials

Paintal, Ajit Singh, *Nature and Place of Music in Sikh Religion and Its Affinity with Hindustani Classical Music*, PhD Dissertation, University of Delhi: Department of Music, 1972.

Scott, Cyril, *Hymn of Unity*, Libretto, 1947.

Scott, Desmond, "Cyril and Percy," Paper presented at the Grainger seminar, British Library, London, February 20, 2011.

Index

Printed in the United States of America